W9-AYE-366

ALSO BY JONATHAN NOSSITER

Feature Films
Resident Alien, 1991 (New Video)
Sunday, 1997 (Lion's Gate)
Signs & Wonders, 2000 (Strand Releasing)
Mondovino, 2004 (Think Films)
Rio Sex Comedy, to be completed in 2010

Series and Short Films
Searching for Arthur, 1997 (Lion's Gate)
Making Mischief, 2001 (Strand Releasing)
Losing the Thread, 2002 (New Video)
Mondovino, The Series, 2006 (Kimstin)

LIQUIDMemory

LIQUID Memory

WHY WINE MATTERS

Jonathan Nossiter

FARRAR, STRAUS AND GIROUX

New York

FARRAR, STRAUS AND GIROUX
18 West 18th Street, New York 10011

Copyright © 2009 by Jonathan Nossiter
All rights reserved
Distributed in Canada by D&M Publishers, Inc.
Printed in the United States of America
Originally published, in different form, in 2007 by Bernard Grasset, Paris,
as *Le goût et le pouvoir*
Published in the United States by Farrar, Straus and Giroux
First American edition, 2009

Library of Congress Cataloging-in-Publication Data
Nossiter, Jonathan.
    [Goût et le pouvoir. English]
    Liquid memory : why wine matters / Jonathan Nossiter.— 1st American
ed.
        p.   cm.
    "Originally published, in different form, in 2007 by Bernard Grasset,
Paris."
    Includes index.
    ISBN 978-0-374-27257-9 (hardcover : alk. paper)
    1. Nossiter, Jonathan—Anecdotes.   2. Wine writers—Anecdotes.
3. Wine and wine making.   I. Title.

TP547.N67A3 2009
641.2'2—dc22

                                                          2009010183

Designed by Cassandra J. Pappas

www.fsgbooks.com

1   3   5   7   9   10   8   6   4   2

To my wife, Paula,
and our children, Miranda, Capitu, and Noah Bernard

Contents

LIQUIDMemory

Introduction

THE LIBERTY OF TASTE

This book is a highly personal journey through the liquid looking glass, an insider-outsider view of the world's most mysterious, contradictory, and jubilatory drink. It's an attempt to understand wine in its relation to culture (and even movies) and why that can bring pleasure to people who never even imagined putting a glass of wine to their lips (or for those who do drink but are, rightly, loath to talk). It might be a surprise to those justifiably wary of winespeak and wine snobbery to imagine that wine could be as powerful an expression of culture as books, paintings, cinema, music, baseball, and sex. Through an intimate examination of the relationship between taste and power as expressed in wine, I've hoped to uncover something of how wine expresses that relation in the world at large.

For those who've seen a film I made about the wine world, *Mondovino*, please note that this book is not a continuation of *Mondovino* by other means. While the film traces a kind of comic anthropology of the wine world, it barely brushes on the fact of wine itself, its taste, its use, its physical existence, and what has always fascinated me the most: its profound relation to the general culture. I grew up drinking wine by the finger drop at the age of two, courtesy of my expatriate American parents in Paris and their efforts to pacify four boisterous sons. As an adolescent in London, I spent my allowance on wine, in a quixotic attempt to improve my chances in the dating lottery. By my mid-twenties, I was making wine lists for restaurants in New York and sporadically writing wine articles, which were even more sporadically published. But because filmmaking has been my primary craft for the last twenty-five years I've always been an outsider in the clubby, sometimes mafioso, and always culty world of wine. And this may be my one advantage for the lay reader.

At a dinner in Paris not long ago I was introduced to film director and formidable Parisian gadabout Anne Fontaine. Having heard I had some association or other with the wine world, she turned to me as I went to take my seat, sipping blithely from her wineglass: "Men who speak about wine at table are instantly condemned," she hissed. "Death! The guy is done for. Conversation about wine is anonymous. A man isn't speaking to me when he speaks about wine. He's trying to prove something to me, but it has nothing to do with conversation. I think to myself: he's a little macho shit trying to show off his power. Talking about wine is unbearably mediocre." While this may be no more than one snob's preemptive strike against another, I have to admit that I share her fear of the dreaded *winespeak*. Though it seeks to describe an innocent object of pleasure, I often have the feeling that the language of wine deployed by critics, sommeliers, restaurateurs, and the dreaded self-appointed wine connoisseur has most in common with Orwell's vision of the willfully abusive inversion of language in totalitarian regimes.

Most winespeak—in any language—is designed not to enlighten or enchant but to exclude, bully, and belittle. What are we to think, for instance, if a critic assures us that we should spend $115 on a Washington state Cabernet because, as Harvey Steiman wrote in the *Wine Spectator* of July 2008 (the highest in circulation of the world's rash of wine magazines), it's "richly aromatic and brims with dark berry and currant aromas and flavors, shaded with espresso and dark chocolate overtones set against somewhat gritty tannins. A meaty note adds extra depth as the finish lingers on and on against the tannins. Best from 2010 through 2017"? Does he mean to say that our considerable investment will net us a substantial, if not entirely complete meal, beginning with the fruit cocktail, followed by a mystery meat, a chocolate dessert, and a postprandial coffee? And all of this with a mathematically determined shelf life, as scientific an exercise as predicting the eventual life-span of a child of two. Another wine writer at the same magazine describes a wine from the venerable Châteauneuf-du-Pape region in France like this: "A very grippy style, with lots of sweet tapenade, tobacco, hot stone and braised chestnut notes weaving through a core of dark currant and fig fruit. There's a nice twinge of lavender on the structured finish. Best from 2010 through 2028." Two thousand twenty-eight? Surely we've plunged through a ("dark berrylike") hole and find ourselves, like Lewis Carroll's Alice in Wonderland, trying to comprehend the Mock Turtle's school curriculum, caught between "reeling and writhing" and "laughing and grief."

Moreover, like the queens in *Through the Looking Glass*, there is, contrariwise, a diametrically opposed school of thought: the self-proclaimed populists, determined to dumb down wine at any cost. They urge us to "just say what you like and that's what's good," like those signs in front of tourist mall art galleries that reassure us that "art is what you like." With one insouciant phrase, they discount several thousand years of cultural and agricultural experimentation that have made wine interesting in the first place.

This book is an attempt to transmit something of the sensual and intellectual delight that wine has brought to me since childhood. It is intended for people who prefer not to be condescended to and yet who are rightly skeptical of jargon, defensive snobbery, or any use of power that obstructs the uncovering of one's own taste. I don't believe there are either rules or shortcuts to the acquisition of taste in relation to *any* subject of value and complexity. However, a few well-timed kicks to the rear end of the wine world (the part, alas, that leads us all by the nose) might help us appreciate why wine can in fact be a subject of universal value, whether or not we drink—or even think about it. A reappraisal of wine might also lead us to reconsider how and why we acquire a sense of personal taste (in wine, the arts, politics, anything) and how we might be able to affirm that crucial liberty without fear of intimidation by those who profess to know all—or, worse, by those who proudly profess to know little or nothing.

PART I

The (None)sense
of Place

1

WHY WE'RE NOT DOGS

Terroir Is Where You Come From. Or Where You're Going

The term globalization is frequently misused. This is particularly disturbing for me, a child of the globe. My father, Bernard Nossiter, an American journalist, moved our family from Washington, D.C., to Paris when I was two. I grew up across the cultures of France, Italy, Greece, India, and England, as well as the United States. So, where do I belong? A German filmmaker, Thomas Struck, told me that while riding his bicycle through the vineyards of the Rheingau, he stumbled across Stuart Pigott, one of the world's most experienced drinkers of German wines. He asked Pigott, an Englishman who lives in Berlin, "What is your *heimat*?" Pigott paused before responding to this peculiar German term, which means, variously, "roots," "origin," "home," or "homeland."

"My *heimat*?" he repeated. "German Rieslings."

I couldn't agree with him more. Of course, my own *heimat* would include not just the Rieslings of the Rheingau, Mosel, or Franconia, but equally the wines of the Loire's Vouvray or Burgundy's Volnay. My *heimat* is globe spanning. It would also include the Aglianico del Vulture from the Basilicata region of southern Italy, which I drank recently in Rio de Janeiro, where I now live. Part of what makes it my *heimat* is that I drank this "Vulture," a 1998 vintage from the producer Paternoster, in the company of my neighbors and fellow film directors, Karim Aïnouz and Walter Salles. Why is that a part of determining my *heimat*? Because the force of a wine—or any cultural expression (or expression of love, for that matter)—is also dependent on the context in which it's understood. It was only in explaining the origins of the bottle to my film world friends that I remembered that this fiercely dry, earthy, and bittersweet drink is made not far from the dramatically barren rock formations of Matera where Pier Paolo Pasolini shot *The Gospel According to St. Matthew*. And this film gives the three of us a common heritage. In fact, we can go further. We could each one of us say that Pasolini—and *Gospel* especially—is our joint *heimat*. And this is the best explanation of what allows three such radically different filmmakers to sit down happily together at a dinner table.

It's a strange film to link the three of us, just as it is strange that we three are linked. Through the story of Jesus, Pasolini made an uncompromisingly personal effort to reconcile his own devout Catholicism with a kind of exuberant homosexuality and Gramscian Marxism (an Italian humanist vision of utopian social justice). I wondered what Pasolini would've felt, knowing that *Gospel* (miraculously endorsed by the Vatican in 1963) begat three such disparate followers. What would he think of Karim, a half Algerian from the hardscrabble Northeast of Brazil, making *Madame Satã* (a radical, tender portrait of a boxing Rio transvestite); Walter, a debonair French-educated son of a Brazilian diplomat, launching his career with *Terra Estrangeira* (a delicate story of Brazilians adrift in Portugal); and me, a secular, rootless American Jew, shooting *Mondovino* (a black comedy about wine, shot on three continents)? It doesn't matter.

Although we may all claim Pasolini as a *heimat*, he bears no responsibility for the claim. And it's precisely this notion of claiming a *heimat*, without the *heimat* claiming you (or, like a country, having any claim *on* you), that is most essential to me. It has shaped my greatest pleasures in cinema and wine, and it's this distinction from "belonging" or "nationalism" that is at the root of my understanding of *terroir*, the sin-gularly French expression of *heimat* that I grew up with. *Terroir* formed my sense of taste, wherever I happened to be living. And it's the reason for writing this book.

Without *terroir*—in wine, cinema, or life (I'm happiest when the three are confused)—there is no individuality, no dignity, no tolerance, and no shared civilization. *Terroir* is an act of generosity. The last thing it should be is sectarian or reactionary. In fact, the often willful misun-derstanding of this concept led me to a number of fights during the release of *Mondovino*, because of knee-jerk anti-Americanism in Avi-gnon—where reactionary locals misread *terroir* as an exclusively French birthright—or because of the smugly disingenuous political correct-ness of San Francisco's affluent liberals with a vested interest in denying substantial value to Old World *terroir*. A true expression of *terroir*—say, a Meursault Luchets from Jean-Marc Roulot in Burgundy—is a very precise means to share the beauty of a specific identity, a specific cul-ture, with the rest of the world. It is using the local not to exclude, but to include any one of us in the mystery and distinctive beauty of an "other." Any other. It is an affirmation of difference in fact in many ways. Not only will the Meursault Luchets of Jean-Marc be distinct from that of his father, Guy, but each year his own expression will evolve, as his understanding and the soil and climate also shift.

In cinema, these notions are readily accepted. It's a given that when someone sees Ira Sachs's *The Delta*—one of the rare American films of the last twenty years that conveys the emotional and physical texture of a peculiarly American psyche, seen through the lens of misfits in Mem-phis, Tennessee—they feel included in the experience of American life. And America becomes more human and comprehensible. When you see Wong Kar-wai's *Fallen Angels*, where an idiosyncratically Taiwanese spirit meets Hong Kong reality (a dumping ground at the time for global kitsch), a certain conception of "Chineseness" becomes intimate without losing its otherness. Though it's very interesting to see how this quality of otherness has shifted in the decade since Wong Kar-wai made that film: how he's repackaged it in subsequent movies for Western consumption on the back of his international success, losing, in my opinion, both his films' intimacy and their otherness.

So why should wine be any different? The defense of *terroir* is not a reactionary, unquestioning clinging to tradition. It is the will to progress into the future with a firm rootedness in a collective past, but where that rootedness is left to evolve freely and continuously above ground, in the present, to create a sharply etched—and hard-earned—identity. It's a way to counteract the relentless homogenization of certain global forces. It is the only way, I believe, to progress forward ethically, to respect and place oneself in relation to, but not to ape, the past.

Terroir has never been fixed, in taste or in perception. It has always been an evolving expression of culture. What distinguishes our era is the instantaneousness and universality of change. Before, the sense of a *terroir* would evolve over generations, hundreds of years, allowing for the slow accretion of knowledge and experience to build into sedimentary layers, like the geological underpinning of a given *terroir* itself. Today layers are stripped away overnight, and a new layer is added nearly each vintage. "Why is this dangerous?" ask those genuinely eager for progress and modernity, as well as the conscious (or self-deluding) profiteers of this new world order. Because it risks wiping out historical memory, which is our only safeguard against the devastating lies of marketing and the cynical exploitation of global markets, culture, and politics.

So the fight for wine's individuality, for the survival of individual taste in relation to the homogenizing forces of impersonal power (especially when wielded by a very individual person) is a fight (as much as that in cinema) that concerns all of us. But if these differences, these expressions of diversity and cultural identity, these vital links to the past are being threatened, who decides what to preserve, what to safeguard? Who says what should survive? Why should a Burgundy Volnay be safeguarded as something distinct as opposed to, say, a Uruguayan Tannat, a wine that only recently began to assert its identity and almost as quickly seems to be losing it? But what should its taste be, and who gets to judge? And what does it mean when we express our taste? And are we sure that it really is our own taste, when we do express it?

For that matter, what is taste? It *could* be described as the expression of a preference between, say, A and B. But what distinguishes taste from mere opinion is that such a preference emerges from a sensory, emotional reaction with the subsequent ability to intellectually decipher that reaction for the self (and, if really necessary, for others). But ultimately, the defining characteristic of taste is the coherent relation of that preference to one's own conduct, to an ethical relation to oneself and to the world.

Taste and Memory

THE ART OF MEMORY HAS BEEN FORGOTTEN

I'm convinced that wine is among the most singular repositories of memory known to man. If historical memory is the essential quality by which we are distinguished from beasts, that which gives us shape and purpose and ethical structure, as the historian of Vichy France Robert Paxton said to me in an interview for the research of *Mondovino*, then it's worth considering wine's relationship to memory. Without cultivating memories of our dead parents, of acts of history, of our own prior conduct, we are lost and become prey to all evildoing, lies, and exploitation, especially our own.

A museum contains works of art that are fixed expressions of a specific sensibility, a specific memory, no matter how rich and varied our responses and our understanding of that sensibility. A novel is the same. And while one might argue that the patina of a building reflects both the original expression of a memory and the visible traces of that memory across time, it is still inert matter. Its fixity clings to it, even once decayed, restored, or buried underground.

Why is wine unique in its relation to memory? Because it is the only animate vessel of both *personal* memory—that of the drinker (or maker) and the subjectivity of his experience and the memory of that subjectivity—and *communal* memory. That is, it is communal to the extent that a wine is also the memory of the *terroir*, which the wine expresses as an evolving, active taste. As communal memory, it is above all an expression of place as a communal identity, the history of the civilization of that place and the history of the relationship to its nature (especially soil, subsoil, and microclimate).

A well-made wine from a *terroir* of some complexity, when the grapes are *born* healthy and the wine is allowed to develop in further salutary circumstances (i.e., when the process is chemical-free, organic), can live about the same life span as a human being, sixty to eighty years (this is also, perhaps not coincidentally, the life span of a well-cared-for vine). Consider further that the wine itself is constantly evolving in bottle, from its birth to its death (i.e., its consumption). The wine's expression of "memory" is in perpetual, biological evolution, just as ours is. The memory of a wine is the closest thing to human memory.

In fact, nothing so complex, so dynamic, and so specific, nothing that links both nature and civilization, can be said in relation to memory in literature, painting, cinema, music, architecture: any of the other records of human civilization. However, precisely because neither *terroir*, nor nature, nor men are fixed, and because a wine itself is destined to be consumed—to vanish—a wine of *terroir* is by its nature, an ultimately indefinable, unquantifiable agent of memory. This is a curse for relentless rationalists, unrepentant pragmatists, and all the busy codifiers of this world, anxious for absolutes. And a blessing for the rest of us.

Since the beginnings of Near Eastern civilizations, since the Greco-Roman civilizations that have circumscribed (until recently) our own culture, across the entire Judeo-Christian tradition (and even a dash of the Moslem), wine has been a singular expression of who we are and, equally important, what we hope or pretend to be. Wine is bedrock truth, blood of the earth, but also a heightened agent of pretension, snobbery, and a double agent of deception (because, when false, it beckons us with promises of precisely that truth). The evolution across thousands of years of taste in wine has revealed fundamental things about the people who expressed (and repressed) those tastes.

Frances Yates, legendary historian of the art of memory, writes that when Charlemagne wished to restore the educational system of antiquity to the Carolingian empire after hundreds of years of barbarism, he summoned the scholar Alcuin, who wrote the following dialogue:

> CHARLEMAGNE: What, now are you to say about Memory, which I deem to be the noblest part of rhetoric?
>
> ALCUIN: What indeed unless I repeat the words of Marcus Tullius that "memory is the treasure-house of all things and unless it is made custodian of the thought-out things and words, all will come to nothing."

From Homer through Primo Levi, we've learned that if there is a sacred trust that passes from one year to another, from one generation to the next, it is that testimony to experience, no matter how gruesome, is essential for our moral survival. Bearing witness and preserving memory is the bedrock of civilization. Wine is memory in its most liquid and dynamic form.

Taste and Power

Simonides of Ceos, the sixth-century BC pre-Socratic poet, said to be the inventor of the Greek art of memory, was asked by a queen whether it was better to be born rich or a genius. He replied, "Rich, for genius is ever found at the gates of the rich." Taste is always subservient to power—though the great irony is that whenever true taste is expressed, power is subverted. The expression of taste is an expression of freedom. The moment you abdicate responsibility for your own taste is the moment you voluntarily abdicate your freedom. When you rely on others to largely determine your tastes, you are undermining your own liberty. Kant, among other philosophers, believed that judgments of taste are an expression of human autonomy, symbols of moral freedom.

The time we live in is quite peculiar. It seems to be distinguished by the voluntary, mass relinquishing of this liberty, from cinema to politics, from wine to academia (political correctness is nothing less than a voluntary suppression of one's own tastes). We speak of the "taste for power," but often that taste for power is merely power itself and is in fact a substitute for the absence of taste. One generally seeks power because one has no taste. That is, one doesn't have the means to make taste an expression of one's power. Power naturally accrues to those who do have taste. The difference is in the seeking of it. This distinction in wine and cinema is apparent everywhere.

Film producers—those responsible for the financing and administration of film production—can express this division quite clearly and brutally. They are anxious to be around artists, writers, directors, actors, people who try to express their taste for their living. But insecure producers can become deeply resentful of the power that gathers around these people because of their taste. They sometimes seek to *unproduce* as their only available means of expression. They look to undo, sabotage, actually undermine their own film productions, in an attempt to assert power over the artists, out of the rage of knowing either that they have no taste or that they lack the courage to express it if they do. And at least in this way, they insert themselves in a venerable tradition of arts patronage.

After my second feature film, *Sunday*, catapulted me, briefly, to Hollywood's attention, my new agent explained to me, "The only rule you'll need to know here is this: studio executives and their producers are in the business of saying no, of *not* making films." "Why?" I asked naïvely. "Because the minute they say yes to a film, their taste and reputation, their job, is on the line. The clearest path to being a successful producer or studio executive is a career of saying no to movies." Those in power often fear taste. Because the expression of taste devolves power back to the self, away from the voice of authority, the corporation, the institution, the state.

I recently saw Ettore Scola's *La Nuit de Varennes* for the first time in many years. From my first viewing as an eighteen-year-old through later viewings in my twenties, I thought it was a slight, if charming entertainment. This was my inexperience. Its depth and brilliance are subtly disguised behind the lightness, the ludic tone (much like a high-acid, impossibly low-alcohol Riesling from the Mosel Valley). Twenty-five years on, I now understand that *Il Mondo Nuovo*, as it's called in Italian, is a profoundly graceful meditation on the irreconcilable tension between notions of liberty and matters of taste. Scola is surely one of the most underrated of the great Italian directors, author of at least four masterpieces (in my opinion): *Nuit de Varennes, The Most Wonderful Evening of My Life, A Special Day*, and *We All Loved Each Other So Much*. I think his reputation, in fifty years' time, will eclipse that of Visconti, De Sica, and Rossellini . . . and he'll be viewed alongside Pasolini and Fellini as part of the great Italian cinema trinity. (If, at the very least, this last phrase hasn't provoked some disagreement of taste with the reader, then one of us isn't doing our job.)

The twinned heroes of *Varennes* are Jean-Louis Barrault and Marcello Mastroianni, two of the most charming and complex masculine presences in the history of French and Italian cinema. Here Marcello is a physically decaying but cuttingly aware Giacomo Casanova, a deliquescent aesthete hovering on the periphery of radical political change. Barrault is Restif de la Bretonne, witty and libidinous chronicler of his times and someone more sympathetic to the demands of the people as they hunt down the fleeing Louis XVIth in the spring of 1791.

What emerges from their adventures from Paris to the border town of Varennes is a delightful expression of the struggle between taste and justice. While Mastroianni-Casanova is himself a victim of power (he's in fact fleeing from his role as court jester to German nobles), his sympathies as a fop, a dandy, a lover of pleasures, a man of consummate good taste—and unquenchable tastes—lie completely with the collapsing ancien régime. He remarks acidly to Barrault-Bretonne, as they take a midnight pee side by side, that "The play has changed. The audience has taken over the stage from the actors."

Is he a defender of aristocratic taste and privilege (or of *terroir*)? Is he an apologist for the status quo? Yes and no, since Mastroianni-Casanova—part of the genius of Scola is to induce us to view actor and character as twin spirits—is a radical and a libertine, a subversive, a maker of tastes as much as a follower. He is also enough of an outsider and permanent alien, as he freeloads off the various European courts, never to feel at home with any established order. His taste is therefore both for and against progress—or rather, like all tastemakers, he is for progress when it coincides with his taste, and against it when it does not.

Barrault-Bretonne is more clearly radical, but no less ambiguous. He is by his own description a chronicler or journalist, a voyeur, a filmmaker, as it were. He is someone who wishes both to observe and to participate, in a perverted sort of way (the only plausible definition of a film director). His taste perhaps could best be described as in opposition to any status quo. When he is with the aristocrat, played by the incomparable Fassbinderian muse, Hanna Schygulla, he argues for the rights of the people; when with the people, for the delight of the refinement of the ancien régime. Above all, he is against "la pensée unique"—any orthodoxy.

But the nostalgia that Barrault-Bretonne seems to feel as the king's person and authority crumble, a nostalgia for the *dolcezza di vivere* (of which he took less than the crumbs) is contradicted by his instinctive sympathies for anyone denied his liberty, denied power. Seemingly against his own taste, his better judgment, he joins the people at journey's end. It's bittersweet, the sentiment that we're left with—Scola's and Barrault-Bretonne's—a haunting suggestion that we cannot have liberty *and* refinement, justice for all *and* good taste. It touches on one of the essential paradoxes of what constitutes democracy in taste, one of the other central pursuits of this book.

This Is Not a Guide (nor a Pipe)

Wine is intimate. After sex, wine, like food—as Bill Buford points out in *Heat*, his hilarious and profound rumination on our food culture—is the most personal contact the outside world can have with your body. Your taste in and of wine becomes an essential—and literal—part of your identity.

This book is not a guide. I'm against wine guides and against a culture that induces us to submit our own tastes to the perverse rule of self-proclaimed experts. After all, would you leave your sexual tastes in the hands of a guru? Though this book is adamantly not a guide, it *is* the product of more than forty years of drinking wine. And as Paris has been—repeatedly—my base for traveling the world, I thought to take you on a tour of its wine shops and restaurants as a launching point for wine travels together across the globe, from Rio de Janeiro, where I now live; to New York, where I used to live; to Madrid, where I've never lived. Inevitably, I'll lead you to the wines that have given me the deepest satisfactions and provoked the greatest indignation. (It's not me, wine *is* anthropomorphic.)

So you could call this an involuntary guidebook, from not so much a reluctant guide as a guide with no pretense other than to offer a tour of his personal experience. I am not the voice of authority. My judgments, while I hope considered and grounded in experience, are not in any way definitive. This book in some ways is a polemic against all those critics and arbiters who purport to speak with authority and are taking most of the fun and almost all the culture out of wine these days. But in order to offer a credible questioning of their taste and authority, I have to expose my own taste, while inviting you to question my authority (a classic ruse, I know, for imposing it more forcefully).

Ultimately, this journey is an invitation to discover your freedom to taste.

2

LEGRAND

The Old Curiosity Shop

Liquid Madeleines

Wine bottles to me are not inanimate objects. And not just because the liquid inside them is biochemically alive. The shape of the bottle, the label, with its carefully printed place names, family names, and year of harvest, both evoke deeply human stories that remain vital even once the contents are consumed. When I see a wine bottle, I travel in space—of course to the place the wine comes from (if its identity and personality have been respected), but also to the place, people, and circumstances where it was consumed.

The bottle becomes the intersection of at least two strands of memory. I travel in time, in a way that is multiple, mutable, and unique. And not just because of the year of the harvest printed on the label, or the passage of time—if the wine was allowed to grow up, to age into wisdom or senility (or both!). A wine bottle is also time travel because it not only records the memory of its origins, but also evokes the memories of its destination. And not necessarily cloudy, nostalgic ones. The more precise and detailed the wine, the more complex and lucid is the association when that bottle is encountered a second time.

When I enter a wine shop—a magical place for me since adolescence (an arrested adolescent replacement for the childhood delights of a toy shop?)—or when I scan a restaurant wine list, I feel a surge of excitement, like someone arriving at the doorstep of a potential love affair. A tour of places in Paris where wine is critical—wine shops and restaurants—becomes for me a kind of triple Proustian journey. I might go back in time with one glance (a bottle last drunk or seen years before), forward with another (there are millions of bottles that are unknown to me that I hope one day to meet), and rooted in the present with a third turn of the head (because the choice of wines is like a choice of friends: it instantly reveals character and taste).

So in order to give concrete form to the following tale, I decided to spend several weeks back in Paris, visiting some old wine haunts and discovering potential new ones, in order to see how my liquid madeleines were faring.

Ghosts of Wines Past

On a bitingly cold November morning in Paris, I cross the halfhearted excuse for a park where the Les Halles market used to be. The unhappy medley of trees and concrete has been redesigned a number of times, but always with the same purpose: to hide the new "Les Halles" from sight. But the tawdry multilevel underground shopping mall extrudes from its grave anyway. In fact, it's a double grave. Or an upside-down grave. Because this sprawling, lifeless subterranean mess was built in the 1970s in the area *underneath* the home of the legendary outdoor market of Paris.

I remember coming here as a small child with my mother in the mid-1960s, when it was the mecca for produce and meat for the entire city. People from all classes—housewives, bohemians, traders from the nearby stock exchange, and restaurateurs—flocked to this geographical center of Paris bursting with (above-ground) life. Les Halles was the belly that fed the bellies of Paris. My earliest memories are of the rustic, Chardin-tinged colors of the fruit and vegetables, much less bright and shiny than today's produce, but rich and varied in detail and tone—infinitely fascinating for a little boy of three, four, five.

Just as captivating were the earthy, acrid smells of the surrounding cafés and the bitter, acidic, ruby red wine that the men in blue overalls were swilling from early morning on. The sharpness of these smells was consistent with the sharpness of taste I knew from the finger measures of wine my parents fed us four boys at home. My palate adjusted early to acidity, tartness, lightness—wines that were neither better nor worse than the global *vin ordinaire* of today, but were much less heavy, less obviously pigmented, and less sugared.

Laborers from the Middle Ages onward drank a thin, tart red wine during their lunch breaks. It was often no more than 6 or 7 percent alcohol (as opposed to the 12 to 14 percent that is now standard from the Loire to New Zealand). It was always a safer choice than water up until at least the nineteenth century. But I often wonder if they chose wine over water because in those lighter, tangier wines there wasn't also more energy, a brightness, a spur to reaction, a dynamism. Seeing the Les Halles workers knocking back their *verre de rouge* at any hour, I took in with my own eyes the notion of *vin comme carburant*, wine as pick-me-up.

You could say that amid frequent trips with my mother—an avid cook and an untethered, if not entirely free spirit—to the sharp-edged, pluralistic rough-and-tumble of the marketplace, with all its character-istically Parisian hidden passageways, my palate, my sense of wine, was formed by mystery, acid, and a certain notion of democracy.

The Caves Legrand Today

But the biting cold of a recent November morning doesn't remind me at all of my childhood. This kind of extreme temperature is the pure product of twenty-first century global warming. So I leave behind the ghosts of 1960s Les Halles and cross the Place des Victoires, into yet another century, where the forbidding Louis XIVth façades seem equally closed off against the gray-blue chill. I enter the rue de Banque and try the front entrance of the Caves Legrand, one of Paris's most venerable wine shops (though from this side, it looks more like the antique grocery store it used to be). The gates are pulled shut.

I walk farther up the street and duck into the Galerie Vivienne. Built in 1823, this enclosed shopping arcade is one of the bourgeois jewels of the Empire style. It's also one of the rare places of great architectural charm that's resisted either a soul-removing renovation or the inevitable mummification that occurs when a building is reduced to a tourist attraction. Running the length of a city block, but narrow and elegant in its interior arcade, it houses not only the Caves Legrand wine shop but also restaurants, clothes shops, a hairdresser's, and a used-book shop. In other words it's an active, absolutely contemporary shopping "mall," but with vital links to its remembered past, a place as much for locals as for visitors, history in action: yet another possible definition of *terroir*.

From the interior gallery entrance, the Caves Legrand with its Beaux Arts woodwork untouched since 1900, is so "authentic" that it actually appears fake. It seems exactly like what a tourist—or a transatlantic film director—would conjure up for a wine shop. It reads "Ye Olde Paris," a quaint museum piece, an image for sale. But that's totally misleading. In fact, the Caves Legrand has such vitality that, like the surrounding "Galerie," it's absolutely contemporary.

Why? Because the choice of wines is so astutely selected that it remains of a piece with (the best of) its era. Actually, the wine shop has reflected (and sometimes created) contemporary trends in a continuous evolution since Lucien Legrand took over from his father in 1945 and converted it from a grocery store. To the bags of store-roasted coffee beans, Lucien added barrels of wines he bought at the Bercy wine depot in the eastern end of Paris. (Bercy itself was torn down and turned into an office complex and shopping mall in the 1980s.) He bottled all the wines himself from barrel, adding the label "bottled by the master grocer." For the next forty years, Legrand was a meeting place for neighborhood wine lovers. They would sit at a table off to the side, drinking and gossiping and sampling the new wines that Lucien would uncover from his trips to Bercy and to the vineyards themselves (including the first samples in Paris of Aimé Guibert's now internationally famous Mas de Daumas Gassac).

Lucien's daughter Francine took over the shop in the mid 1980s. By this time, with most of the better vignerons* (winemakers) bottling their own wine, she shifted the emphasis to more conventional bottle sales. In 2000, diagnosed with cancer, she sold the Caves Legrand to one of her dad's regulars, Gérard Sibourd-Baudry and a partner, Christian de Châteauvieux.

Legrand: First Time Around

I don't remember the first time I went to Legrand, but it must have been in the mid 1980s, when Francine had taken over. I was a beginning filmmaker and a marginal sommelier in New York (whereas today I'm a marginal filmmaker with the spirit of a novice sommelier). When I would return to Paris twenty years ago it was as a semi-impoverished visitor. But like all wine lovers, I always spent, on wine, way beyond my means. I'd hunt down less-known bottles or wines from less-ballyhooed vintages—even downright lousy years—but from the best vignerons. This in fact is a buying strategy I've continued happily to this day. The principle for me is that a so-called mediocre Fellini is always going to be better than even the greatest Luc Besson (however overheated the press and marketing get on the latter's latest release).

But the wine shop attendants at Legrand always intimidated me a little, with that inevitable soupçon of contempt. I thought at the time it

---

*I will use the term *vigneron* in this book instead of *winemaker* or the even more awkward, if more suggestive, *winegrower*, because it more accurately expresses the craft of those who are responsible for the making of the wine but who view their work as farmers in the field tending to the vines as equally if not more critical than the vinification process. They also believe that their contributions are an extension of the work of the *terroir* and of nature and therefore find it presumptuous to be called "wine*makers*."

was because of my age, or because I was a foreigner (even if a virtual native French speaker). Today, having been bullied into and out of choices from New York to São Paulo, I understand that wine shop arrogance is "democratic" and ubiquitous. But my thirst for good wine always outweighed my anxiety in the face of social intimidation. At Legrand, on my frequent visits, I'd find a lot of the great (my great) vignerons at relatively terrestrial prices; the Volnays of Montille, the Meursaults of Lafon, the Chambolles of Georges Roumier, the Jura wines of Puffeney, and the sublime, singular Chinons of Charles Joguet.

Both a farmer and a painter (one way or another, a guy who gets his hands dirty), Charles Joguet is an archetypally French bon vivant and gleeful rule-buster, and the spitting image of the great actor Michel Simon, star of many Jean Renoir films, including *Boudu Saved from Drowning*. Single-handedly, Joguet restored the reputation of the wines of Chinon, probably for the first time since native son François Rabelais sang its praises in the sixteenth century. What happened to Charles Joguet himself, the tragedy of his estate and the bottles that surfaced over the following years at Legrand, would acquire a fablelike aura during my current tour of Paris wine shops.

But when I came to Paris in October of 1996, I was looking for the finishing funds for my film *Sunday*. It had already been shot and edited but lacked the financing necessary to complete it (much like a finished wine without the means to bottle it). But my love story among marginal New Yorkers and the homeless struck as inaudible a chord with French production companies, as it did in the United States. A two-week round of the more progressive distributors yielded the typical independent filmmaker's harvest: a tattered ego and a backpack filled with personally recuperated homemade copies of the film. I remember that I avoided even going to the neighborhood of Legrand, for fear of spending money I didn't have. I think I must have felt just as precarious emotionally as financially. Not up to confronting the Parisian "wine police," it occurred to me that buying wine can sometimes be as daunting as trying to finance a film.

I have better memories of Legrand linked to my next film, *Signs &*

Wonders, though ironically that film only existed thanks to *Sunday*'s eventual reversal of fortune. A few weeks after my disastrous trip to Paris, I found out that *Sunday*, a fiction film made without money or powerful backers, had been selected in competition at the Sundance Film Festival. For an independent film, that's like getting an Oscar nomination. And when *Sunday* most improbably won the Grand Prize for best film and best screenplay, my life as a filmmaker was transformed. The film world finally opened up to me after ten years of struggles as an assistant director (including a delirious stint as assistant to Adrian Lyne on *Fatal Attraction*) and a first feature, *Resident Alien*, about the last days of New York's bohemia, that remained as marginal as its subject. After Sundance, I got an invitation to Cannes (even though the film had been rejected by the august French festival pre-Sundance win), excellent distribution deals across the globe, agents in Hollywood (two of them!), and a contract with Fox Searchlight to make a new film with my writing partner, James Lasdun. Exactly the same people who had pronounced *Sunday* "without interest and without a future" six months before were now spouting phrases like "instant classic." If I was able to avoid being duped by these sirens of power masquerading as judges of taste, it was in great part thanks to wine.

Escape to New York

Ironically, at exactly the moment that I no longer needed to earn my keep as a sommelier, this parallel career also started to take off. In addition to working with small, homey downtown dives like Rice, Ñ, and Il Buco (the last, relatively undiscovered at first, was "divey" in origin and intent), I was given the chance by Keith McNally, legendary New York restaurateur, to do two lists, a small-scale, high-end one at his then-fashionable supper club Pravda, and an ambitious lineup at Balthazar, a Parisian-inspired brasserie of gargantuan scale. From the time that it opened in the spring of 1997, and for at least four years thereafter, Balthazar was not only one of the most sought-after tables on the jet-set circuit, but it also sold more wine per capita than any other restaurant in the city. The biggest miracle was that McNally allowed me to do something unheard-of in New York at that time: a substantial list devoted entirely to artisanal producers of largely organic wine, from the humblest to the mightiest names in France. Furthermore the list was classified by region and *terroir*, whereas most wine lists in the United States are composed according to grape variety, just as most films are sold according to their star, not their story or their author. Even more radical, the list was 100 percent French. And this, it seems, was shocking, since even the most refined and snobby French restaurants in the city yield not only a lot of room to the pressures from the Californian wine industry but often extra space for Italian wines (in part to accommodate the Mafia-dominated wine trucking network, a fellow sommelier once quipped).

Balthazar's business manager told me and Keith that given the $5 million already invested before the doors opened, an extensive and exclusively French list, and one not defined by the star system of grape varieties, was a form of financial suicide. Funny how these words echoed those of the film distributors who first saw *Sunday*, an equally starless, artisanal production. But Keith is not only one of the canniest and most innovative of New York's restaurateurs, he also happens to be an independent filmmaker himself. Son of a London cabbie, he built up a succession of clubs and restaurants in the eighties and nineties that were always a step ahead of the latest hipsters. He began with Odeon, which announced the slicker (but still edgy) reinvention of Warhol's Downtown in 1980, continued through Nell's—in my experience the last truly, unpredictably glamorous and heterogeneous club in the city—to Pravda, the first of the yuppie-chic lounges (but the only congenial and eclectic one) that marked the 1990s era of intolerance under Mayor Giuliani, the man who transformed New York from a city of heterodox culture into the most orthodox of shopping destinations.

The cultural glory of the city had always been rooted in its unapologetic cosmopolitanism, the fluid exchange between all classes and all levels of achievement. The friction between its financial and media power and the constrictive geography of Manhattan made that power subject to a democracy of taste. I lived this New York, the city my father grew up in, intermittently from the late 1970s up through my first wine list, made in 1988 for a restaurant on the corner of Avenue C and Ninth Street. At the time, that slab of the East Village was still considered dangerous by nonresidents, and it's true that drug dealers prowled most parts of the sidewalk. The restaurant where I worked was called Bernard's, owned by a beefy Gérard Depardieu knockoff who was among the first chefs to realize he could sell to uptowners the concept of "organic" as downtown chic. But seduced by the local (street) wares, he abandoned the restaurant and disappeared from sight. I then organized the staff, found an investor (thanks to Keith McNally), and reopened as Métèque, a socialist cooperative where everyone down to the illegal Mexican dishwashers would share in the profits—had there been any. Alas, this utopian venture, like others of its kind, lasted six months, closing just after our Un–Bastille Day celebration, when we honored the cuisines of France's ex-colonies. The closing was a slap in the face for more than just my political ideals. It also served as a classic first comeuppance for any young person with creative ambitions.

I acquired my love for the taste of wine as a small child when it was first dropped into my mouth or mixed in a glass with water. I then cultivated that taste as an adolescent—doubtless, for dubious social reasons: out of snobbery as well as the search for ever more effective means of finding—and then keeping (aloft)—a girlfriend. But wine also became a teenage passion because I discovered that it was as intellectually and historically complex a subject as painting or literature. And my appetite for the pleasures of the mind was almost as large as for those of the flesh. And certainly at that age, more easily fulfilled.

I spent the following years writing down the name, region, vintage, and author of every wine I tasted, attempting also to describe its character. For a long time, I fell into the prolonged pubescent trap (carried into adulthood by most so-called wine professionals) of describing the wines by association with every conceivable fruit, flower, and organic matter—I at least stopped at the inorganic—but gradually the absurdity and narcissism of this exercise led me to locate a given wine in the context of how and where and with whom I drank it. The specific sub-jectivity of the wine-drinking experience became clear to me, though it didn't mean that taste and perception were infinitely relative. That's a postmodern position as fatuous as the eternal adolescent notion of applying definitive judgments. But by always writing about the human and environmental particularities surrounding the tasting of a given wine, I did begin to see the joy and freedom of complex and mutable judgments. I also ended up with a diary of the evolution of my own taste that, however callow, trained my palate and my mind to work together. Even as I studied the wine authors I still admire today— Kermit Lynch, Hugh Johnson, Oz Clarke, Stephen Brook, even Matt Kramer (for me, Kramer is among the most lucid and talented, even if ethically questionable, of American wine writers*)—it allowed me to appropriate the experience of drinking wine for myself.

By the time I did my first wine list at Bernard's, in my midtwenties, I had more than just a cursorily gained sommelier's certificate. I had an entire childhood's worth of suppressed desire to communicate my taste to the world. As with many first-time novelists, my first effort at public expression was self-consciously radical and entirely solipsistic. Only the tiniest winegrowers from the least recognized regions would do, wines that no one had ever heard of (and few would eventually buy). I tracked down the few organic wine suppliers of that time. One in particular became a friend, Michael Skurnik. A shaggy-haired, rock-and-roll garage musician from Long Island, Michael would drive up to the cor-ner of Ninth and C and pull sometimes refermenting, rather skanky samples out of the back of his old station wagon. The skankier the bet-ter was my mantra, as I hauled the frothing symbols of rebellious taste into the restaurant. It's a tribute to Skurnik as a taster and a business-

---

*Kramer's *Making Sense of Wine* is one of the rare wine books that never dumbs down but does make skillfully intelligible even the most abstruse of wine notions. It may be the best wine primer in English. On the other hand, what are we to make of his critical judgment given his self-proclaimed friendships with the people he writes about as a journalist, most notoriously with Lalou Bize-Leroy, banished former co-director of the famed Romanée-Conti estate, gray market speculator in her own wines and creator of Burgundy's most brand-driven and ostenta-tiously *hedge-fund*-priced bottles?

man, as well as a sign that there are many hugely positive developments in the current wine world, that twenty years later he's the most commercially successful of all the high-quality wine importers and distributors in the United States, and that he and all of his comparable colleagues now sell a majority of organic (but no longer skanky!) wines.

At any rate, the Bernard/Météque chef Chris Gaddess's commitment to organic produce was as sincere as mine was to wine. The restaurant, in both its incarnations, was a pioneer in combining a conviction about the ethics and origins of food with a sophisticated execution. Our customers included locals and uptown folk, many of whom, terrorized by their only contact with the notorious neighborhood, ran to the front entrance from the taxi or limo that dropped them at the curb, providing us with a nightly comedy loop. Artists from the neighborhood included fabled documentary filmmaker (and equally legendary ladies' man) Emile de Antonio, Robert Rauschenberg, NYU students, their Tompkins Square neighbors Iggy Pop and David Bowie, and disoriented musical novices who'd drift down from CBGB looking for sustenance of one kind but who were usually happy even if they ended up with just a plate of our food. The vibe was so tolerant and eclectic that semi-impoverished kids felt as at home in the restaurant as any star. Or rather, the reverse. Bowie could be sure to have a bite at Météque (née Bernard) without feeling like he would be gawked at. We all shared the same city.

The *terroir* of New York, its soul and sense of place, unlike say a Burgundian *terroir*, was dependent on a continuous and radical reinvention of its past. This reinvention in fact was its *terroir*. And it's hard to imagine a more fertile one anywhere. This was true as much for established rockers like Iggy Pop as for any struggling young musician. But when Giuliani came to power, everything changed. Or, rather, he fixed things such that the constant democratic change and reinvention could no longer occur. He systematically eradicated all of the heterodox vitality of the city, expelling the homeless—I used to watch cops at the start of his regime literally scoop them off the Little Italy streets where I lived—allowing real estate speculators to destroy much of the complex patina of the city's marginal, yet culturally essential, neighborhoods, and creating a Disneyworld not just on Forty-second Street, but also up, down, and across town. He created an island ghetto for the rich in an ever increasing sea of faceless high-rises, a vast commercial mall for the omnivorous consumer of power, for the *consumer* of taste, edging out the last dissenters who believed that the *creation* of taste was sufficient power in itself.

Struggling artists, musicians, and journalists no longer have the means to live in Manhattan (aka New York). They're now dispersed across the vast swaths of Brooklyn, Queens, and New Jersey. This is a phenomenon with two effects. Those who stay, who have already "made it," can no longer be nourished in the same way by waves of new kids, and each day become a little more complacent. The kids who come to New York, those still in search of the legendary ferment, are so dispersed across the flatlands that the historic friction that created Manhattan can no longer goad them. Only now when I look back at *Resident Alien*, my first feature film, which I shot around the East Village in 1988 and '89, do I realize that it was an unconscious elegy to the end of the bohemian dream, the end of a personal notion of New York authenticity. And I suppose it's not accidental that this Grail-like search for *terroir*, for the "authentic," continues through my love of wine.

Already in 1997, when Balthazar opened in the last remains of Soho (before the area's total transformation into branded outdoor mall), I wasn't sure that wine redolent of place and conviction could find a home. But luckily Keith McNally's business savvy is matched by a romantic spirit. He was intrigued by the idea of a wine list as a personal expression of taste, as an homage to a vibrant and chic but profoundly democratic New York that he also felt was disappearing. He was happy that a fashionable place could be accessible to those with taste but little money, and his door policy tried to encourage that eclecticism even as it was eroded from the city around him. It obviously amused him as well that a list of extremely fairly priced organic wine, by now from recognized producers of the highest artisanal quality—$12 a bottle for a Muscadet, through $30 red Burgundies to a (comparatively cheap because of its rarity) $2,000 1945 Chambolle-Musigny Blanc—would be served up to Madonna, Richard Branson, Woody Allen, and the revolving waves of jet-setters and hipsters. During the subsequent years, without even realizing it, those people accustomed to the most cynical gastronomic gestures on the planet (it's axiomatic that those who spend the most will be the greatest victims of the cynicism of others in matters of taste) would unconsciously be imbibing some of the world's purest, most quixotic wines at nonexploitive prices.

And if Keith maintained the list much as I made it, even once I'd gone off to Paris and Greece to shoot my next film, it's maybe because the notions of "ethical wine" and economic success are not incompatible. We're so accustomed nowadays to make a cynical distinction (or worse, the opposite: a confusion) between acts of commerce and acts of culture that wines of *terroir* offer a provocative counterexample. An honest engagement with the earth (free of chemicals) and a wish to express the character of a place (over the simple expression of ego) that is at the heart of *terroir* wines allows us—city dwellers everywhere—to construct an ethical relation with not just the product itself, but perhaps even one another. The thousands of bottles sold each month at Balthazar (and the weekly attempts at bribery from a legion of wine distributors to place even a few wines on the list) were proof that this is no utopian fantasy.

Legrand: Second Time Around
SIGNS & WONDERS

Despite my post-Sundance contract with Hollywood to write *Signs & Wonders*, an ironic psychological thriller inspired by Polish writer Witold Gombrowicz's blackly absurdist novel *Cosmos*, it became clear to me after six months that the cultural divide—despite sincere efforts on both sides—was insuperable. I went out several times to Los Angeles with my co-screenwriter, James Lasdun, the very fine British poet and prose writer living in New York, whom I'd co-opted, with great luck, into the world of movies. We tried to see if we could find a common language for the script with the executives at Fox. Each time, I was struck by the parallel between their vision of film and my understanding of Californian wine. In both cases, the "California taste" can be admired for its intelligent design and consistency of purpose. But it's also clear that this model leaves little room, in wine and cinema, for the kind of accidental pleasures and historical dimension that are essential for my happiness.

So in the spring of '98 Marin Karmitz, legendary—even notorious—producer of European cinema for five decades, offered to have his French company, MK2, take over the production of *Signs & Wonders*. I then moved to Athens to begin the preparations for the shoot, but I often went to Paris for meetings and casting, including a memorable first meeting with eventual lead Charlotte Rampling. I showed up (inexcusably) late for our first lunch and was astonished—and thrilled—to see that she had already ordered a bottle of wine (a solid Médoc) and blithely had it already opened and served. Having just come from Los Angeles, where no actor could afford to be seen drinking a light beer at a casting lunch, I sensed that I'd made the right choice in opting, in a sense, for taste over power, predilection over ambition. This was confirmed, when the other lead actor, Stellan Skarsgard, made only one condition for accepting his part: that I bring sufficient cases of French, Italian, and German wine to soften the shooting conditions in Athens, an unabashedly abrasive, brutal, noisy, and polluted city (and a strange echo of New York in the seventies).

So each trip back to Paris would mean a visit to the Legrand wine shop, which in turn meant that the anxious atmosphere of our psychological thriller could be relieved nightly by bottles of Jean-Marie Raveneau's Chablis, the Rieslings of Zind-Humbrecht, and the last vintages of the supremely talented Loire Valley vigneron Charles Joguet, especially from his magical vineyards in Chinon, the Clos de la Dioterie and the Chêne Vert, the latter with its old vines planted around a regal seventeenth-century oak tree. I didn't realize it at the time, but these were the last wines made by Charles Joguet still on the market. By 1998, he'd already been forced to sell not only his vineyards but also his name, a tragic event for the wine world that I would later get a taste of first-hand.

Legrand: Third Time Around
FILMING *MONDOVINO* WITH YVONNE

In October 2002, during the filming of *Mondovino*, the feature film about the world of wine that I made after *Signs & Wonders*, it was Yvonne Hégoburu, a seventy-six-year-old vigneronne from the Pyrénées mountains who would bring me back to Legrand. She had organized a tasting of her delicious Jurançon white wines at the venerable wine shop, and I came by to film a little atmosphere.

I'd met Yvonne only once, eight months previously. But it was a memorable meeting. A young sommelier in a restaurant in the southwestern city of Pau had mentioned her one evening as a colorful local figure. I called her the next morning at eight and arranged to drop by to see her in her vineyards right after, planning to spend an hour with her on a kind of casting session before moving on to meet another three or four potential vigneron protagonists for my film. I left her magical mountainside property nine hours later, having been so enchanted that my casting test was transformed into a full shoot day with one of the eventual stars of *Mondovino*. Dressed in sneakers, jeans, and a woolly sweater, bounding around the steep slopes of her vineyards with her huge sheepdogs, Yvonne seemed like a woman twenty years younger than her age. As she plunged her hands into the clay and limestone soil, caressing each vine like a distinct being, her commitment to the land and organic farming was so palpable that I couldn't help but be seduced. Here was a woman intensely "of the earth." So, what a shock to see her eight months later, dressed in a form-fitting Chanel suit, wafting around the chic Galerie Vivienne of Legrand among a crowd of Parisians equally attentive to their image.

While I was at the property, something of her paradoxical nature had already emerged. Yvonne planted her fourteen acres of vines in 1985, six months after her husband, René, died of lung cancer at the age of sixty-five, an explicit homage to him and to his career as a journalist. They had met, she told me, in 1944, while he was an active member of the Resistance against the Nazis. After the war, he went to work for the local newspaper in the nearby city of Pau and became, by her account, a muckraking investigative reporter and an active member of the Left. Or at least he considered himself a socialist until François Mitterrand and the Socialist Party finally came to power in 1981, their first victory since the war. A freethinker at the end of the day, more than an ideologue, in a robust journalistic tradition, René Hégoburu believed his job was to challenge any expression of power. It took this fierce Basque, said Yvonne, a half day of seeing the socialists at work to declare himself "once again, in the opposition."

As Yvonne told me about her husband—laughing at him, at herself, going off on tangents to talk about the challenges of farming land without the aid of herbicides or pesticides—there was something in the tender self-mockery of her manner and the transparency of her feelings that reminded me of my own mother. There was also something uncanny about the parallels between her husband and my father, not least of which that my dad was a progressive but fiercely iconoclastic investigative reporter who died of lung cancer at the age of sixty-six. A trained economist and committed Keynesian, his experience of Roosevelt's New Deal provided him with an intellectual and social foundation for his career as a reporter. But across five books and thousands of articles for the *Washington Post, New York Times,* and magazines including *The New York Review of Books, The Progressive,* and *The Nation,* he prided himself on his ability to gore sacred cows of the Left as often as those on the Right. My father believed it was a journalist's moral obligation to question all uses of power and to fight any restraint on absolute freedom of expression. I grew up in an era in which I believed that these ideals belonged exclusively to the Left. I now understand that it's an ethical engagement that exists in the place of ideology.

So I was especially moved that fall afternoon at Legrand when

Yvonne introduced me to her son, Jean-René, child of a fiercely combative independent journalist father and of a free-spirited, hyperbolic mother. And despite the somewhat prim wine-tasting crowd that overran the wine shop into the covered gallery, I imagined that I was shaking hands with someone with a common *terroir*. But the forty-five-year-old Jean-René, an accomplished corporate lawyer, seemed less than eager to chat about our possible commonality. It reminded me, as he shuffled back into the crowd, that the *terroir* that one recognizes for oneself is not necessarily obliged to reciprocate the feeling. Yvonne took me aside and explained that Jean-René's reticence that afternoon had much to do with his having no intention to leave his Paris law practice to take over the family winery in the Southwest. This of course is a perfectly reasonable position, but as Yvonne spoke, it reminded me of the problem that haunts the Charles Joguet winery, a problem that seems to me fundamental to an understanding of the human and cultural complexity of wine.

It's of course not uncommon for a father or mother, from artists to doctors, to wish for their children to follow in their footsteps. But in most cases the only thing at stake is what the person from each generation wants for himself. For the work of an artist or filmmaker to survive, to have meaning and value beyond his own life (we'll leave discussions of posterity aside, pace Orson Welles*), it's in no way dependent on his children or anyone else continuing and developing the work itself. With winegrowers, on the other hand, their work will disappear when the last bottle from their last vintage is gone. Or if, upon the vigneron's death, the winery is taken up by someone with fundamentally different values, his life's work will also dissolve. A vigneron's opus, constructed across years of activity, cannot survive a succession by someone who doesn't share a profoundly common ground (sense of *terroir*) or who is incapable of reinvention without destruction (much like traditional New York).

---

*It was Orson Welles who said "the only thing more vulgar than working for money is working for posterity."

In the case of Yvonne, her current situation is both better and worse than domaines with long histories. It's better precisely because if she has no successor, there will be a loss of only twenty odd years' work, comparatively modest in comparison with, say, the Joguet domain, with its several centuries of (agri)cultural transmission. But her situation seems to me at the same time more dire precisely because she has courageously created a sense of *terroir* and identity practically ex nihilo at the end of her life. And her titanic struggle to survive economically—she's been in the red and fighting off her bankers for virtually every year of the winery's existence—only makes this ageing widow's costly and risky commitment to organic wines of great quality that much more admirable. And unless her only son changes his mind, all this will evaporate on her death or the day she can no longer do the work herself. And still, lest romantic souls trip over themselves too quickly, the situation is paradoxical. Because what would it mean even if Jean-René decided to take over the property? After all, he has no training or culture as a vigneron or farmer. Would he be the right person to reinvent for a new generation, even if this vineyard is the most literal of expressions of the love between his parents?

I wondered why in these circumstances Yvonne continued to fight at her age, what kept her motivated to continue to create what would quite possibly end with her end? In what relation to life did these vines, planted in memory of her husband's death, now place Yvonne? The more I watched her mingling enthusiastically with the Paris crowd, the more she reminded me of my own mother, even though at that time my mother's energies had been greatly dissipated. I thought I saw in Yvonne (as I imagined I found in the taste of her wine) a similar fabulist streak, a certain awkward charm that was so pronounced it became graceful and, at the same time, a terribly touching, troubling fragility.

As I watched Yvonne thrive in her role of "artist at her opening," I had no idea that my mother, Jackie, the same age as Yvonne, had barely another three months to live. In fact my mother's death, while I was shooting in the farthest-flung regions of northern Argentina, brought an abrupt end to the three-year-old cycle of shoots for *Mondovino*.

After the funeral, on my return to New York, I immediately set to work editing. The editing process itself became a kind of active mourning, the emotion of the edit an homage to the spirit of my mother. And this felt like a good balance, since the act of filming often seemed like an unconscious dialogue with my father and his work.

That day, Yvonne continued to work the crowd. I noticed how her son edged himself into a corner, avoiding both his mother's gaze and the casual, probing eye of my camera. A waiter carried a bottle of one of Yvonne's sweet wines past my gaze. I saw the label: "Cuvée Marie-Katalyn," named in honor of her only grandchild. I couldn't help but do a quick calculation. Marie-Katalyn was born in 1993. She'll be twenty in . . .

Legrand Times Four
EDITING *MONDOVINO*, WITH AND WITHOUT JOGUET

I went back to live in Paris a year later, in October 2003, trying to finish the editing of *Mondovino*: five hundred hours of raw material, roughly six times more footage than any other film I'd made, took me two years to edit. I found a loft in the tenth arrondissement, on the rue du Faubourg du Temple, where I could work and live thanks to the spontaneous generosity of the landlady, Alexandra de Léal, an inimitable Parisian bohemian who became one of the cash-strapped film's guardian angels by reducing our rent to a manageable sum. The improbable altruism of Alexandra, whom I'd never met before, and the unpredictable energy of our multiethnic neighborhood—Algerians, Moroccans, Senegalese, Thais, Chinese, and Turks side by side with artists, filmmakers, and other urban conmen—made me feel like I'd stepped back into the New York I knew from the early eighties.

To fuel the Herculean—sometimes Sisyphean—editing labors and to assuage the anxiety of having devoted four years of my life already to a project with virtually no backing and fewer prospects, I used to open a bottle of white around six at night for whoever was slogging away with me. Principally I relied on the talents and energy of my young assistant, Laurent Gorse, a half Egyptian American, half French recent college graduate who more than honorably filled the role of cinema Sancho Panza. The editing table also saw frequent visits from my principal collaborator on the film, fellow filmmaker Juan Pittaluga, a Uruguayan living in Paris for the past fifteen years; and from my future wife, Paula Prandini, a Brazilian photographer. In fact, in an inexplicable gesture at the beginning of our relationship—proof of her love, of course—Paula was the only person to sit through a first cut that ran over six hours.

If the editing day extended beyond ten at night, I usually felt the need to open up a bottle of courage-sustaining red. Depending on the psychological balance of the day's work, we might have earlier drunk a bitingly dry Aligoté from Aubert de Villaine, an essentially dry but subtly perfumed Jurançon from Yvonne, or a soothing but still energetic off-dry Vouvray from Philippe Foreau, all of which cost less than eight euros. And during the first months, I'd still find at Legrand some of the legendary spirited, wholly original Chinon reds made by Charles Joguet himself, from the 1992 and 1993 vintages. But the stock soon ran out, and so one day I gave in and tried a few of the more recent vintages, 1998 and 2000. I brought these bottles back to the loft with some ambivalence. The labels were identical to the emptied bottles of the '92 Chinons propped on the shelves above the hundreds of editing cassettes. They carried the same name, the same *terroir*, the same visual designations. Any wine lover who'd heard of the magician Charles Joguet would have been happy to see this bottle of 2000 Chinon.

So why was I so anxious? Because the potential drama that underlies Yvonne's estate had already played out for real with Joguet. Without any children to take over, and deeply in debt, Joguet had sold the winery in 1997. The name of a vigneron who represented the apogee of artistic individuality had become reduced to a brand when the new owners kept the Joguet name. When I recently spotted a young man in a Tokyo wine shop with a bottle of 2002 Joguet in his hand, I thought, "Another innocent victim, ten thousand miles away." The wine drinkers across the globe, from Paris to New York to Tokyo, who now buy the wines of

"Charles" are in fact buying nothing more than the branded represen-
tation of the artisan, an increasingly common problem in every facet
of life.

However, it's important to point out that having tasted them
numerous times, I wouldn't say that the wines now labeled "Joguet" are
bad. But without the touch of the artisan-artist, the Joguet Chinons
have become banal. Which may be more dangerous. Even from his
greatest vineyards, the "Dioterie" and the "Chêne Vert," the wines lack
the detail, the complexity, and, above all else, the unpredictability—the
thrilling contradictions—that emerge only when there's a profound
symbiosis between man, vine, and *terroir*. This of course is true of any
art form. The magic of expression emerges only when the artist is able
to seize on—and transform—the accidental. In wine, it's certain that
neither monthly visits by a consultant enologist (the wine world's man-
agement consultants) nor weekly visits by a property owner (a factory
boss visiting the shop floor) nor daily observation by a technician (the
shop floor worker trying to design the company products) will allow
for the capture of ephemeral grace. The "post-Joguet" Joguets have simply lost their character: the scintillating edginess of the wines' textures,
the mysterious depths of their flavors.

And this absence of the artist is in fact a doubly painful irony.
Joguet, son of a peasant vigneron, managed to propel himself to art
school as a young man, studying in both Paris and New York, and
began a promising career as a painter before his father's death obliged
him to take over the modest family winery—and pour his artistry into
winemaking. But the state of these wines today would be as if we
walked into the Museum of Modern Art in New York to find efficient
copies of the Jackson Pollocks and the De Koonings. Worse, it would be
like presenting these copies as authentic. And imagine that this would
be legally sanctioned. You could be sure that the visitors to the galleries,
out of fear of asserting their own taste, of listening to their own reactions, would observe the flat and lifeless pseudo Pollocks and De Koonings and murmur "how great . . ."—if without much enthusiasm. In a
climate marked by the *fear of being mistaken*, people become unsure of

their own tastes. And so they abandon their tastes. Or, perhaps, they might say before the lightless copies: "I don't feel anything, but it must be me my fault because I don't know anything." And in this way, we understand how subtly the public's taste can be undermined. By subtle, unseen gestures, those in authority slowly strip people of their confidence to locate their own taste, their affirmation of their own individuality, their liberty. This is how Mussolinian propaganda functioned in the 1920s and '30s. This is how small- and large-scale corporate rebranding of previously human activities and products functions today.

One late night, in mid-January 2004, desperately trying to cut the edit of *Mondovino* down from five hours to a length presentable to the film's best hope, the Cannes Film Festival selection committee, I took a break for a bite. I made a sandwich and opened a bottle of '99 Clos de la Dioterie "from" Joguet. It was rich, but not heavy, concentrated but not inelegant. But the wine, though without faults, was also without a story to tell, without words at all in fact. I wondered, am I not in a receptive state? Is my sense of taste too influenced by what I know about the winery's fate? Or had the other disappointing bottles produced after Charles Joguet retired in 1996 prevented me from tasting this bottle honestly? Perhaps.

But I think my palate was tasting accurately. I later learned that the "Domaine Charles Joguet," bought by his ex-financial partner and local property owner Jacques Genet, which had been twenty-four acres at the time of the sale, had nearly quadrupled in size, to eighty-five acres, a few years later (an impossibly swift and large expansion for maintaining the quality and specificity of *terroir*). Worse, not only were the wines bearing Joguet's name now mostly made from *terroirs* that had no connection to him, but the majority of those parcels came from the poor-quality flatlands. And the biggest coup from the new "Joguet" brand? The most mediocre lands of all—and those least expressive of any identity—provided the wine for a bottling they now labeled, with no sense of irony, "Cuvée Terroir."

So what to think of this wine drinker's cautionary tale, especially given the great debate about what most influences a wine, the vigneron or the *terroir*? Charles would probably be the first to say that despite the force of his style, none of his wines is "his own." He would say that the Chinon of "Clos de la Dioterie" is an expression of that parcel of land and its history. "It's the *terroir* that always tells," he's repeated to me many times. But a winegrower is somewhere between a midwife and a magician. Without the magic wand, no *terroir* can express itself. So between artist and *terroir*, how can we choose? The only answer is that we can't. Man without a cultural context is lost, while all culture, without individual expression, is dead.

Today, with no more Joguet-era Chinons left in my cellar, it makes me sad to realize that my three children, born in 2005 and 2006, might never taste an expression of an art that was crucial for the formation of their father's taste.

Legrand Times Five

THE "FONSALETTE AFFAIR"

The day after sampling the Joguet-brand imposter, I consoled myself with an old friend: a 1997 Château de Fonsalette, a delightfully aromatic white wine from the Côtes du Rhône. This wine, like the even more coveted Château Rayas, is made by Emmanuel Reynaud, the nephew of the legendary Jacques Reynaud, a vigneron as notorious for his monarchist leanings as for his talent in expressing his *terroirs*. Jacques Reynaud oversaw both châteaux from 1978 until his death in 1997. He himself had taken over from his equally reactionary father, Louis, one of the first artisanal winegrowers to bottle his own wine, in 1920. (The custom until then, in the Rhône, as in Burgundy and elsewhere, had been to sell the grapes off to a large broker who would then construct the wine in a centralized wine facility.) I always feel ambivalent when I drink the Reynauds' wines because of their makers' politics. But then why, for instance, if I feel no guilt when I read the anti-Semitic French novelist Céline (author of the bleak masterpiece *Journey till the End of the Night*), should I boycott the Reynauds' wine? Should our judgments of taste be influenced by the ethics of an artist's character or the odiousness of *his* taste?

At any rate, Fonsalette is a name with deep resonance for me. I remembered a 1962 Fonsalette white that I'd brought to Athens from New York (after I'd found it at a Chicago wine auction) in 1991. It was for my girlfriend Evi Mitsi's birthday in June of that year, when both she and the wine turned twenty-nine and we were living in Athens. When we opened the bottle at a fish taverna, the savory odors that wafted up from the still-vigorous wine seemed to echo the piney scents from the surrounding Lycabettus Hill. Or was it just my imagination that fused the two odors? It doesn't matter. The fact that the wine was still so radiant and energetic that it provoked the association was already sufficient proof of its powers.

I also remember a 1987 Fonsalette white that I unearthed in a store in San Francisco in 2000 for only ten dollars. The risible price was a reflection of the *fact* that everyone *knew* that '87 was a catastrophic year in France. But the wine was far from a catastrophe. Yes, it was thinner and more acidic than usual: the grapes had been a bit diluted by the rains preceding the harvest, and its acidity was more aggressive due to the lack of sunshine during the summer. But just as with people, it's in moments of stress that a wine grape's nobility can show most plainly. This bottle may not have been the most openly seductive of Fonsalette whites, but it was certainly among the most admirable and transparent.*

So, four years later, at the end of January 2004, I opened the Legrand's bottle of 1997 Fonsalette with Paula for two reasons: to erase the previous evening's taste of the counterfeit Joguet wine and also to celebrate the fifteen minutes of finely edited material I'd thrown away

---

*Though not wishing to bore the reader with a technical discussion of wine, there is a simple way to think about the structure of white and red wines. White wine can be imagined as a triangle, with acidity, alcohol, and fruit constituting its three points. Every white wine in the world will seek its own notion of balance between these three elements. Red wine can be thought of as a square, in which the three elements of the white are also present, complemented by a fourth point, tannin, a form of acidity mostly found in the skin of the grape, and the decisive element that gives red wine a more imposing structure and texture.

that day (progress in film editing is determined by the number of favorite scenes a director is able to cut from the film). But the bottle was a terrible disappointment. It wasn't "corked" (a contamination of the cork by chlorine molecules that produces a sometimes subtle, sometimes overpowering taste of moldy, wet cardboard). Nor was the wine oxidized (soured by air attacking it, generally because of poor storage or a faulty cork) or "maderized" (the "cooked" effect from a bottle exposed to heat, which transforms the wine into bittersweet syrup). But the taste I knew so well—I must have tried at least forty Fonsalette whites over a span of twenty years, including the 1997—wasn't there. The wine was dull, diluted; the color was drab, the aroma wan. A strange bitterness dominated each sip. As so often with people we know very well, we know at once when they're ill, whether the exact symptoms are discernible or not. So I decided to take this sick bottle of Fonsalette back to Legrand to have it replaced with a healthy one, as I had been doing for twenty-five years whenever I came across the inevitable dud in wine shops all over the world.

I put it in the refrigerator, just so I could verify my feeling the next day. But with the stress of having to present the film for acceptance or refusal at the upcoming Cannes festival, I forgot about my bottle. Despite a modest reputation gained in the filmmaking world thanks to *Sunday* and *Signs & Wonders* (the latter presented—to strongly mixed reactions—in competition in Berlin in 2000 and suitably toasted, or roasted, with Germany's sublimely restorative Rieslings), I felt under terrible pressure with *Mondovino*. My remaining agent in Hollywood had already abandoned me the previous year because this "little documentary between two works of fiction" had taken over my life and delayed my next fiction film by four years. "You've thrown your career in the garbage," he said with admirable frankness, if no suggestion of real loss.

The film had been shot with two friends; most often I filmed with only one of them, or even by myself. The little money we did have, about €200,000 culled from various French sources, had run out in November 2003. It was our darkest moment; I was afraid the project would never come to fruition, due to lack of financing and of support. In a classic expression of the bravado of those with neither taste nor power, my Parisian "co-producer" had relinquished any notion of actively producing or seeking financing—taking what seemed at times a perversely French satisfaction from his self-proclaimed powerlessness. Miraculously, the film was saved by a genial neophyte Argentinean producer, Rick Preve, who invested enough funds to cover the work loft, pay a survival salary to me and my assistant, Laurent, who had followed me from New York; and provide a few good bottles of wine each day (the sine qua non for even an impoverished wine film). After four years, this project had become an enormous risk for me—personally, financially, and professionally. Given the idiosyncrasy of the film's style (I shot it with a highly reactive and spontaneous, some might say drunken, camera) and the improbability of its subject for a feature film, I knew that without the benediction of a selection at Cannes, the film world's most important festival, it would never see the light of day in France—one of the last countries where cinephilia in general and foreign filmmakers in particular are still prized—or anywhere else in the world, for that matter.

But that bottle of Fonsalette white that I returned to Legrand a month later would set off a tale worthy of a Brazilian soap opera. The story itself was so peculiar, so funny, and so humiliating (for all the protagonists involved, including me) that I felt obliged to go back to Legrand nearly two years later to discuss what happened with the proprietor, Gérard Sibourd-Baudry.

Legrand: Round Six

"F FOR FONSALETTE—OR FAKE"

I find Laure Gasparotto, the wine historian and freelance journalist assisting me on my Parisian wine tour by recording and organizing all our conversations, waiting for me on a stool at the cozy Caves Legrand bar. She's sitting with Gérard Sibourd-Baudry. Fiftyish, distinguished, a bit of a dandy and ladies' man (judging by the way he's already enveloping Laure), he greets me warmly, apparently not recalling the "Fonsalette incident" from two years earlier.

He plunges at once into a description of the Caves Legrand's place in the wine world. "Wine no longer plays the same role in the art of living. When you give a dinner party you're no longer praised for the quality of the food, but rather for the prestige of the wine you serve. When I was a child there were no newspaper or magazine articles about wine, no wine writers. What did people used to do when they loved wine? They bought a few casks from a merchant like Lucien Legrand and he scrawled on the bottles taken from the cask: 'Bottled by the master grocer.' Once the cask was empty, they bought another. Wine producers bottling their own wine with their own labels is a recent phenomenon. In the 1960s you could still buy casks of top vintages from top proprietors. But Lucien Legrand's great strength was that he always drove his little car out to the vineyards to hunt around for new treasures. There was no media coverage of wine. Today the press has replaced the merchant as the agent who discovers winegrowers for the public. But before this media explosion, it was Lucien and other merchants like him who uncovered all these wines from the Loire, Alsace, and the Beaujolais. He was the first to breach the peasant defenses of Jacques Selosse in Champagne and Jacques Reynaud in the Rhône Valley and bring them Parisian, and then international, renown."

I sense my chance. "Oh, Jacques Reynaud, the former owner of Fonsalette! That's actually why I'm here today." Do I detect a flicker of recognition in Gérard's eyes? He continues:

"The work Lucien did in the 1950s and '60s was the same sort of thing the art merchant Kahnweiler did with Picasso and Matisse, and Durand-Ruel with the Impressionists thirty years before Kahnweiler. In Lucien's time, almost nobody was discovering the great wine estates. My work at Legrand really is like a gallery owner's. I need to guide the customer toward an understanding of 'Why does this painting arouse more emotion in you than another at a given moment?' Whatever the exhibition, whatever the museum, there is always one painting you can't tear yourself away from."

I look at Gérard, wondering how to lead him indirectly back to the purpose of my visit: "Have you ever been transported by a painting, only to find out later that it was actually a copy?" He looks at me warily.

"I might have been fooled at some point, I suppose," he says, "but as far as I know I've never had that experience. In the appreciation of these things, there are always extenuating circumstances. Is your spirit open to receiving emotion? As with an encounter with a woman. There are times when a woman passes by and, you know, you go after her. Other times, the train passes and it's left the station before you recognize the moment and can get on. To receive emotion you already have to be in a state of grace."

"It's funny that you use the word *grace*," I say. "I believe completely in the religious aspect of wine. It's an act of faith, as you said about painting. Whether you're religious or not. But as with any act of faith, there are many things, even highly implausible ones, that you have to accept. From the beginning to the end of the winemaking and wine-selling cycle, there has to be trust. You have to believe that the vigneron isn't cheating you, even though there are a million ways to do it, from chemical additives to mixing wines from other regions to beef up what they've made. Then there are all the middlemen working between the 'artist' and the wine lover. A vigneron after all is an artist, and you must admit that a lot of artists 'cheat' a little. That's part of creating art. There is no absolute truth—which is actually what I wanted to talk to you about. I admire the work you're doing, but I had an experience here—I don't know if you remember—that really unnerved me. It was almost two years ago."

Gérard's gaze sharpens: "Fonsalette?"

"You remember? I bought a mixed case, a dozen different bottles."

"There was a bottle of '97 Fonsalette white among those, if I'm not mistaken."

"So you haven't forgotten! There was a Lignier, an Yvonne Hégo-buru, a Joguet . . . not a true Joguet, though, unfortunately."

"I know."

"You agree about the Joguet? Interesting." ("And yet you still sell them," I think.) "But let's go back to that Fonsalette white. I've been working in and around wine for twenty-five years. I thought every wine shop in the world would always take back a defective bottle, without tasting it, without asking questions. With wine, the client is always right. I knew from my years as a sommelier that even though one bottle in fifteen or twenty probably has some significant defect, it isn't more than one in fifty that is actually refused—or brought back, in the case of a wine shop—by the client. The client is always right, but the restaurant or shop always wins, as you know."

Sibourd-Baudry gets up from his stool and delivers his reply like a lawyer in court. I'm keenly aware that I have no right to play either judge or jury. Let alone prosecutor.

"A few things . . . with regard to the 'incident.' What was reported to me—what your assistant said—was 'this wine is corked.' So that's what I looked for. Was the wine corked? And the answer was no, it wasn't."

I pick up the thread of the narrative, since I know elements I'm sure he still has no clue of: "Right, and so you didn't take it back, and you called me in the editing room. It was an intern, doing some errands in your neighborhood, who brought the bottle back. He *was* wrong to say the bottle was corked. I explained that right away over the phone. The wine wasn't corked, but the bottle wasn't healthy. As you know, wine can be defective through other causes than the cork. I expected you to give me credit or replace the bottle, as is customary."

"It is true that if a bottle shows a flaw, we replace it. But we, as consumers, also have to accept that a bottle of wine is a living body—it's very subjective."

"Of course. But in this case you refused to replace the bottle, saying that the wine *was* good. I won't tell you just yet why I think it wasn't simply a question of taste, but a real error in judgment. The question of taste or whether there was a defect is secondary in this case. The only thing I have against this shop, which otherwise I greatly admire, is that you didn't have the grace—or, rather, the professional instinct—to replace the bottle right away. So I was irritated. Someone from the shop—I don't know who—told me, 'Four of us have tasted this Fonsalette white, and it's perfect.' I was shocked because I knew what was inside the bottle, though I didn't want to tell him right away. For reasons that I'll explain. Two days after that first phone call, your associate Christian de Châteauvieux called me, since I'd asked that one of the store's owners taste the wine. With undisguised contempt, he told me that 'the wine is a perfect '97 Fonsalette white.' I tried to stay cool. 'Listen,' I said, 'I know the wine isn't how it should be. Please believe me,' but he refused. It became purely a matter of pride. As so often happens with wine."

"It was all a misunderstanding," Gérard says, "made worse by people's attitudes. For us, Fonsalette is no ordinary wine. It is part of Legrand's history. We tend to be a bit defensive about it. It's a gut reaction. But a businessman should be able to rise above his own reactions . . . that's where we failed as businessmen."

"Only as businessmen? Maybe. At any rate, Châteauvieux wouldn't budge. And then he said, mockingly, 'And what if I have the vigneron who made it taste the bottle?' I agreed at once: 'Excellent idea. And I bet you a case of Romanée-Conti that Reynaud won't recognize his own wine.' 'I'll make it happen immediately,' Châteauvieux said. I doubted that he would actually do it. And I didn't hear anything for a month. Then one day he called me. Remember that by now the bottle had been open for more than two months. Your partner told me—quite triumphantly—that the vigneron Emmanuel Reynaud had told him the wine was perfectly sound. I was flabbergasted—and forced, finally, to reveal the secret of the bottle."

Gérard stares at me, gobsmacked. Is it possible that he didn't know any of this? Did his partner never tell him my secret? "It's my turn to apologize to you," I continue, "but not for the reasons you think. I did something that was wrong—even though I did it for reasons I think could be vaguely justifiable.

"I explained to Christian that more than half of the liquid tasted since that first day had not been the Fonsalette wine. Three weeks after opening the defective bottle, I looked in the refrigerator to take it back. I found it half-empty. Paula had used it for cooking, without telling me.

What could I do? It's poor form to bring back a half-empty bottle. Thinking that the bottle would be accepted for return without requiring explanations (standard industry practice), I thought it better to fill it to the brim—so I poured in half a bottle of cheap Aligoté that had been open for two months. So what you tasted was half an entirely different and spoiled wine."

Gérard arches his brow. "What did Christian say?"

I smile back and say that "he refused to believe me; he hung up on me, in fact. It's a crazy story and we were all at fault in our own ways; especially the maker of the wine in question, Emmanuel Reynaud, the owner of Fonsalette, for not recognizing his own child. Or, rather, for recognizing a child that was not in fact his own! It was bizarre. How could a vigneron as talented and experienced as Emmanuel Reynaud be so wrong about a wine that had so clearly been tampered with?"

Gérard slips off his stool, stands up. Places his hands for support on the balcony. "Labels are hugely powerful. I don't even remember now if I tasted the wine myself. Frankly, I don't have a clear memory of the incident. I don't remember." He looks at me cagily. "If I had tasted it I would admit it."

I smile at Gérard. "What this whole thing really showed me is that even the people I admire most in the wine world—wine merchants and vignerons—can be wrong, like me. The beauty of wine is that it leads us to be mistaken in an infinite number of ways. Maybe it's this that makes it most human."

Silence follows, but not an uncomfortable or hostile silence. There is a sympathetic twinkle in Gérard's eyes. A good-humored searching. Each one of us seeks to take stock of the story in his own way. And doubtless each one of us would later offer a different interpretation not just of its meaning but also of the events themselves. The grandest surprise of all, though, the *real* resolution of the Fonsalette mystery, would occur, as if by authorial design, at the last hour of my last day of this book's journey, when I'd return once again to the Caves Legrand before boarding my plane back home to Brazil.

3

LAVINIA

The World of a Multinational

Leaving Legrand, I head to the snooty eighth arrondissement, near the Place de la Madeleine. I've asked my *Mondovino* coconspirator Juan Pittaluga to meet me for lunch at a ballyhooed wine shop and restaurant that is new to the Paris scene. Although I'm skeptical from the outset that a restaurant tacked on to a retail outlet will offer much gastronomic pleasure, I have two reasons for meeting Juan there. I've just arrived from Brazil, where wine is 300 to 400 percent more expensive than in France or the United States (thanks to a knee-jerk antielitism and consequently punitive taxation). So I'm thirsty—thirsty for a great bottle to share with a great friend I haven't seen in a long time. And I know that here I'll be able to choose a wine from the shop's massive selection and drink it at the table for nearly the same price. The second reason is more theoretical. After my visit to the *über*traditional and cozy Legrand, I want to see how a brazenly postmodern conception of wine in Paris works: globalized and large in scale but with a "chic boutique" aura. In theory, it's everything that augurs against a happy home for wine.

It was Juan who first mentioned Lavinia to me—a gargantuan department store of wine, sixteen thousand square feet of bottles and wine paraphernalia sprawling over three floors on the Boulevard de la Madeleine. A multinational franchise of French origin, Lavinia already existed in Madrid and Barcelona. "What a joke," I thought just after its 2002 Paris opening: *lavinia* means "purity" in Latin.

As I now walk through the doors of the glass and steel temple I remember that in February 2002, after filming sporadically for two years in the United States and France, I had come to Paris from New York because I hadn't yet found the vital, complex actors to give life to *Mondovino*, as critical a factor for a documentary as for a fiction film. So I suggested at the time to Juan that we use the remaining $5,000 of funding for a trip to Burgundy, the center of the wine world for me (and many others). If we couldn't find protagonists in that wine Mecca to give direction to the film, maybe I'd better give up.

The red wines of Burgundy unnerve a lot of people—including knowledgeable amateurs and "experts." Why? Because they're the most ambiguous and elusive wines on the planet. They're much closer to poetry than prose: a quality that can only disturb us in the current climate. Consider its historical rival, Bordeaux, for example. The richer, denser wines of Bordeaux have the physical weight of a novel. The "narrative" that a drink of Bordeaux offers is easily recognizable: sequences of clearly defined tastes, sometimes majestic, sometimes banal, but always with a comprehensible beginning (as it first hits the tongue), middle (as it develops in the mouth), and an end (the palate's immediate memory of the texture and flavors it has just encountered— otherwise known as the aftertaste). And their structure is also generally clear and "logical," due to the nature of the Cabernet Sauvignon and Merlot grapes that predominate in the region and to the gravel and clay soils where they grow. With most Bordeaux wines, a substantial physical texture fills the mouth, a soothing feeling, reassuring as much as it stimulates. After a bottle of Bordeaux, you often feel the same kind of "bourgeois" satisfaction as you do when you finish a hefty novel. Is it a coincidence that Bordeaux wines, like the novel, may have reached their apogee (at least in terms of glory and market dominance) in the nine-teenth century, with the (transient?) victory of the great European bourgeoisie? And perhaps it's not a stretch to say that their slow and subtle loss of market share since then can be traced to rival bourgeoisies emerging all over the rest of the world.

The color of a Burgundy, on the other hand, is much lighter and more luminous, the delicate, complex range of tones shimmering deceptively, reflecting rather than absorbing the light. Burgundies are among the only wines that begin their life with clearer, lighter tints and yet become deeper with age; most wines age in the opposite direction, losing pigment and density as they go. The charm of Burgundies stems in large part from their aroma, exuberantly fruity when the wine is young; ethereal, at once savage and sophisticated, when it ripens. In the mouth, they are often sensual and captivating but nevertheless impene-trable—but because of their delicacy, not their strength. The flavors are unpredictable, often seemingly contradictory: edgy acidity and savory qualities coexisting with delicately sweet and fragrant fruit. In their intangibility and their deceptive resilience, they're closer to the experi-ence of poetry, particularly as practiced by the ancient Greeks and, say, the classical Chinese or, not coincidentally, by the modernist poets since the turn of the twentieth century who've sought inspiration in the stac-cato lyricism of the Greeks and in the mellifluous indecipherability of the Chinese.

The most astonishing thing about these ethereal wines is that they are made either by down-to-earth peasants or by bourgeois and aristo-crats with deeply enracinated rustic spirits. It is these people, the least pretentious on the planet, whose wines incite the greatest pretensions in the wine lovers who drink them (of course, including me). The paradoxical beauty and mystery of these wines—and the making of them—are the clearest expression of the idea of *earth*. The people themselves are so transparent in their way of life, in their manner of expressing themselves, that they seem to root their ego and identity in the cultivation of the soil.

But as with all things Burgundian, this affirmation is both true and false. Certainly, no place in the world other than Burgundy has a larger density per square meter of profoundly different soils (marked by the frequent presence of complex layers of limestone subsoils). A singular interweaving of natural and human history has created an ideal situation for the soil and subsoils to express themselves through a single actor: a single varietal for reds and a single one for whites. Only here do the red Pinot Noir and the white Chardonnay grapes express themselves with such complexity and such diversity. Imagine Marcello Mastroianni at Cinecittà, filming with Fellini in the morning, with Mario Monicelli at lunchtime, with Scola in the afternoon, and with Antonioni at night. This, in a sense, is what occurs in Burgundy. That is, the same actor—the grape—is interpreting all the roles, but with an infinitely fine variety of geological and meteorological circumstances (the same basic story but told an infinite number of ways through different scripts), guided by talented directors (the vignerons) in order to bring out the very essence of this *terroir* (the overall story that all these elements together have to tell). And everything happens in an acutely challenging environment, perfectly suited for the life of a grapevine. Between Dijon and Mâcon you will find every type of weather imaginable; a single day can be filled with light that is infinitely variable—and thus infinitely stimulating for the grapes. It's worth noting that many vignerons, unlike most wine critics and pundits, consider the amount of rainfall less decisive in determining a particular vintage's quality, than the nature and *variety* of light the vines receive during their season of growth. There is surely no winegrowing region anywhere with more complex and mercurial light.

The crucial geological and meteorological variations began to be discovered at least two thousand years ago and were painstakingly pursued by the Romans of Autun during the reign of the emperor Augustus, and then by their viticultural successors down to the eighteenth century: from Charlemagne's vassals to the Benedictine monks through various dukes and lords to the Cistercian monks. After the French Revolution, it was the ambitious middle class that picked up the torch. The land was redeveloped, molded, zealously reworked by an ever more fragmented number of tiny plot holders. In a paradox perhaps singular to the French, the petty jealousies and mean-spirited rivalries among small landowners in fact contributed further to the ennobling delineation of subtle differences in identity.

So much for the good news. As for the bad . . . I think very few vignerons of quality in Burgundy will disagree that almost three quarters of the wines in the region, as in all other winemaking regions of the world, are produced with total or near-total cynicism by industrial hawkers, false artisans, or misanthropic (or feud-ridden) family estates. The last are the most dangerous, because they sell the image of artisanal craftsmanship and familial legacy without truly assuming it. In any case, just like everywhere else in the world, the majority of wines are betraying their heritage—*our* heritage. It is as if most of the planet's museums allowed their canvases to rot in damp cellars, or exposed them to the harsh glare of direct sunlight. So it isn't enough, unfortunately, to look at the taste that this or that piece of land is capable of imparting as a particular identity. We must look also within each appellation to see which producers are doing serious work: respectful of the past and of the present, attentive to nature and mindful of man.

Travels in Burgundy—via Long Island City

So I went off with Juan in search of Burgundian growers capable of expressing, through the lens of the camera, the poetry and complexity of their culture: a quest for the Holy Grail. The Monty Python version of course. In the course of a week we visited dozens of wine producers for our casting call. My only criterion was to find people whose work I respected. Which is an excuse to say I wanted to get tipsy by midmorning on the good stuff, while still laying claim to be at work. I'd dreamed of this since I began my film career in 1984. During the filming of *Sunday* in 1996, in the then exclusively working-class, multiethnic borough of Queens, New York, I scandalized my co-producers (with the exception of Alix Madigan, as much a daring *bonne vivante* as a deeply talented producer) by insisting, despite the minuscule budget for the film, on wine for the crew at lunchtime. By the middle of the four-week shoot, everyone could clearly see the superior quality of rushes from afternoon shoots—i.e., after the crew and I had drained modest-sized pitchers of everything from Chianti Colli Fiorentini to Montepulciano d'Abruzzo at our favorite lunchtime restaurant, Manducatis, a pure expression of Queens *terroir*. Founded in the sixties by Vincenzo and Ida Cerbone, immigrants from Monte Cassino, and run by them and their children—especially Anthony, who now runs the floor— Manducatis brought to the formerly modest Long Island City district a notion of Italian restaurateurship that is incomparable. In a cheerfully nondescript setting, they served painstakingly cut handmade pasta; herbs and vegetables from a farm that Ida and Vincenzo started in upstate New York (in the sixties, before it was trendy . . . and costly); fresh buffalo mozzarella from a Campania farmer, flown in twice a week from Naples; a menu that was largely invented that morning by Ida; and . . . a staggering wine list: staggering not just because of the depth and breadth of Italian vintages stretching back to the 1960s and '70s but because the prices hadn't changed since the wines were first bought twenty or thirty years before! Whereas a Manhattan restaurant would charge, in the late '90s, $300 to $400 for a legendary—and virtually extinct—1978 Giacomo Conterno Barolo from the Piedmont, at Manducatis you could find it for, say, $40. Generations of less privileged wine lovers were able to school their palates on the scented glories of old Barolos, Chiantis, and Brunellos, thanks to the ongoing generosity of the Cerbones. Alas, there had been too many of us returning too often and I suspect the cellar has today been drained of these treasures. The last time I was there was on September 11, 2001. Many people walked across the bridges from Manhattan that day to seek refuge in the three spacious rooms of Manducatis. Each one was packed with businessmen, artists, construction workers, secretaries, all seeking solace of some kind within those walls. Vincenzo sat down with me and a friend for half an hour, fed us with pasta and a bottle of bracing Castell'in Villa Chianti, and told us to keep a certain perspective on the unfolding tragedy: "The bombing in Naples in '44, when I was a boy, was even worse. It went on for months."

After the happy but limited experience of wine on my first three feature films, *Mondovino* opened up an exciting world of possible opportunities to drink well before, after, and during filming, in part because the crew consisted only of Juan and me (we'd had a crew of thirty on *Sunday* and around seventy on *Signs & Wonders*). We started in the village of Gevrey-Chambertin, with the atypical Bernard Maume and his son, Bertrand. Atypicality is the norm for good Burgundian wine producers. Maume the vigneron is unabashedly rustic. But Maume the man is also a professor of enology in Dijon. His style of wine is considered raw, untempered, and difficult by some (and demonized outright by admirers of the facile, including the megacritic Robert Parker). I've always loved the "Cassavetes" quality of his wines (as rough, unpredictable, and as intermittently inspired as the great rebel filmmaker): a sense (and soil) of nobility (including Grand Cru vineyard Mazis-Chambertin and Premier Cru Lavaux Saint-Jacques) expressed with a spontaneous, uncontrolled energy. There is always considerable variation in his bottles, and the surprises are sometimes tough to swallow, but Maume creates the rare Gevrey-Chambertins that express—as Juan put it when talking about his taste in films—the singularly exciting tension that can exist between "the sophisticated and the savage." More Rossellini's *Stromboli* than *Journey to Italy*. Of all the villages on the Côte-de-Nuits, I think this tension applies more to the wines produced on the lands around Gevrey than to the highly polished expressions of Vosne-Romanée, the velvety seductresses of Chambolle-Musigny, or the robust, more forthright bottles of Nuits-Saint-Georges.

I first came to know the wines of the Maume estate twenty years ago thanks to a legendary American importer, Kermit Lynch, who is also the author of a book that perhaps most successfully humanizes wine, *Adventures on the Wine Route*. Since the early 1970s Kermit has personified an admirable postwar American tradition that is in part responsible for Burgundy's current renown. During the 1940s and '50s, Colonel Wildman (an ironic title for an American *not* involved in a colonial venture) and Frank Schoonmaker traveled from the United States in search of quality Burgundy wines to import for a new class of American society, one just discovering fine wines. With the geopolitical ascendance of the United States came a new taste for the trappings of power. And as always occurs with an emerging world power, this engendered a thirst for the power of taste in itself. The purchasing might of a whole new class of postwar Americans and a budding curiosity about all things foreign—thanks to the millions of GIs who'd recently been exposed to "abroad"—spurred importers to look beyond Bordeaux wines and their historical status as the consensus wine of the powerful.

What did Schoonmaker and Wildman find in Burgundy in the early 1950s? A wine-producing industry that had not regained its footing since the war. They saw that most of the winegrowers there could not depend on their vines to earn a living, so they were abandoning them, or selling the grapes (crushed or uncrushed) or the finished wine to middlemen—speculators and brokers—instead of bottling their own work on the estate (today the sine qua non of quality). But the intrepid Americans also noted the potential for encouraging the most ambitious and talented of these winegrowers to bottle their own wines, control their own destinies, and stop submitting to the anonymity of a business that produced standardized wines with little personality, despite the potential of the *terroirs*.

Little by little, Schoonmaker, followed by Vermonter Robert Haas in the 1960s, Berkeleyite Kermit Lynch and Becky Wasserman (still the only female American importer in the region) in the 1970s, encouraged a number of artisans, like Bernard Maume, Hubert Lignier, Hubert de Montille, and François Jobard, to bottle their own wines. As they coaxed the Burgundians to value their own heritage, they taught American wine lovers to consider wine as not just a pleasure, but also a form of cultural expression—and created a market for the consumption of Burgundy's most distinctive wines in the process. Given the disastrous effects of American foreign policy since at least the arrival of Ronald Reagan in 1980, we tend to forget that not long before, the same United States, even for the French, was a symbol of tolerance, shared liberty, and cultural curiosity. Ironically, if today's Burgundy is the flagship region for wines of the greatest quality and singularity, a model of the French notion of *terroir* and also of an economically successful resistance to the homogenizing effects of globalization, it's in large part thanks to the historic collaboration of the Americans. And this cross-cultural partnership continues today, spearheaded by the brilliant *terroir* activist Neal Rosenthal, Becky Wasserman (a grand ambassadress for both countries), Michael Skurnik, David Bowler, and other conscientious and talented American importers.

But despite all these reasons (and more) to want to cast Bernard Maume for the film, it didn't work out. Neither his lovely wines, his intelligence, nor the obvious passion and talent of his son, Bertrand, made a difference in front of the lens. In my work in fictional films, I've seen many brilliant actors turn into black holes when they stand in front of the camera; that's just it: *they stand in front of it.* They don't inhabit it from the inside. Who does? There are no rules; what appears vital in front of the camera is a lucky accident of biochemistry, of the alchemy between human nature and technology. Now every time I drink the Maumes' wine, regret mingles with the flavors.

After our Maume visit, we spent the afternoon in the neighboring village, Morey-Saint-Denis, with a man universally acknowledged as one of the greatest vignerons in the world. I had already met Hubert Lignier once before, and I knew he was reserved to the point of impassivity. But his wines are so profound, so transporting for me, that I wanted to see if there was a way to capture these emotions for the viewer of a film about . . . about what, really? I still didn't know what a film about wine should be. The only thing I was certain about was that it had to avoid mind-numbing jargon and *technospeak*, the death knell of pleasure and understanding. Lignier's wines from the adjoining villages of Morey, Gevrey, and Chambolle come from small parcels of an acre or less spread out across various vineyard sites within the different villages, each plot representing a different expression, something like the same director with numerous screenplays who is compelled to reimagine each film freshly each year. In fact, this may well be a measure of how nature's genius, her imagination, outstrips man's. Imagine Billy Wilder trying to remake *Sabrina, Double Indemnity, Sunset Boulevard,* and *Love in the Afternoon* each year! And yet to taste multiple vintages of Hubert Lignier's simple Gevrey-Chambertin and Chambolle-Musigny, his Morey-Saint-Denis "Chaffots" and Clos de la Roche year in and year out is anything but absurd. In fact, it's the opposite. Despite the unmistakable hand of the vigneron and the proximity of each of these vineyard sites and the commonality of the same Pinot Noir grape, each year, and year after year, the experience of these wines is like a bold new interpretation of a cherished (literally timeless) film. But how on earth could I possibly convey this through the eye of a camera? How would I capture the tremendous complexity (and yearly risk) taken by this man in his relationships with his *terroirs*? And how could I possibly find a satisfying cinematic means to convey Lignier's experience within the framework of Burgundy, France, the entire Babel of the world of wine?

Juan was even more pessimistic, convinced we'd go home, as filmmakers, empty-handed. But that was also why I wanted him along: precisely because he was an amateur in the complete sense. He was neither a filmmaker with an entrenched worldview—he'd abandoned his day job working for the Bank for Latin American Development only two years previously—nor an initiate of the wine cult. He enjoyed a glass with a meal, but never made a fuss about it. The son of a Uruguayan diplomat, he'd grown up—like me—across many different countries and languages, from Spanish (he was born in Madrid) to English (his early childhood was spent in Canada) to French (he spent time in Switzerland and Belgium) and Portuguese (he studied political science in Brazil). With Juan at my side, I had a true ally: an intelligent, gentle-mannered, fiercely curious person but with the unjaundiced eye of the neophyte as far as both cinema and wine were concerned. When we arrived in people's homes with our small camera and a discreet boom or with the mike attached to the camera (and later with my photographer friend Stephanie Pommez), we weren't a "film crew." We were simply inquisitive friends and colleagues in search of a human encounter.

When such an encounter occurred, the magic and spontaneity were available to the camera in a way a conventional, colder, and more distancing film crew could never have allowed.

Hubert Lignier received us with his thirty-two-year-old son and partner, Romain. Hubert's father had been among the first small growers to bottle a fraction of his wines in the 1950s. But at the time, even his best wines sold for the equivalent of less than a euro a bottle. It was Hubert's painstaking, almost monastic efforts, beginning in the 1970s, with each of his twenty-odd parcels that changed things. And when his American importer Neal Rosenthal urged him to bottle the entirety of his nineteen-acre holdings, the Lignier estate became known throughout the world.

Romain and Hubert Lignier spent several hours quietly trying to help us understand the complex relationship between the vineyards' subsoils, their exposure to the sun, the drainage that differentiates how much water each plant can drink, the microclimates that can vary every thirty feet, and how all this translates into the distinctive taste of each wine. I was riveted. Juan, much less so. Seeing Juan's flagging attention, Hubert suggested that we go do a bit of tasting in the cellar. It occurred to me, watching Lignier's patient rhythms and eye for each natural detail as we walked back through the Clos de la Roche vineyard, that the pious monks of our era are the farmers, especially the vignerons, who work the earth and who believe in nature with a genuine fervor. It is they who transmit to us—laymen and city dwellers—the symbols of a common ancestral spirituality.

We reached the unadorned, decidedly untouristic cellar. With great tact, the father moved into the background, eventually disappearing from sight, allowing his son, Romain, to lead the new cycle of explanations. For several more hours we drank, talked, compared each of the twelve different bottlings from two vintages, the younger one still kept in oak casks of 225 liters because it was unfinished. Juan and his uninitiated palate were quickly exhausted. Even I have to admit as a general rule that after tasting and spitting a dozen wines, my palate grows quickly less acute and sensitive. If wines are indeed like people, then even a considered and leisurely tasting like this could be compared to a cocktail party in which you meet dozens of new people, chatting with no one for more than ten minutes. The energies of even the most experienced and talented diplomat would begin to flag after the tenth person. By the twentieth, how could he not be on autopilot? What do we make, then, of today's wine critics, from France, Portugal, Italy, the United States, and everywhere else, who pride themselves on giving us definitive assessments of two hundred wines tasted on the same day? And this repeated several times per week throughout the course of the year!

Juan told me later in the car, as we drove back to our hotel in nearby Beaune, that he grew up with a diplomat father who "drank only Bordeaux, which meant, in the sixties, good but simple and inexpensive." He inherited his father's taste for Bordeaux, he thinks. Burgundies, even the Ligniers' comparatively robust and structured ones, seemed to him on this day—and during the first months of filming—incomprehensible. Not bad or unpleasant, but in a register that hovered out of his reach. He explained to me later that the Burgundy wines he was discovering seemed less "present" to him (because more light bodied and mercurial) than the Bordeaux he believed he knew. I understood his position, but I felt certain that there was a serious confusion on both the analytical and sensorial levels. I suggested to him that the Bordeaux his father drank, the ones he tasted as a child in the 1960s, were much less rich, less alcoholic, less structured, less sweet, than the Bordeaux of today. So he might have inherited a psychological bias toward the notion, rather than the actual taste, that Bordeaux is powerful. My father and mother had the same habits; they drank mostly modestly priced (at the time) Bordeaux, particularly Saint-Emilions. My memory is of wines with a certain power but also an acidity and litheness that have nothing to do with contemporary Bordeaux.

Nine months later, after two weeks spent tasting a hundred Bordeaux wines and filming hours upon hours of the Bordeaux wine culture, Juan exclaimed, "Eureka!" In the Bordeaux village of Saint-Julien, in front of the venerable Château Beychevelle, he stopped the car and turned to me excitedly: "I get it! The Bordeaux of today—most of them—have a childish taste! They are sweet and treacly. Kids' wines. But I don't remember Bordeaux tasting like that when I was a kid. My father's Bordeaux didn't taste like that. Maybe they weren't good, but they weren't like this." I told him that this change is the result of an American influence, opposite in its effect to what Americans provoked in Burgundy. Since Bordeaux has historically produced wines of status, principally for export, it was logical that by the 1980s, when American wine consumers' power reached its apex, Bordeaux would look to adapt their style to suit the flood of new customers. And these new American (and American-influenced Asian and Latin American) consumers, brought up on hard alcohol and soft drinks, had already become accustomed to wines from California, Australia, and Chile: sweetly fruity, densely textured, and highly alcoholic (alcohol bringing both greater structure and weight and a sweeter impression on the palate). Bordeaux was only too happy to oblige, devising myriad techniques to produce beefier, sweeter, plusher wines—more unabashedly Napa-like in character and decidedly less determined by historical qualities of *terroir*—to please the world's new consumers, as Château Mouton Rothschild's director of marketing, Xavier de Eizaguirre told me unapologetically during our Bordeaux shoot.

But despite Juan's situation on this February day in 2002, when he thought he knew Bordeaux and he believed Burgundy still unknowable, he was as touched as I was by the delicacy of the relationship between Hubert Lignier and his son, Romain. We both noted their obvious love for each shift in soil and for the history of their land, their humility in the face of their achievements, and their mutual but unspoken respect. I found it even more interesting when I thought of the tension that had marked the morning spent with Bernard Maume and his son, Bertrand. When I asked the question (a provocative but essential one) "Who creates the wine?" both Maumes had answered me at the same time: "I do," they said. And then they corrected themselves, this time one after the other: "The *terroir* does." I imagine that the tension between the Maumes—vital, natural, somehow courageous—invigorates their wine, expressing itself in the unpredictable, rough, and tensile quality of their Gevreys—whereas the harmony, the solidity, the restraint, of the Ligniers' Gevreys or Moreys, I think (I imagine) I can sense in wines dating from 1991, when Romain began to take the reins from his father. With the Ligniers, you have to wait patiently for them to reveal themselves, just as you have to wait for their wines. Unfortunately film, which has a complex relationship with time, not always impatient but always demanding, paradoxically will not let us wait for them. The Ligniers, alas, despite their extraordinary qualities, proved no more able to anchor a film than the Maumes. That night I told Juan we might have to give up on *Mondovino*. He was in complete agreement.

Back at Lavinia
(TO BETTER ROAM THE WORLD)

These memories, discussions, and past anxieties return to Juan and me piecemeal as we sit down at a table in Lavinia's second-floor restaurant, almost four years after our first trip to Burgundy, and a year and a half following *Mondovino*'s miraculously unexpected official selection in Cannes (miraculous because only two other documentaries were selected for competition in the fifty-year history of the festival and because a selection in competition—the international equivalent of an Oscar nomination—is generally allotted to films with stars, powerful distributors, and producers). We decide to buy our wine in the shop first and then order our meal according to what we chose (usually a more successful strategy than the opposite one). The restaurant space isn't very clearly separated from the store—a winning strategy for keeping consumers in a permanent state of consumption. We get up from our table and walk down a long corridor lined with hundreds of wineglasses and decanters, following the stairs down to the first-floor entrance, which, from a distance, resembles a Madison Avenue clothing boutique franchise—at an upscale airport. Behind the sleek veneer, we already feel the ruthless model of globalizing efficiency. Lavinia houses an enormous range of wines, a visible investment of considerable capital. But the investment is not one of time; there are no old vintages here, no patina-marked woodwork. The investment is simply in the scale of apparent choice, making it a candidate for the already classic supermarket or chain store con: where every aisle offers an enormous array of products that disguise the fact that the only actual choice is between the packaging and the attendant marketing campaigns.

But as I start to examine the bottles, especially the extensive section of Italian wines, including the Piedmontese vignerons of universal repute, La Spinetta, Clerico, and Giacomo Conterno, I realize that Lavinia in fact is perhaps the only place in Paris where there is a *real* choice. That is, there are not just French but also international wines of quality. It's a notion that now goes without saying in Tokyo, São Paulo, and New York (where wine lovers have probably never had such a dazzling choice of true wines of *terroir* from all over the world), but it isn't part of the French self-conception. And until there are more places like Lavinia in France, the loss of its shares in the global market will surely continue. *Terroir*, to be vital, must be local but not parochial.

We then come across several shelves of German wines, something unimaginable anywhere else in Paris. Despite my instinctive hostility toward this undisguised temple of consumption (because more personalized wine shops—from jazzman David Lillie's Chambers Street Wines in New York to Vila Viniteca in Barcelona to the Caves Legrand in Paris—are traditionally places for wine lovers to meet, drink, and chat *as well as* buy), I have to admit to Juan that there seems to be a rigor and an ethic in Lavinia's selection. Other than France, Germany is the country that possesses the greatest number of historic *terroirs* of finesse and complexity. Internationally renowned until the early twentieth century, German wines were especially prized by the English throughout the eighteenth and nineteenth centuries—not coincidentally when England's imperial supremacy also set the standard for the world's wine taste. But the two German-instigated world wars of the twentieth century and the dissolution of the British Empire relegated the sublimely delicate and noble white wines of the Mosel, Rhine, Pfalz, Nahe, and Franconia to comparative obscurity.

For our lunch, given my Brazil-generated thirst, I'm tempted by bottles of the Riesling master worker of the Nahe region, Donnhoff, particularly given the startling modesty of the prices (between thirteen and thirty euros). I also see Mosel wines from the legendary producers Dr. Loosen, Johannes Selbach, and J. J. Prum. My mouth is watering at the thought of all these profoundly different expressions of Riesling, this most regal, complex, and graceful of white wine grapes. Crackling with world-record levels of acidity because of its position at the northernmost latitude possible for fine wine grapes, the best Rieslings of the Mosel are Audrey Hepburn–like: impossibly lithe and delicate but irrepressibly bright, daring, and enchanting. Thanks to perilously long growing seasons that court the risk of frost and ruinous cold climate damage, the vines are forced to fight for every last bit of sun-ripening grape sugar. This epic struggle produces a gravity-defying delicacy of structure, an intensity of taste, and an overall balance among the dramatic acidity, the hard-won ripeness of the fruit, and ridiculously low levels of alcohol (sometimes as little as 7 percent) that is utterly unique in the world of wine.

Passing into the Rheingau section—a region that produces wines that are more structured and sober—I'm amused to see a bottle of Franz Künstler, made by his son Gunter, an excellent young producer from the village of Hochheim (incidentally, one of Thomas Jefferson's favorite *terroirs*, from which he even brought back vine cuttings to America). I had met Gunter Künstler at his estate in 1993 when I was visiting nearby Wiesbaden for an alternative film festival that showed *Resident Alien*. The clarity of Künstler's wines undoubtedly stems from his obsession with cleaning his wine cellar, which he hosed down with a high-pressure jet for what seemed like hours in my presence, all the while explaining the need to maintain purity and hygiene in the wines. Fassbinder was alive and well, I thought, in this manically determined (and strapping) young man.

I now turned to Juan: "I'm very impressed to see such a cosmopolitan selection. This is a new France. And a welcome one. What do you think?" But Juan—who eats nothing but meat—is much happier with reds. I ask him what he wants to drink to celebrate our reunion. "Burgundy," he answers unhesitatingly. I think of his attitude toward Burgundies when we first started filming *Mondovino* and hide a smile.

The New Boys from Brazil

As we head toward the stairs leading down to the Burgundy section, I see a bottle from "home"—that is, from Brazil. Wine production is so new there that I'm astonished to see any of it here. "Wow, Lavinia really is the France of the future," I say to Juan. But then I pick up a bottle from the producer Miolo and add ruefully, "Wait. Here's a bottle of a (putative) Brazilian wine, an exotic object in all ways, in a place, Paris, that I've called 'a home'—though not 'my home'—since I was a small child." But now that I live in Brazil, married to a Brazilian woman, with my three Brazilian-born children (Miranda and Capitu, twin girls born in April 2005, just after our arrival in Rio, and Noah Bernard, a son born in June 2006), I feel like I'm observing a wine from home put on display in a foreign land. This feeling of paradox, if not downright contradiction, is intensified by the fact that the lone representative of the fragile Brazilian wine industry is, in my view, the least possibly Brazilian wine on the market, a cannily crafted product of nascent Brazilian marketing forces and cynical French globalizing practices.

Why would someone in Paris want to buy this Michel Rolland signature wine other than for the fact that its label says Brazil? Since Rolland, the world's most ubiquitous and powerful wine consultant, began to work for Miolo in 2004, he has spearheaded a movement, as he did in Argentina fifteen years ago, to create technically well-made, globally palatable, interchangeable "wine products" of no perceptible origin or identity. With consummate showman's skill, he's been able to cultivate the most successful of the world's wine critics to ensure a global media validation of the Rolland trademark for his more than hundred clients on six continents. Why is this "Brazilian" wine in Lavinia? Should they know better, given how rigorous the selection of German and Italian wines is? Does it mean anything that Lavinia's press attaché, Jean-Pierre

Tuil, is also the press attaché for many of Rolland's clients? Is this globalization? I would vividly remember this feeling of disquiet months later when I was asked to take part in an evaluation of the new harvest in the state of Rio Grande do Sul, where the Brazilian wine industry is concentrated.

Two hours drive from the city of Porto Alegre, in the southernmost state of Brazil (hence one of the coolest), lies the small, innocuous city of Bento Gonçalves and the Vale dos Vinhedos ("Valley of the Vines"). In the late nineteenth century, tens of thousands of Italian immigrants—mostly from the Veneto region—settled these prettily undulating hills that evoke, without too much imagination, the countryside around Verona. That the nineteenth-century version of the Veneto dialect is still alive in the Rio Grande do Sul is testament to the long isolation they and the region have experienced up to the present. The immigrants brought with them grapevine cuttings from home, and for the next hundred years, countless families made wine for family consumption while a few cooperatives churned out industrial-quality wine for the millions of Italian immigrants of São Paulo. There was no commercial wine culture to speak of, especially as the vast majority of the population in the rest of the country had little or no cultural connection to wine drinking.

But starting in the 1970s, a few of these Italian immigrant families, Dal Pizzol and Valduga in particular, decided to increase their production and commercially bottle their own wine under the family name. No one seemed to pay any notice as they struggled to combat geographic and climatic conditions that were hardly favorable to fine wine production. The soils were sandy, the rainfall was heavy (making it difficult to get fully mature, balanced grapes), and national consumption remained negligible. But still, Antonio and his brother Rinaldo Dal Pizzol experimented with different grape varieties, including the Tannat from the Madiran region in France (which arrived via Basque immigrants to neighboring Uruguay in the 1880s), Cabernet Sauvignon, Riesling Italico, Trebbiano, and other varietals, producing quirky but earthy, edgy, and subtly characterful wines. Quietly cultivating a clientele in São Paulo (the wealthiest and largest city in Brazil) and in Rio, but absolutely unnoticed by the outside world, they produced highly drinkable, low-alcohol (10 to 11 percent), high-acid, food-friendly wines that unwittingly went against the growing global fashion in the 1980s for rich, sweet, high-alcohol monster wines. It was naturally the style of wine that this emerging *terroir* could produce, and the two Dal Pizzol brothers merely sought to enter into a dialogue with the *terroir*'s potential. The Valdugas were more ambitious and commercially astute, and by the midnineties, they'd built up their winery to an 800,000-bottle capacity. (Dal Pizzol has remained around 50,000, the size of a modest Burgundy estate.) Though João Valduga was producing some wines of generic quality for larger consumption, he was also crafting a number of wines of real character, including a surprisingly biting Chinon-like Cabernet Franc, a perfumed Malvasia (in homage to his deceased mother), and a world-class sparkling extra brut from the '99 vintage (still alive and complex in 2007). Alas, Valduga even more recently seems to have fallen under the Miolo-Rolland spell, and their wines appear each year to be more generic.

Perhaps as a result of the distant echo from the world-wine boom, a few more small- and medium-size producers began trying their hand, including the very talented Mario Geisse, a recent Chilean immigrant who produces excellently herbal reds and a remarkably elegant, tensile sparkling wine from his forty-three acres. Slowly, old immigrant families and young Brazilian entrepreneurs and then larger corporations all started to develop the region, if with hugely variable results. Technically many wines are shaky, the result of entrenched provincialism and the climatic challenges that continue to present real difficulties for achieving sufficiently ripe grapes. Nonetheless a few dozen pioneers are searching honestly for the qualities of their *terroir*, searching to allow its defects to coexist alongside its virtues. If the outside world gives it time to develop, exchanging information and trading equitably with these vignerons, permitting them to slowly build a local, then national, then regional, and eventually an international market, perhaps Brazilian *terroir* will one day represent something singular in the world wine culture.

At least this is what I thought until I headed down to Bento Gonçalves to join a jury judging the year's vintage, shortly after the sighting of the Rolland-Miolo bottle in Lavinia. Of all the reds prese-lected for our evaluation, I was surprised not to find a single wine from Dal Pizzol, Valduga, or Mario Geisse. As the tasting and oral evaluation got under way, I was further shocked to realize that we were drinking almost exclusively rich, sweet, oak-flavored, high-alcohol marmalade wines—typical of Argentina and Chile, with their vast export markets, but until recently unknown in Brazil. And right in the middle of the tasting, what was the poster child for this brash new style of highly manipulated wine? A 14.5 percent alcohol Michel Rolland Merlot made for Miolo (a company whose production rose from fifty thousand bot-tles in the late nineties to five million today). It took Rolland less than ten years to radically change three hundred years of winemaking tradi-tions in Argentina; why should I be surprised that it took him less than two years to change the thirty-year-old neophyte Brazilian culture?

Even more disturbing was to see how the panel of Brazilian wine critics and industry people appeared delighted that Brazil could now produce a globally interchangeable product, even if second tier in qual-ity. When it was my turn to speak, I tried to be diplomatic but I made clear my concern. A silence fell across the vast conference hall of eight hundred people. After the tasting, I slowly made my way toward the luncheon. A clean-cut, baby-faced young man stopped me and intro-duced himself. "I'm Luiz Henrique Zanini. I'm only the president of the 'Provale' winegrowers association by default. I was the glorified secre-tary, officially the vice president. But the president quit in disgust at the direction that we're heading in. I'm actually a vigneron with a twelve-acre farm." He thanked me for questioning the direction of these cari-catural, intensely concentrated, super-rich fruit bombs in the Rio Grande do Sul and explained how distraught he and other artisanal vignerons were at the sudden shift in the Brazilian wine industry.

We grabbed some food and sat to the side of the vast luncheon. He offered me a few bottles of wine made by people not even considered for the evaluation, because so opposed to the instantaneous fashion. We began with a delightfully rustic and expressive white wine made in the neighboring state of Santa Caterina, a Peverella from Cave Ouvidor. It's a slightly oxidized style of white wine reminiscent of its Veneto Malvasia origins, made by Alvaro Escher, a former historian and economist recently turned winemaker. Somehow he has managed to capture something distinctively local: salty, earthy, mineral. We also sampled two reds: a Barbera and a Teroldego from the Angheben winery, another fractional production from a subregion near the Uruguayan border that Luiz Henrique described as "off the beaten track, but filled with promise for the future." The Teroldego grape is a conscious effort by Eduardo Angheben to commune with his Trentino immigrant past, to resuscitate a little-known grape and observe how it will behave after its own "immigration." Equally peasantlike in its roughness of texture and execution, it is nonetheless fully alive, riper and richer than many of the traditional bottlings, but with provocatively bitter flavors. I could see why this complex, but decidedly "unslick" drink had little chance to pass muster at a national showcase trying to invent an internationally consensual posture. It would be as improbable to imagine the idiosyncratic Peverella or the peasant-style Teroldego among the finalists as it would the head of a Hollywood studio green lighting the deliriously raw emotion and raw filmmaking techniques of John Cassavetes's subversive masterpiece of the 1960s, *Faces*.

Luiz Henrique looked around the room nervously, aware that he was being seen with a known maverick, a potentially uncomfortable position for the accidental president of the largest growers' association. In low tones, he explained to me that "Whether they're big or small, most 'family wineries,' unfortunately, are prostituting themselves. There are virtually no more genuinely family-run companies in Brazil today—except maybe Dal Pizzol. Suddenly, they're all trying to produce fourteen-, fifteen-, even sixteen-percent-alcohol wines to cater to a latent market that's already been brainwashed by 'new products' that are all the same. There's a pressure that pushes people to become very egotistical and to forget even their recent past as they jockey to get ahead in this new market. The only thing they preserve is the label of 'family' with a cute photograph of Grandpa. Globalization has arrived in a terrifying way here . . . very different from what I imagined. The ability to work seriously, ethically, authentically in Brazil—to find *our terroir*—ironically is going to be the responsibility of people with no significant family wine history. It's a paradox, but the only hope for the Brazilian wine industry lies with nonindigenous people who have a passionate desire to preserve—or, better, discover—what's authentic."

A few weeks later, tasting his superb wines made under the Vallontano label from his wife's family vineyard, I was delighted to see that his deeds matched his words. As I sipped his lean and muscular Tannat in Rio (a market, like São Paulo, to which he and his artisanal friends have had virtually no access), and his enchanting, delicate 7 percent alcohol sparkling Muscat (a Brazilian Moscato d'Asti), I remembered that Miolo-Rolland bottle back at Lavinia. I wondered about the irony of what determines who is a foreigner—and what is foreign—in a native land, and who is native in a foreign land. I thought about the paradoxes of those on the inside looking out, as much as those on the outside looking in.

The Belly of the Beast

I set Mr. Rolland's bottle of "Brazilian" wine back down in its display rack and we head down to the basement, where the full, dazzling array of French wines are stored. On the one hand, the trendy lighting—a kind of lulling high-amp glow from upscale clothes shops—makes me want to run straight for the exit. On the other hand, with each step, it seems that Lavinia accomplishes what no wine shops in Paris even try and few elsewhere succeed at. There are bottles of interest for every palate and pocket—including those (many) people in search of Rollandomania—all clearly visible. The instinct of the old French (and

English . . . and even some old-line New York) wine shops is to play on what is hidden, to make the client ask questions of the "expert," to compel him to submit to the power of the retailer—or to accept the crumbs scattered in the windows and on the few display racks. Here, everything is accessible; all the regions are clearly indicated, and every French region and subregion is represented in breadth and depth. It's radical—democratic, in fact. Even if the prices are slightly higher than in a number of smaller, specialized wine shops, the markups are still reasonable. More impressively, Lavinia has made the effort to price many excellent *vins de terroir* at between five and twenty euros. In the back of the basement, there's a sort of "VIP room" reserved for the most expensive, rare, and aged vintages. Though this gesture may appear gratuitously elitist, it's significant that the room is surrounded by standard-priced wines and balanced by the "bargain" wall on one side and a prominent section of reasonably priced organic wines on the other. Wine, indeed, is democratic—because you can buy a good bottle of wine for €2 just as you can for €200—but not Marxist; not all wines are equal, and they cannot be treated the same way.

We continue our search for the right bottle for our reunion. We pass Alsatian wines—a kind of fuller-bodied stepping-stone to the more filigree German classics—including the Zind-Humbrecht estate's sublime Rieslings, Pinot Gris, and Gewurztraminers (literally "spiced grape of the south Tyrol" in German). Olivier Humbrecht was one of the first, and remains one of the most radical, proponents of full-scale organic farming and winemaking in the region. Happily, his wines have not been relegated to the "organic" ghetto but exist in their regional subdivision. Although I'm happy to see a wall advertising organic wines, it's also an identity trap if applied indiscriminately. It occurs to me, as a Jew, that it's critical that there are communities and institutions that function as public displays of Jewish culture but it's equally critical for me that Jewish identity isn't an all-consuming and all-excluding denomination. In the bin next to Zind-Humbrecht's wines, I see stacks of bottles from one of their principal Alsatian rivals for international glory. The "femmes Faller" of the Domaine Weinbach are undoubtedly the best known and most esteemed female vigneronnes (a rarity in itself) in France. Their wines and their story are indeed seductive. When Colette Faller lost her vigneron husband, Théo, in 1979, their two daughters, Laurence and Catherine, were still children. Everyone in the town of Kaysersberg expected her to sell the Weinbach estate, because, they reasoned, what could a woman alone with two young daughters do with these beautiful *terroirs* on the steep slopes of the Schlossberg and Fürstentum vineyards. Despite the intensely chauvinistic and reactionary culture of rural Alsace, especially thirty years ago, Colette decided to keep the property. Her neighbors, it's said, gave her six months before she'd be forced to sell, eagerly awaiting her collapse. But she hung on, and in less than fifteen years she succeeded in making the Domaine Weinbach one of the most famous white wine producers in France, with her daughter Laurence eventually taking over the winemaking while Catherine managed the estate. This was a formidable achievement, not only for women in general in the internationally sexist world of wine, but also because she and her daughters, along with the Humbrechts, created a new recognition in Alsace for Burgundian-style delineations of *terroir* expressed by genuinely artisanal family efforts.

It was an irresistible and infinitely photographable story, especially given the three women's physical beauty and pronounced charm. And it seemed throughout the 1980s and '90s that few did resist: from *Paris-Match* to Robert Parker, from *Libération* to the *Times* of London, from Tokyo to Antwerp. The press coverage of these women and their vines hasn't ceased. But what now? There's been no scandal, no betrayal. I think the wines are as finely crafted today as they were fifteen years ago. In fact, Colette and her daughters welcomed us with boundless generosity during the filming of *Mondovino*. But . . . but . . . Juan and Stephanie Pommez (the third member of our crew, when the crew swelled to its maximum of three) walked away with the sensation that we had been welcomed by expert welcomers, people so exposed to, and by, the media that each gesture seemed somehow rehearsed or previously reproduced. Although I shared their sentiments, I also felt guilty since we were the beneficiaries of nothing more than the Fallers' considerable hospitality and talent. But when you're used to paying eight euros for a humble Muscat and twenty for a grand cru Riesling and then, all of a sudden, you're faced with twenty-eight euros for the Muscat and sixty for the Riesling, you can't help feeling a bit squeamish—independent of whether they merit these prices. Because the value of a wine, for a wine lover, for the vigneron, or for the market constitutes three distinct and often contradictory realms. And I'm fully conscious that in a media-saturating culture, where money is the final arbiter of value, these calculations of "what something should be worth" become even more difficult.

Staring at these bottles on the rack in Lavinia, I tried to think why they provoked discomfort in me, despite so many beautiful wine-drinking memories. Do I really feel they've sold out? Have the Fallers' wines (and purses) become distinctly richer and more concentrated than they were ten years ago? And if so, is that a bad thing? Certainly not for the current market, which values richness and immediate intensity above other qualities. But for wine drinkers like me, who prefer elegance, a graceful vivacity, and finesse, these more concentrated, more structured, more *come-hither* wines are actually less seductive. Just as a diluted wine will not have the substance to express the depth of a great *terroir*, wines that are too rich will mask the complexity—the mineral subtlety—of the same *terroir*. Imagine a talented athlete too thin and weak to exercise the range of his skills or the same athlete so well fed and self-satisfied that he won't push himself to reveal his full array of talents. I'm the first to admit that it's entirely possible that the style of the wine has remained the same, and that it's my palate that has changed (saturated, maybe, by the past ten or fifteen years' sampling of too many saturated wines).

Moving past the Fallers, I glance at the wines of Trimbach, one of the biggest wine merchants in Alsace, an industrial output of almost a million and a half bottles per year. Ironically, I'm not sure that the Trimbach wines don't more cleanly express the Alsatian *terroir* than the more intense and discernibly complex wines of *les femmes Faller*.

Yes, the Trimbach wines are less artisanal, less elaborate and detailed—
especially the vast majority of their production, which are varietal
denominated rather than geographically denominated wines. (Traditionally, Alsace is the only region in France where the name of the grape
features more prominently on the label than the place of origin.) These
wines are indisputably less rich and robust than the wines of the Fallers
or Olivier Humbrecht. But in the sleek-bodied acidity and transparent
mineral flavors of the Trimbach wines—Sylvaner, Pinot Blanc, Riesling,
Pinot Gris—there is a singular demonstration of just how graceful a
white wine can be, impossible to reproduce in any more southerly
region in the world. I ask Juan, "So, in making less self-consciously
'individualized' wines, is the mass merchant Trimbach actually producing wines that are more typically Alsatian? It's a lovely paradox that
points up how difficult it is to determine what criteria are necessary to
determine what is finally culturally authentic or distinctive in wine."
Juan just looks at me and says, "What about our bottle of red Burgundy
for lunch?"

4

LAVINIA AND BURGUNDY

A Cosmopolitan Exchange

Two parallel themes emerged forcefully during the Burgundy casting trip in 2002: the roots of *terroir* and the roots of man. At every encounter, we felt the tension—and the beauty—of the transmission from earth to people and from people to their children. I'm reminded of this as we head toward the Burgundy section of Lavinia. To my continued surprise, the store managers have not used their considerable financial resources to impose the most easily supplied and marketable of Burgundy wines (in general, from mass merchants and bottlers rather than artisans with limited stocks). Instead, they've put together the sort of idiosyncratic lineup I might have selected. As we stroll down the Burgundy aisles, I feel like I've arrived at a party where, having been afraid I wouldn't know anyone (or want to run into anyone I do know), I find instead only friends and people I respect from a distance. Immediately, I spy among the whites the highly prized Meursaults of Jean-Marc Roulot, as well as his excellent generic white Burgundy (i.e., not from a specific village but from the less distinguished plains at the edge of villages). These wines tend to have less definition and depth but in the right hands can be delicious drinks at a modest cost. Next to these is a wonderful selection of six or seven different *terroirs* from within the Meursault village appellation from Roulot's neighbor François Jobard. An excellent vigneron I've followed for many years, thanks to Kermit Lynch's vigorous importation to the United States, Jobard gracefully declined to appear in the film, as he declines most media encounters: an honorable, and doubtless intelligent, choice.

Jobard's understandable reticence reminds me of someone else's during our casting trip. Through the intermediation of Kermit Lynch, I had contacted Aubert de Villaine, co-owner of the mythical Domaine de la Romanée-Conti, universally considered the most sacred of the world's wine estates. But it was less the glory of Romanée-Conti that made me want to meet de Villaine than his personal reputation. Those who know him always spoke of a profoundly democratic man, respectful of all expressions of *terroirs*, eloquent and active in the fight on behalf of wine as cultural heritage. But I was skeptical when the grave and resonant voice of Mr. de Villaine explained to me over the telephone that he wouldn't agree to be filmed without meeting us beforehand. This seemed the typical reflex of powerful men afraid to expose themselves to anyone outside their carefully cultivated network. Given the reputation of Romanée-Conti, it seemed a clever ruse to democratize our meeting and invite us to his home in the modest village of Bouzeron, and not at Vosne-Romanée, the headquarters of the majestic estate.

Driving through the pitch black of a late winter afternoon, already feeling bleak because of a rapidly developing head cold, I felt sure we were wasting our time. We pulled up to a pleasant but unostentatious stone house in the middle of the small village. Aubert de Villaine opened the door himself and led us through to the kitchen. Very tall, in his midsixties, he had a long oval face lined like a patch of well-worked earth. His gestures were calm and careful, but his gaze was sharp and subtly intimidating. We dawdled in the kitchen while Aubert gathered glasses for a bottle he was to share with us. I saw the label: a Bâtard-Montrachet from Romanée-Conti. Given that the three thousand bottles of the estate's Le Montrachet are considered the rarest and among the most expensive white wines in the world, what were we to make of this gesture? The Bâtard-Montrachet he was offering us is made in such small quantities—less than five hundred bottles—that it isn't even sold. I was moved. And surprised. And angry with myself. Not only was it obvious that we were in the presence of one of the true "gentlemen" of the wine world, but thanks to my head cold, I'd be unable to appreciate this Grail-like bottle. At that moment, for a wine lover like me, it seemed like a tragedy. But Aubert de Villaine was so courtly and hospitable that today I have wonderful memories of the bottle as well as the meeting.

And of course the invitation to Bouzeron rather than to Vosne-Romanée wasn't a political maneuver at all. At least not in the sense I'd imagined. It turned out that Aubert de Villaine was the mayor of the village and had just returned from a town hall meeting. In fact he divides his time between Romanée-Conti, forty-five kilometers away, and Bouzeron, where he and his American wife, Pamela, live and make their wine under the de Villaine family label. It's significant that the most august figure of the Burgundy hierarchy—and probably the most prestigious vigneron in the world—has chosen to live in one of Burgundy's most low-key villages, producing under his own name the region's most humble wines. It's especially ironic that the flagship wine of his and his wife's estate is the most ill-regarded grape in the pantheon, the Aligoté, generally so tart and light-bodied, it's considered useful only for mixing with black currant liqueur to produce a Kir.

But the de Villaines' Bouzeron Aligoté is so precise, so elegant and delicate that it rivals august Chardonnay-based Burgundies of five times the price. As we settled around the large fireplace that dominated the book-lined living room, it was clear that de Villaine was much more excited to talk about his Aligoté and red and white Mercurey village wines than Romanée-Conti. Above all, he was eager to share his vision of the historic complexity of Burgundy's *terroirs* and how the hand of man has been as critical in determining the characteristics of each parcel of land as the more traditionally invoked geological and microclimatic factors. As he explained how the Cistercian monks painstakingly delineated the Burgundian *terroirs* over the course of five hundred years, de Villaine began to take on the aura, even more so than Hubert Lignier, of a monk himself. It's not only that his ascetic appearance belied an intellectual fervor and a latent physical vitality, reminiscent of a character from Robert Bresson's *Diary of a Country Priest* or Carl Dreyer's *Joan of Arc*. There was something monastic in his fundamental conception of the role he plays in the agricultural passion play of vine into grape, grape into wine. "I'm a midwife, rather than a creator of the wine," he said to us. "The creator is the *terroir*. In Bouzeron just as much as in Vosne-Romanée." De Villaine searched for a way to explain this paradox between man and nature. The Cistercian monks gradually worked the land, attentive to its natural contours and underlying "shapes," he suggested, in much the same way that the anonymous artists at the great Incan site of Machu Picchu in Peru created their sculptures in relation to the mountain's natural rock formations.

This search for something both terrestrial and mystical—that we could call the *inner narratives of nature*—led de Villaine to convert Romanée-Conti from simple organic farming to the more radical process of biodynamism. This ultra-organic practice in the wine world is at once cutting-edge and also deeply rooted in ancient principles. Inspired by the late-nineteenth-century Austrian philosopher Rudolf Steiner and his holistic "anthroposophism" (a belief in the inseparability of the personal and the universal), biodynamic agriculture seeks to address any given plot of land as a unified organism, in which all living elements—soil, plant, and animal—are to be mutually self-sustaining. It encompasses such medieval concepts of pruning a vine only during certain phases of the moon, the use of phytohomeopathic cures (like fermented herbal and mineral preparations) in the place of any chemical or artificial fertilizer. Above all, there is an underlying belief that all living energies, from the tiniest microorganisms, are interdependent and therefore sacred and that the soil, the grape, and the resulting wine will reflect this holistic exchange. While skeptics may deride this as mystical claptrap, many of the world's most scientific and empirically

driven vignerons, from chemist Noël Pinguet and his Cartesian ration-
ality at the Huet estate in Vouvray, to Dominique Lafon in Meursault
and Frédéric Lafarge in Volnay, pursue their personal version of biodynamic farming. All of these vignerons, it should also be added, are so
highly respected that they could easily dispense with such arduous,
risky, and unprofitable work. Two weeks after visiting de Villaine, when
I met Yvonne Hégoburu in the southwestern city of Pau, I was intrigued
to learn that she, too, with her deeply mortgaged six hectares, felt it a
moral obligation to nature to work her vineyards biodynamically.

At the same time, Aubert de Villaine is careful not to become an ideologue of any kind. "Everything is a source of questioning for us," he
said. "We don't know where we are going, or how to best express the *terroirs*. Besides, there is no one *terroir* truth. It's like in Plato's cave . . ."
His words reminded me of two personal axioms. The first is that my
wine world experiences led me to believe that all film school students
should spend six months learning their craft . . . at the side of a
vigneron. The second is the belief that my own university training in
ancient Greek had given me a solid base for the craft of filmmaking
(because the ascetic rigor required to learn the language leads to the
most sensual of freedoms once the daunting texts can be decoded in the
original). De Villaine's words strike a deep chord within me—even if
my studies of ancient Greek focused on the playful fantasies of Homer,
while de Villaine's were anchored in the rigor (and illusions) of Plato.

We would film later that year with Aubert de Villaine, in a situation
of trust and simplicity, among the vines of La Tâche and Romanée-
Conti. It struck me that the laser-sharp precision in the tastes and textures of all his wines, Romanée-Conti and Bouzeron alike, can be traced
to roots that are not simply nourished by the mineral nutrients of the
earth. So why isn't this man with admirably photogenic (photosyn-
thetic?) charisma in the final version of *Mondovino*? After over a year of
editing, it was apparent that de Villaine's relationship with his *terroirs*
(and thus with time itself . . . since a *terroir* is also the historical development of a relationship between man and nature) belonged to a
rhythm too far outside my (syncopated, kinetic) pace for a theatrical

release film, featuring a global cast of hundreds. It was then that I realized that I'd have to find a different film format for him (and others) outside the narrative requirements of a traditional feature-length movie. Slowly I built up, in parallel to the feature version of *Mondovino*, a ten-part series of hour-long episodes in which de Villaine could emerge, at his own pace, as one of the film's protagonists. With the series, I'd imagined an invitation to the viewer to search for pleasures closer to a nineteenth-century novel—the Burgundian apostate searching for Bordeaux-like redemption?—in which the viewer could "read" the narrative at his own pace, perhaps giving it a half hour's attention sporadically over the course of a few months, or, maybe sick in bed, do a ten-hour marathon over the course of two days. This different and in some senses more antiquated conception of narrative film storytelling—a DVD release of a ten-chapter interlocking tale—ironically became for me the most original and resolutely progressive expression of my film's *terroir*.

The *Terroir* of Others

The next day we headed to the nearby village of Volnay to see a great friend of de Villaine's, Hubert de Montille, whom I knew slightly already. I remembered the man as the exact mirror of his wines: caustic and suspicious at first, but capable of dazzling wit if he felt there was an open spirit before him. I'd been drinking the Volnays and the Pommards of Montille since the early 1980s, in France, England, and in the United States. The wines were always surprising, often pushing a wine drinker's preconceptions or expectations to the limit. None of the vintages made by Hubert de Montille, from the midfifties through the late nineties, were ever easy at first sip, and their development in bottle was rarely logical from year to year. Many wine drinkers were put off by the wines' unpredictability, orneriness, and elusive complexity (often bitingly acid when young, even though always elegantly textured). Which was why I always liked putting these wines on restaurant wine lists: provoking drinkers to rethink what was in front of them, inducing a dash of anxiety to spice the pleasure. I had met Hubert de Montille only once, in 1999, with my brother Adam and his wife, Sharon. Now a foreign correspondent for *The New York Times*, Adam was then living in Vichy, where his first son, Franklin, was born, named in tribute to an important influence on our family. Adam was writing a book at that time, *The Algeria Hotel: France, Memory and the Second World War*, about the maddeningly contradictory invocations of Nazi occupation memories by the French. His reflections on the ethics of historical memory—a fusion of W. G. Sebald's blurring lines between desire and fact and the more pitilessly ironic judgment of documentary filmmaker Marcel Ophüls—would later provide me with a critical framework for imagining *Mondovino*.

On a soft September afternoon in 1999, Hubert and his wife, Christiane, received my brother, his wife, and me—three unknown American visitors—with a measured cordiality. However, I sensed a change in Hubert's demeanor within half an hour. We were obviously wine enthusiasts, curious about the history of the domaine, but in no way self-proclaimed professionals or "connoisseurs." I think it was this latter quality, more than anything else, that led Montille, before his retirement a highly regarded lawyer in the nearby city of Dijon as well as a talented vigneron, to fetch a precious bottle of '85 Volnay Taillepieds from the depths of his dark and chaotic wine cellar. The greatest pleasure for me, beyond the generosity of the gesture, was to see the pleasure that Montille himself took in drinking this delicious wine, and to see that he felt comfortable enough with three strangers not to hide the feeling. "In Bordeaux," he said to me, refilling my brother's glass, "they show, but they don't drink. In Burgundy, we hide, but we drink."

Three years later, on a February morning in 2002, Hubert welcomed Juan and me alone. We had parked our car in the courtyard of his eighteenth-century limestone manor, next to the barn that was used for fermenting wine three months out of every year. I had told him I would be filming during this (first real) encounter. "I've been retired for six years now," he'd told me on the telephone, laughing, "so do what you like with me." Born in 1930, Montille walked more gingerly since the stroke in 1996 that forced him to retire, but his mind was still agile and engaged. A former president of the bar in Dijon, he came from a long line of judges. "We've been judges in my family since the seventeenth century, when we were elevated to the nobility, but really we're just glorified bourgeois. Go see the de Vogüés [highly reputed producers of wines in Chambolle-Musigny] if you want to see real aristocrats. They're from one of the most ancient and noble families in Burgundy." His comments resonated with the feeling of the house. Despite its scale, it felt more provincial bourgeois than landed gentry, a comfy village home put to multiple family uses.

He decided that the most interesting place to show us would be the Tallepieds vineyard, two hundred meters from the house. If the Volnay wines are considered the most delicate and fine of the Burgundy reds, this *premier cru* (or "first growth") Tallepieds is the prince of elegance. The wines are more subtly complex, complete, and refined than the other *premiers crus* of the appellation's fairly steep hillside vineyards. The Taillepieds' seventeen acres are split unequally among at least fifteen owners, with one tenth of it belonging to Montille, yielding on average about thirty-five hundred bottles a year. Overall, the Montille family produced sixty thousand bottles in 2002, from about a dozen different vineyard sites across two villages.

"What sets the Taillepieds apart from other vineyards in Volnay?" I asked him.

"Difficult to say. We *could* talk about the favorable exposure to the sun [a necessity for ripening the grapes in sun-deprived northeastern France], the optimal mid-slope drainage [critical for keeping the vines from drowning in the constant rains], the complexity of the chalk and limestone subsoils, or the care given to the vines for centuries by people who cared about quality and refined taste." He looked at me with a sly smile: "But the truth is, I can't tell you, exactly."

I gaze at this lawyer known for his dazzling courtroom arguments and I wonder if this laconic reply isn't just another canny vigneron's ruse to avoid revealing the secrets of the *terroir*—or worse, confirmation of the view trumpeted by many New World vignerons and critics that *terroir* doesn't exist, that it's a fabrication of French marketing. But Montille's strength lies in his transparency. This is the opposite of marketing. He simply stated what he feels in an entirely unguarded way. Ambiguity and contradictions in no way occlude truth or belief.

Hubert contemplated the denuded but not desultory landscape, the austere grays and browns of a Burgundian winter. "I remember when I would come to play here as a child. It always made me happy to play among these vines." Then he slowly bent down and buried his hands in the earth. He pulled out a handful of rocks and pebbles of various sizes and explained how they pressured the roots to search deeper in the subsoil, thereby extracting ever richer layers of minerals and nutrients for the plant and so increasing the complexity of the grape's character. He seemed equally at ease playing the role of the peasant, the bourgeois, the intellectual, and the provocateur. He seemed indifferent only about playing the part of the man of privilege and power (always the most winning strategy, in fact, for inhabiting that role with conviction).

All of a sudden, his nose started bleeding. I noted that even he, a native, was affected by the punishingly dry cold of this February day. I didn't know if it would be impolite to say anything, so I quietly looked at Juan, who also seemed unsure what to do. Montille remained oblivious as the bleeding continued for a few moments. I then rummaged in the camera bag and handed him a Kleenex. He stuffed a small wad of paper in the offending nostril without breaking off from his discussion, obliging us to keep filming with the tissue sticking prominently out of his nose. And so, by example, he'd invited us to "screw appearances"— as he would say—and be as transparent as he.

Montille spoke about his struggles alongside his friend Aubert de Villaine to relocate wine in a larger cultural and historical context, followed by a subject he seemed to relish even more: his relationships with his children. His description of Alix, his vigneronne daughter, who works outside the family domaine, was suffused with tenderness and respect, for her rebelliousness as well as her talent. But his tone changed radically in discussing Etienne, his only son and the overseer at the family estate since his retirement. Etienne, forty at that time, had only recently abandoned his career as an international corporate lawyer, suffering, said his father "from a fucking banker's mentality. He has a head for business, not poetry." Montille's surprisingly harsh phrase was softened by the twinkle in his eye: "Of course, he makes good wine anyway." The oldest child, Isabelle, he then told us with a chuckle, had managed to avoid following in her father's complicated footsteps. The conversation with Montille, above all, revealed a man not in the least afraid of *being*. The often brutal—and self-denigrating—honesty of his words left no doubt about that. Nonetheless, his years spent concocting defenses for his clients had taught him that one cannot "be" fully without also mastering the art of "appearing." And it's for this reason that in Montille I'd found a true actor and the eventual star of *Mondovino*.

After our morning shoot, Hubert's wife joined us for lunch at the one (quite mediocre) restaurant in Volnay. It was fascinating to watch how Christiane, who had evidently suffered his caustic stream of consciousness for forty years, punctuated by outbursts of irascibility and charm (the latter quality most often directed at others), had learned to survive by the side of this outsize character. Throughout the lunch, Hubert sought to provoke all three of us, notably with a blind tasting of two bottles he'd pulled from his cellar and brought to the restaurant. Each bare bottle had only the numbers '89 scrawled in chalk on the sides. Hubert explained that they were both from the 1989 vintage (a ripe, sun-basked year), but it was up to us to discover whether they were from Volnay or Pommard, and which of the dozen or so Montille *terroirs* they came from within those two villages. As the lunch progressed, Juan and I felt we were being given a master class in identifying tastes that linked to origin. One bottle was softer in the mouth, less acid but fuller bodied. Wouldn't this lead us to the neighboring village of Pommard and its clay soil component? Maybe, said Hubert, but what of the mineral delicacy and fragrant fruitiness of the wine? Of course, I said like a too-eager pupil, those qualities are considered more characteristic of Volnay and its higher limestone content. But with careful attention to the evolution of each sip, he led us fifteen minutes later to find the soft lining inside the wine we'd originally thought sharper.

Hubert occasionally baited his wife, mixing sarcastic remarks characteristic of long-surviving couples with a quiet admiration for her no-
nonsense descriptions of the aromas, tastes, and textures she knew so
well. "This one feels more complete. Long, biting finish," she said. After
two hours and with both bottles now emptied, we turned to the old
peasant-lawyer-Socratic-dialogue-maker. "And so, is the first bottle a
Pommard Rugiens and the second a Volnay Champans?" (The latter
vineyard is a fruitier, less earthy, mineral *premier cru* than the
Taillepieds vineyard we'd just visited.) Christiane thought so, and I felt
inclined to agree—or ill equipped to dispute her judgment. Montille
smiled for a long time, while his wife released a tiny, almost impercepti-
ble sigh. Juan and I waited for the oracle to pronounce a verdict. Finally
he spoke: "You may be right but I can't tell you for sure, since I lost the
records a long time ago." And he meant it.

Terroirless in Gaza

En route back to our hotel in the town of Beaune, Juan and I discussed
the peculiarly Burgundian attachment to *terroir* and the contrast with
our shared deracinated status (the *sans terroirs?*). Among the Maumes,
the Ligniers, and the Montilles, we'd discovered a relationship unique
to the world of wine, but with universal repercussions. We all ask:
"What do our fathers owe us? What are our obligations to them? What
do we owe our past? How do we affirm our identity, our individuality, without sinking into solipsism?" In the articulation of *terroir*, a
vigneron finds a singularly concrete expression of the problems of heritage and transmission. Whether the land that is worked is ancestral or
newly acquired, it's surely both a privilege and a burden to be con-
fronted with one's heritage every day. Each generation of vignerons has
a physical relationship with his past. In the case of long-standing family
operations, the vines they nurture as a "parent" have also been nurtured
by their fathers and forefathers in an act of multiplied parenting. If
they're first-generation vignerons, they are placed in an undefined but
nonetheless filial relationship with the person—known or unknown—

who worked the land before them. To understand the relationship of vine to soil and climate, books can be no help. A *terroir* wine that is fully expressive of a place and its history can emerge only from empirical experience: the experience of the vigneron to be sure, but also the accumulations of experiences of his forebears or the vineyard's previous caretakers. Although many New World and neophyte vignerons would dispute the notion (for obvious vested interests), I'm convinced that there is an incomparable complexity and mystery embedded in wines of long-standing *terroir* precisely because of these generational exchanges and their cumulative effect on the wine.

But let me be clear that this is not an argument that only families with hundreds of years of experience can make wines of the greatest complexity. Rather, to achieve the maximum expression of the interlocking relationship between land and man, there can be any number of combinations of historical interaction, from an ancient familial relationship to a specific plot of land, as in the case of Aubert de Villaine in the Burgundy village of Vosne, to three generations' worth of exchange, as in the case of Charles Joguet in the Loire town of Chinon, to a first-generation relationship to a vineyard, as in the case of Yvonne Hégoburu in the southwestern Pyrénées appellation of Jurançon. What these instances have in common, however, is a centuries' old skein of interactions among land, vine, and man that gives a context for current and future engagement. It's as if the land itself, like the rings of an ancient tree, has a palpable memory of what struggles and triumphs each growing season brought.

Consider the vineyards in Yvonne Hégoburu's fifteen-acre Domaine de Souch. Planted no later than the fifteenth century (and probably well before that), these steep slopes were worked continuously until World War II, when the vines were abandoned (and left to die) because all of the available men went off to war and women were considered incapable of working the treacherous hillsides. But forty years later, the intrepid Yvonne, at the age of sixty, replanted the whole vineyard area she had recently bought. Although a first-generation nonnative urbanite (she comes from the nearby city of Pau), simply by assuming responsibility for the land itself, she immediately entered into a dialogue with that land's memories of past plantings—including, in the literal sense, trace elements in the subsoil of hundreds of years of dead roots, rootstocks, vine leaves, grapes, and vine composts, all of which contribute to a physiological land- and timescape. At the same time, this dialogue with the *terroir* includes her own theoretical and empirical reconstitution of previous farmers' understanding of the land, leading her to the philosophical decision to work the vineyard according to the precepts of biodynamism, thus allowing the natural "history" of the land to express itself without the toxic interference of chemicals and other agents of memory erasure. To be sure, how much of this is perceptible in the taste of either her fragrantly dry or finely sweet Jurançon white wines depends on the palate and belief system of the taster.

These questions of belonging and heritage led Juan and me to discuss our common culture of uprootedness and the premature deaths of our fathers. Both Juan's and mine died while in the prime of their professional lives (mine at sixty-six, his at fifty-three, when the dictatorship in Uruguay was making it impossible for his diplomat father to continue his work). Both our fathers were of the same generation as Montille, when a certain paternal severity was considered essential for the formation of one's sons. I thought I recognized my father's voice in Montille: authoritative—sometime authoritarian—blunt, often indiscreet, but always with a skeptical glint. But unlike with the Burgundian lawyer-winegrower, my father's authority was never directed as conflict toward his sons. This allowed me to transform his bullish, crusading force into a stimulus for my own development (or so I'd like to now think). But at his death, I'd just turned thirty and had barely begun my career as a film director; I hadn't yet entered into a fully engaged dialogue between his work and mine. Nonetheless, during these encounters with Burgundian fathers and sons, I came to realize that my work was an unconscious continuation of a dialogue with the memories of my father, long after his death. The danger, of course, is that a *dialogue* with one's own memory veers dangerously close to a monologue. But if one is able to keep the memories from being static by avoiding any saccharine glorification and by a ceaseless effort to reconstruct and reevaluate the nature and purpose of those memories, then it remains vital and productive for the future. It, of course, occurred to me that this is exactly how many winegrowers view their relationship to their *terroir*.

Driving from estate to estate, we, the *sans terroir*, asked ourselves if a Uruguayan expatriate and an ever more deracinated American-born Jew could lay claim to an idea of *terroir*. Could our *terroir* simply be the consciousness of our own pasts, constantly worked and reworked? Could the effort to enter into a dialogue with our fathers, to establish an ethical relationship with our past, to trace the roots of our uprootedness, constitute a *terroir* in itself? Could our cosmopolitanism in fact be considered a *terroir*, on an equal footing with the Taillepieds vineyard: a civilized counterweight to the barbarism of the new globalization? Were that the case, I'd feel a particular satisfaction given that the term *cosmopolitan* has historically been employed as a derogatory synonym for Jews and other suspect outsiders. Aubert de Villaine's notion of man's relation to his *terroir* returned to me with even more force: "We are nothing more than caretakers of our *terroir*," he said. "We are midwives for each successive vintage." One thing at least was clear to me. The *terroir* of others is what allows us to understand our own. So even the Burgundian *terroir* of the most entrenched peasant has as much universal as local resonance. Or, as Miguel Torga, the mid-twentieth-century Portuguese poet, wrote, "the universal is the local without the walls."

The Cellar of Memory

As Juan and I searched Lavinia for a bottle of Burgundy to drink with lunch—a lunch that must have seemed like an illusion to Juan at this point, after an hour's worth of meandering ruminations in the belly of the shop—we had the impression of reliving the beginning of our adventure of four years earlier. We didn't find any bottles of Maume.

"Too radical for a luxury shop," I thought. We'd have to go to a more decidedly artisanal and idiosyncratic wine store, such as Les Caprices de L'Instant, for such an ornery expression of *terroir*. But Lavinia did carry the wines of Alain Burguet and Joseph Roty from the same village of Gevrey-Chambertin: two producers whose wines are as expressive and vital as those of the Maumes, if in a more obviously seductive style. And given that these bottles run between thirty and fifty euros a bottle in most Parisian wine shops, there is a shared ethic in terms of pricing that is increasingly rare in the highly speculative world of wine.

It's especially astonishing given that the global market allows start-up wineries in start-up *terroirs* to charge €100 to €200 a bottle, from the Languedoc to California to Argentina, only because their proprietors feel they can get away with it. (Consider these monetary values the wine world's equivalent of hedge funds and derivatives.)

We pass Montille's bottles, including the Pommard Rugiens '99, a beautiful iron-laced *terroir* (*Rugiens* = "ferruginous") in the neighboring village to Volnay. Juan and I look at the simple, elegant label: an off-white background with delicate cursive lettering. The name of the proprietor, with characteristic Burgundian restraint, is in tiny letters at the bottom, while the name of the *terroir* is most prominent in the middle of the label. But then I see the price. "Caramba!" I exclaim. "Eighty-five euros!"

"And Hubert's name isn't anywhere on this label," says Juan.

"Funny. I hadn't noticed. It's gone from 'Domaine Hubert de Montille' to 'Domaine de Montille' overnight. Etienne has already kicked his father upstairs, while he's still alive. This is an unusually aggressive move on his part."

"Filial revenge, for all those years of humiliation at his father's hands?" asks Juan with a sneaky smile, remembering Hubert's public hectoring of his highly market-conscious son. "But who sets the prices?" he adds.

"When it left the wine cellar, this eighty-five-euro Volnay cost around thirty euros. So the Montilles aren't getting *that* rich, either. But when the wine arrives in Paris or New York (strangely enough, before

the fall of the dollar, the prices were often the same in both cities), it's at
least twice as expensive as it was when the vigneron sold it. So the steep
hikes are due to the middlemen and the wine shop."

It's important for understanding the context of these prices to note
that even with more commercially minded proprietors like Etienne de
Montille, this is still only a fraction of the cost of comparable Bordeaux.
A Bordeaux château similar in prestige and historical significance to a
Pommard Rugiens—let's say a "2eme Grand Cru Classé"—will make
five hundred thousand bottles in an average year, against five thousand
for a typical vineyard holding in Burgundy (such as the two-acre Montille piece of the Rugiens vineyard). And yet a similar Bordeaux wine,
say, the Château Pichon-Lalande 2000 that I see in the adjoining Bordeaux aisle, runs €170. This is more than twice the price for a wine,
however similar in complexity, that is one hundred times less rare. Furthermore, while not wishing to persecute Bordeaux (whose wines have
been precious to me since childhood, including the delicious and still
honorable Pichon-Lalande), there are other factors that make this comparison even more unsettling. While the Pommard Rugiens is a vineyard that historically has been confined to an area no greater than
twenty acres and cannot ever be significantly expanded to include
less favorable lots of Pommard vineyards, Château Pichon-Lalande is
merely a brand name and not a delimited *terroir* at all. It's the name of
the winemaking estate that lies within the *general appellation* of Pauillac. Today the château owns 185 of the 3,000 designated vineyard acres
in Pauillac. But when the wine was classified in 1855, along with the
other Bordeaux châteaux, its vineyard area covered less than 100 acres.
How could a specific wine, considered a *terroir* for its individual identity, expand so significantly in Bordeaux, while it cannot in Burgundy?
The answer simply is that the rules for Bordeaux give the power (and
the pride of place on the label) to the brand name, like Château Pichon-
Lalande, whoever happens to be the owner and however much that
owner wishes to dilute the specificity of his *terroir*. This doesn't mean
that the wine is bad and it doesn't mean that a Château Pichon-Lalande
Pauillac, even if they end up buying all three thousand acres of Pauillac

land, can't be a legitimate wine. But we've seen the effects of franchising of every type and level of restaurant in the world and what that means for overall quality and care. Of course, as previously noted, since its inception as a wine-producing region of prestige in the twelfth century, when Aquitaine became an English dukedom, Bordeaux wine has been designed for foreign consumption, with every successive generation attentive to the dominant global power of its time and eager to cater their wines for that market. The style of wine has swayed back and forth across the great Anglo-French conflicts up through the early nineteenth century, defined in price, style, and prestige by the British in the 1855 classification at the height of the British Empire. It shifted abruptly—and briefly—during World War II to the German occupation, and since America's ascendance in the wine world in the 1980s, it has radically altered its style to that taste and market. With the almost certain decline of American consumer influence in the coming years, it will be interesting to see whether there will be a consequent shift away from the sugary sweet and alcoholic Napa-style Bordeaux of the last twenty-five years. It will also be interesting to see if the concurrent wild price speculation in Bordeaux will also abate.

Juan, thirsty and at wit's and palate's end, gestures me back to the Burgundy aisle. "How about the Chambolle-Musigny from Christophe Roumier? And it's only thirty-seven euros! Incredible!" He's put his finger on one of the poster children of the new generation of Burgundian vignerons (along with Jean-Marc Roulot and Dominique Lafon in Meursault, Frédéric Lafarge in Volnay, and Romain Lignier in Morey, and many others), who not only make biodynamic, organic, or chemical-free wines from the greatest *terroirs* in Burgundy, but who also insist on ruthlessly ethical pricing (despite the subsequent speculation among gray-market merchants and unscrupulous resellers). Many of them also insist on the clarity of a relation to their past. Roumier's label still states, in discreet letters at the bottom, that the wine is issued from "Domaine Georges Roumier," the name of his grandfather. In each case, their fathers transformed estates of modest size and reputation into names of a greater prestige. If one thinks of any other creative profession, from painting to literature to music, it's extremely rare that a child matches, let alone outshines, the father. However, in the case of each of these winegrowing estates, the children and grandchildren have outstripped the parents in quality, sophistication, and renown, and yet they have all maintained their peasant rootedness and commitment to an ever more precise expression of *terroir*. To my great surprise, Lavinia appears to be a merchant's expression of this same positive development.

Juan shoots me a pleading, famished glance: "All right, if we don't choose a bottle and have lunch now, I'm going across the street to a café for a beer and a sandwich." The ultimatum produces a swift glance toward the perfect bottle: a 1998 Gevrey-Chambertin *premier cru* Les Combottes from the estate of Hubert Lignier. Even though I feel a twinge of deep sadness, I can already anticipate the pleasures its contents hold in store. I look at the label and think of the twelve-acre clay-and-limestone hillside where the vines are planted and the quietly shared determination of Hubert Lignier and his son, Romain, to extract the finest details that the Combottes vineyard can express through fermented grape juice. I imagine that the greatest pleasure for me and for Juan will be the homage that drinking this bottle will make to all the father-son relationships in Burgundy. And it will be a true and complete homage because it will transmit equal parts of pain and joy. Romain Lignier died of brain cancer in 2004, at the age of thirty-four, leaving not only devastated parents but also an estate of universal cultural value without its carefully nurtured successor. The old theme of transmission has returned, but in a cruelly inverted form.

We take the bottle up two floors to the restaurant. We think of the sincere young man we'd met for just one afternoon. We think of the discreet father who slipped away from the cellar to let his son take pride of place during our filming. I look at the bottle and imagine the fragility of the memories contained in this liquid: those that belong to us, those of the father and son vignerons responsible for the contents, and those contained in the two-thousand-year-old Combottes *terroir* itself. And I think of the memories this particular bottle of memories might now produce, as the waitress pulls the cork from its neck. During the course of this luncheon reunion between two old friends, the wine becomes a welcome third person at the table with us. The Lignier Gevrey-Chambertin Combottes is alive and fully reactive, even after its liquid form has disappeared from inside the bottle. The energy that we give to a bottle of wine is as important as the energy it offers itself.

PART II

What Do We Talk About
When We Talk About Wine?

(with apologies to Mr. Carver)

5

L'ATELIER DE JOËL ROBUCHON

The Taste of Democracy

The next day I cross the Seine to see how wine behaves on the Left Bank. Historically the more bohemian half of Paris, the Left Bank in the last twenty years has become as gentrified and commodified as New York's West Village. The Boulevard Saint-Germain, its main thoroughfare for contemporary consumption, owed its previous bohemian fame to the cafés Les Deux Magots and the Flore. Meanwhile *the* restaurant since the turn of the twentieth century for the trendy, artsy, and literary has been the Brasserie Lipp. Despite service that is abusive even by Parisian standards and food and wine that would shame the most cynical airline caterer, not to mention the omnipresence of cockroaches (which the Lipp manager was recently compelled to acknowledge publicly), the restaurant remains a magnet for media climbers. Which surely says as much about them as about the restaurant. But today locals and visitors with more gastronomic ambitions head to the Comptoir de L'Odéon of Yves Camdeborde, one of the most talented younger chefs in Paris, or to L'Atelier de Joël Robuchon, a concept restaurant created by the man the French have proclaimed "the chef of the century." To get a seat for lunch at L'Atelier, you have to show up by eleven thirty in the morning, a notion worthy of the deliriously bleak Polish surrealism of Witold Gombrowicz: a passion shared with my lunchmate on this day, Manuel Carcassonne, husband of my adjutant Laure and French editor of some of Gombrowicz's work. In an effort to give haute cuisine a more democratic spin, Joël Robuchon, like Alain Senderens and other Michelin-anointed three-star chefs in Paris, has decided to forego the high-brow comfort of three-star dining. In Robuchon's case, he has even abolished a reservation system. Given the catastrophic economic (and qualitative) state of three-star restaurants, this seems like a logical attempt at survival as much as a social gesture. At any rate, I was curious to discover what kind of space Robuchon had accorded to wine in the restaurant concept he describes as "gastronomy of the future." By reducing the price of "luxury," the former chef of the mythical three-star Jamin seems to be offering us the idea of refined taste with a less elitist spirit, a luxury free-for-all, a gastro-utopia.

With every surface lacquered red and black, the space is a cross between a Westerner's idea of a Tokyo sushi bar and an out-of-state re-creation of a New York diner. I take a seat with Manuel and Laure and ask for the wine list. While we wait for it to be brought, I scan the food menu and see that it's dominated by bite-size tapas-style presentations, that most humble and democratic of Spanish traditions. And while we're certainly not in the dizzying three-star heights of eighty-euro entrées, I am surprised to see that these "haute tapas" run between twenty-five and fifty euros each. Considering that you'd have to order at least two or three per person to equal a normal dish, I already wonder what this new notion of upscale democracy is all about.

Haute cuisine is predicated on a notion of supreme refinement in the art of living, and Joël Robuchon has reached the most sophisticated level possible of his art. As the celebrated philosopher-king of French cuisine, he famously refused in the 1980s and '90s to open a subsidiary in New York, despite the lure of easy dollars and greater celebrity. His equally publicized departure from the complex rigors of three-star dining seemed consistent with this purist attitude. The infrastructure alone of a three-star restaurant must be unbearably limiting for an *artiste des fourneaux* ("artist of the ovens"). I could well imagine that David Lean, having made *Lawrence of Arabia* and other epic films, must have dreamed of being able to make a movie on sixteen-millimeter film with a crew of two.

The wine list, after a lengthy delay, finally arrives. It weighs a ton. But I notice that there are numerous wines offered by the glass, a genuinely populist gesture. A wine by the glass in some sense is the ultimate democratic comfort for diners, allowing them to avoid the fateful decision of choosing an entire bottle, which involves a significant expenditure made often without knowing what the wine will actually taste like. With a glass, the aesthetic and economic risk is severely reduced, and it offers a strategy of freedom and flexibility for any table with competing desires. This has to be a considered a boon given that wine is the subject of profound anxiety (unlike cinema, for example). Everyone recognizes his or her own right to have an opinion about a film, to clearly state likes and dislikes. Thirty years ago, the same could be said of books (and if that's no longer the case, it's only because very few people read anymore). But wine, even for someone with a sophisticated understanding of other arts, generally provokes fear and discomfort.

In the case of the Robuchon list, I'm happily surprised to see twelve reds and twelve whites by the glass, and many of them from extremely modest appellations. But then I look at the prices. I'm flabbergasted. A Haute Côte-de-Nuits white, one of the simplest appellations in Burgundy, from Jayer-Gilles, a producer who few would argue is anything more than run-of-the-mill, runs €17 per glass. *Per glass!* It's scandalous. The restaurant has paid about €8 for the bottle, and therefore less than €1.50 a glass. The price for the customer has been inflated by more than 1,000 percent (while the norm is 250 to 300 percent). I see an Alsatian Pinot Blanc from Albert Mann, an excellent producer of wines of depth at extremely reasonable prices. This particular bottle costs the restaurant less than one euro a glass. But what are they charging the customer? Thirteen euros a glass! A 1,400 percent markup! In the new gastro-utopia it appears that wine has been singled out for peculiarly punitive and nondemocratic action. The restaurant's strategy seems to be: take advantage of people who don't know any better and mock those who do. Though I shouldn't be surprised, since this is a fair reflection of what often passes for democratic politics across the globe.

Why do so many people line up here well before noon to eat lunch after one? The restaurant was designed and marketed as a refuge for those with taste but limited purchasing power. The idea was to offer contact with this legendary chef's talent in a more universal and exper-imental spirit. But why seduce us with the notion of liberty in the kitchen only to take us hostage with the wine? Wine is immediately stigmatized as an object of pure luxury, banished from the democratic paradise, excluded as an agent of easy exchange. It seems doubly sense-less because it's easy to make very good money with wine in restaurants without these extortionary tactics. A waiter reclaims our wine list. I ask for another so I can keep reading. The waiter answers without even looking at me.

"There are no wine lists available at the moment, sir."

"Why not?"

"There are only two lists for each of the two rooms."

"You've got only two wine lists? You're joking! We had only five min-utes to look at it. How are we supposed to choose from a thirty-page list in five minutes?"

"Sorry, but that's just how it is."

"Is the sommelier here? Can we talk to him, please?"

He walks away without another word. Already by noon every seat is occupied, the restaurant groaning with local and foreign voices. But it's hard to tell if the Babel is of excitement or anxiety. The sommelier, or the man who claims to be the sommelier (it isn't clear even once we ask him what his exact function is), arrives behind the counter after a long wait.

"Obviously a lot of work went into developing the wine list," I say to him. "You've got a wide range of producers from many regions. Why not allow people the pleasure of reading the list at leisure? I've never seen a restaurant of quality where there aren't wine lists available for each table when they want them. The server grabbed it from us after only five minutes."

"We don't have the table space for clients to keep the wine list," replies the sort-of-sommelier laconically.

"So it's a question of efficiency, of turnaround? The restaurant can't afford for people to stay too long. So the customers' decisions need to be made swiftly. Don't you think it's a pity that the people who come here for a memorable gastronomic experience have to choose their wine under pressure?"

"The brands are clear. We have something of everything for everyone."

"In that case, please bring me back the list so I can take part in this democratic exercise."

The sommelier leaves. The waiter brings the two glasses we ordered. I ask him: "These glasses are from bottles opened today, right?"

"No. Yes. Well, I don't know. But it doesn't matter."

"It doesn't matter? Are you sure?"

"Yes."

"But that's like saying to a filmmaker, 'You can project your film on the sidewalk instead of a screen. It doesn't matter.' Wine oxidizes rapidly once it's opened. The character changes completely. Very often it isn't even the same wine the next day. It might not even be drinkable."

The waiter leaves. He doesn't take my bait. But this seems to be because he doesn't really register our presence except to take our orders. I taste the first glass of wine, from the Hérault region in the south of France: heavy, charmless, alcoholic. The "sommelier" passes us. Laure asks him:

"What do you think of this wine? Do you like it?"

"I like it a lot with some dishes; the advantage is that it's very bold—rich and round, with touches of acacia flowers and lavender honey, not too citrusy but with just a hint of pink grapefruit and Anjou pear . . ."

Unable to respond to this mechanically delivered shopping list of apparently personal metaphors (a kind of corporate marketing recycling of the Proustian madeleine), I try to engage him practically.

"I'm sorry but I can't imagine what I would drink that with," I say to him. "The acidity is almost nonexistent. With food it will seem even clumsier, more alcoholic—"

The sommelier walks away in the middle of my sentence. Of course he's probably right. I'd flee a customer like me, too. I try the other glass, a Chardonnay Colombette from a little-known region, the Libron. It's just as heavy, alcoholic, and charmless. How on earth in a country with thousands of the most vibrant, vividly food-friendly white wines can they even think about serving up two chunky acidless, alcohol monsters, characteristic of countries with too much sun?

I open the wine list to order a bottle. Right away I notice a page of Italian wines—a sign of modernity in Paris, and of a certain yuppified, self-consciously antitraditional posture. Is this page of Italian wines an expression of cosmopolitanism or globalization? I look down the list and see a modest Chianti from Castello di Fonterutoli, made in a style a little too spit-polished and sweet for my taste, but a well-made wine. Then I look at the price. Though it originally cost €8 a bottle (it would surface on most lists between €28 and €35), it is sold here for €104. Where do those extra hundred euros go?

The two bite-size dishes arrive: "veal slivers with morels" for €28 and "green Provence asparagus with hermit crab in citrus oil" for €32. The dishes are perfectly pleasant and reasonably executed. But nothing is remarkable. That is, the food leads us to remark nothing. We have been dulled into submission. It has the trappings and the ingredients of sophisticated adult cuisine but with the intention of baby food. It feels like the taste of the food was planned so that no one could be "against" it. It is "luxury" reduced to the broadest consensual level. Spurious democracy. Specious elitism. The worst of both worlds. Does the political echo sound familiar? I don't think it's accidental. This "Atelier" ("workshop" in French) is a purveyor of consensus, efficiency, and a kind of ersatz globalized democracy. Most of all, though, I feel there's a deliberate strategy to provoke buyer confusion (an often fruitful business practice for nonessential products). By creating an ambience and a system that pressure the consumer to react quickly—and here they are clearly consumers who've been bluffed into believing they're aficionados—the restaurant subtly stresses the customer, progressively diminishing his ability to spend money reasonably, according to his real tastes.

It occurs to me, as I fidget ever more uncomfortably at my counter stool (another detail that has been well thought out to keep any customer from lingering) that it's impossible to talk about wine without talking about money. Though the price of wine varies even more peculiarly than the price of fine arts, a given bottle's price is supposed to be a reflection of its intrinsic value. Whether it's the producer who sets the initial price, or the importer, distributor, or end seller, each time the price of a wine is fixed, an ethical decision has been made in relation to the wine's origins and contents. That's why Lavinia impressed me so much the previous day. And that's why I am so disgusted with L'Atelier de Joël Robuchon today. Wine is inextricably linked to money, like all objects of desire in a capital-driven world. This relationship has been consciously worked since at least the Romans, but it was the English, at the height of the capital expansion of their empire, who managed to create a financial—and social—calculus of wine not only for the aristocracy but also, crucially, for the bourgeoisie and the nouveaux riches. The famous classification of Bordeaux wines in 1855, which ostensibly was a celebration of the singularity of French *terroirs*, was in fact a purely mercantile exercise in determining a hierarchy of market pricing for the English-dominated "claret" market. Inevitably the American economic empire of the 1960s, '70s, and '80s created a new socio-monetary (which is to say, by contemporary reckoning, "spiritual") classification.

Curiously, at the moment that money acquired a religious value (arguably beginning with the Dutch in the seventeenth century, and the English thereafter), wine's intrinsically ethical relation to the world has only been reinforced (if often by inverse example). Wine as an object of supply and demand is similar to other art objects. The price of a bottle in fact is only partly linked to its inherent value (which in itself isn't necessarily a matter of taste) and only partly a question of scarcity or rarity. It's inevitable that the price of wine today is determined less by a *not-so-free* market as by the manipulations of those in power. This is true for a wine multinational in Chile that controls distribution and marketing throughout Brazil, Peru, Venezuela, and Ecuador, as for an American critic who serves the needs of the rapidly expanding Bordeaux market in Asia, as for the restaurant of a world-renowned chef that sets its wine prices according to its own whims.

A young Japanese couple looks perplexed before what must seem like a French con to them. It's easy to imagine why true Japanese food buffs come here. Many of the most refined connoisseurs of Burgundy are Japanese. This is not surprising, because much of Japanese culture is predicated on an attention to the tiniest detail as a means to achieve the maximum complexity and mystery and by the belief that there is no single truth. I look at the modestly dressed young couple and wonder if they had decided to splurge their Paris budget on this one lunch at the "authentic" Parisian version of Joël Robuchon, international celebrity of French *terroir*. But during the hour and a half they spend next to us at the end of the counter, I don't see even the subtlest sign of pleasure. Two young Americans are seated to my right. I overhear snatches of their conversation. Self-described "food groupies," they dive into their "tapas tasting menu" with zeal. But without ever saying anything negative about the food or the modest bottle of Saumur-Champigny (modest, that is, in everything except its ninety-eight-euro price), they clearly lose all enthusiasm for the experience. As young and perhaps of as limited means as the Japanese couple, they are spending a fortune. Is it that fact that prevents them from more openly expressing their disappointment? Or is it the myth of "Robuchon, chef of the century"? Or, worse, are they intimidated by the vestiges of an American myth that all Frenchmen are food and wine experts? What are they afraid of?

Fear, alas, is as critical an emotion in the psychology of wine as desire. In fact, everyone is capable of being intimidated by the mythic and religious force of wine, by its profound links with the Judeo-Christian tradition. But ironically, in both the Old and the New Testament, amid the hundreds of enthusiastic references to wine, there is in fact only one that places wine in a negative light, and even then the culprit isn't wine itself, but its misuse. In the Book of Amos, the prophet criticizes the wealthy and the powerful who amuse themselves by inebriating the Nazarenes in order to have these impoverished sages say only what they wish to hear—more shades of contemporary politics? Under any circumstance, wine has been historically charged with a power that is unique in the alimentary world. But it has also engendered a fear that is equally singular because of its association with connoisseurship and power.

Wine has been a symbol of prestige since the earliest Greek civilizations (as sacred for Troy's Priam as for the Argives's Agamemnon). It's inevitable, therefore, that money is a critical element in making wine an object of anxiety as much as one of pleasure. For those not inducted into the cult of wine knowledge, the relationship between wine and money must seem irrational and incomprehensible. After thirty years of association with wine in one semiprofessional form or another, I've arrived at the same conclusion. But there's another factor today that induces a state of terror before this liquid that is supposed to bring us only grace and pleasure: the so-called professionals' discourse about wine, the words employed by wine professionals other than the vignerons themselves. Technicians, consultants, marketers, and critics have passively conspired to create a discourse so impenetrable and nonsensical that even some vignerons are cowered into adopting it for the sake of their financial survival. Like in the Marx Brothers' *Horse Feathers*, when Groucho is forced to submit to Chico's continuous reinventions of an equally invented club's passwords, the only purchase in the world of wine it seems is to adopt the irrationality of its discourse. Of course this eventually requires that reality become correspondingly invented. The more a wine salesman—in the guise of a sommelier or wine shop owner—concocts far-fetched flavor associations ("Anjou pear, lavender honey," et alia) and wields a technician's jargon, the more easily he's able to dominate you and prevent you from formulating your own reaction, your own taste, your own curiosity about the wine's cultural dimension, your own pleasure. Very few people have the courage to say that a given wine "bored me" or that its taste is "not to my taste," even though this is the most natural thing for us to say about a person, a movie, or a book. Interestingly, most people have already lost the ability to make these natural pronouncements about works of plastic art, since the plastic arts have become in the last thirty years hermetically sealed off from the culture at large.

Auction sales of fine wine have come to closely resemble auction sales of contemporary fine arts. Before the current economic crisis, during a lunch at filmmaker and magazine publisher João Salles's house in Rio, I was seated next to Stephen Lash, the visiting director of the U.S. branch of Christie's. I asked him if art-world buyers' taste and their expression of power have changed significantly in the past twenty years. "Absolutely," he responded. "There have never been so many people with so much money to spend and with such a finite number of objects to buy. Obviously prices have exploded, and there's been a boom in the contemporary art market. Why? Because that's one area where it's possible to create a supplementary stock of luxury objects. The Old Masters and the Impressionists are fixed in quantity. It was necessary to create a new 'Old Master' market." He looked at me as if my question were rhetorical, a sly strategy to extract some other less obvious point. "I mean, people do have to express their social ambitions somewhere."

I asked him if he considered this phenomenon different from the efforts of Joseph Duveen and Bernard Berenson, the great art impresarios at the turn of the twentieth century who set the standards of taste (and price) for all of America's robber barons (and hence the future foundation for most American museum collections).

"Yes of course. Because in the late nineteenth and early twentieth century there were simply many fewer people with disposable wealth who could get in on the game. Today it's much more democratic."

Having given up on the two wines by the glass, I (hurriedly!) scour the wine list for a plausible bottle (i.e., a wine that excites some desire at a nonpunitive cost). But I can't see past a €70 Beaujolais, a €93 Coteaux de Languedoc, or a Spanish wine, Pingus, for €803! "Why 803?" I wonder. For anyone ready to yield up that extravagant an amount of money for a highly suspect wine that was invented out of whole cloth only a few years ago, the extra €3 seems deliriously arbitrary: a Gombrowiczian—or Duchampian—touch on top of a Marx Brothers gesture.

In 1998, Joël Robuchon very publicly announced his retirement. It was as culturally resonant in the French media as Michael Jordan's first retirement announcement in the United States. And it proved as glitteringly short-lived. Quickly Robuchon created a restaurant in Macao (between business affairs in Thailand and Brazil), two "Atelier" restaurants in Tokyo and New York (giving the lie to his equally publicized refusal to "ever open a subsidiary in New York"), and numerous other business ventures marketing the Robuchon name. Having also announced "the death of three-star luxury restaurants," he then opened a third Atelier and a "three-star restaurant," both in Las Vegas. Perhaps he felt his French brand name could remain under the radar at home by opening at the MGM Grand Hotel. How curious that the man who declared a "new era of the democratization of luxury" in France, would feature a menu at $400 a head in his newest venture in Vegas.

Here at the "L'Atelier de Joël Robuchon" Paris branch, we are at the epicenter of a multinational's conception of productivity. It's bracing to observe such an efficient model of rapid turnover. The *antireservation* system prevents the restaurant from losing even five minutes of its valuable time and space, while the small portions at high prices and the speed of a counter as opposed to tables keep productivity at a peak. And the coup de grâce? The consumption of wine, thrust onto the pedestal of high luxury, stripped of any relation to pleasure and discovery, becomes a remarkably brazen expression of psycho-mercantile intimidation bordering on theft. The Atelier is indeed a contemporary workshop: a powerful work in progress of the global transformation of rarefied pleasure into ruthlessly efficient consumer product, the inversion of luxury and exclusivity into the cynical simulacrum of luxury for the masses. Both Adam Smith and Karl Marx (not to mention the great nineteenth-century *luxury* tastemakers John Ruskin and Walter Pater) are turning over in unlikely synchronicity in their graves.

After all, customers at the Atelier are being fed the same product they can recognize elsewhere, but secure in the knowledge that it's better here because it's apparently more exclusive and certainly more expensive. This restaurant, which ostensibly is a celebration of an individual's singular talent, is indistinguishable in intent from the mass-market chains of Subway or Red Lobster. "One day," I say to my lunch companions, "we'll find Robuchon-endorsed food products in the Leclerc supermarket chain." Manuel and Laure laugh. "They're not at Leclerc, but at its rival, Carrefour. And they're already on sale," they say. When I go home, I look up on the Carrefour Internet site to see a category of luxury items advertised like this:

Quality for everyone! Joël Robuchon has established his top ten products for you, called "Reflets de France [The Mirror of France]."

"Berg" (as Gombrowicz would say).

6

WITH (AND WITHOUT) ALAIN SENDERENS

The Luxury of Having Taste

In late 2005, the widely respected newspaper *Le Monde* reported an important event in the world of haute cuisine: "One of the principal actors in the creation of nouvelle cuisine during the 1970s, Alain Senderens, caused a sensation by declaring that he was renouncing the three stars awarded him for his Lucas Carton restaurant by the Michelin Guide for the last twenty-eight years, in order to make an "un-frou-frou" cuisine suited to today's world. He even went so far as to say that the "pressure" of the Michelin Guide's recognition prevented him from offering sardines to his clientele." Sound familiar?

A few months later, Alain Senderens (who, along with Joël Robuchon and Alain Ducasse, forms the most famous trio of chefs in France), gave an interview to *L'Entreprise* magazine: In response to the question "Why haven't you opened a second restaurant somewhere else like some of your colleagues?" Senderens responded, "If I had changed my location, people would have said I'd opened a brasserie. And that's not what the change is all about. I decided to stay in the same place, but to modify the spirit. Lucas Carton was luxury. The new restaurant 'Senderens' is a new way of being. My team and I have been taking advanced seminars in 'contemporary luxury' with an absolutely top-of-the-line specialist."

I cross the Place de la Madeleine, casting a nostalgic glance at the Verger de la Madeleine, a tiny wine shop with thousands of bottles buried in its cellar, at least a hundred of which offer untold pleasures at reasonable prices. But Laure and I are heading to Senderens, the former Lucas Carton, wedged in one of the opulent corners of the august square. Laure had scheduled our meeting with the famous chef three months earlier. He's granted us an hour, from 3:30 to 4:30 sharp. We enter the (transformed) temple of haute cuisine. When the chef separated himself from his stars, the wood-paneled walls of his restaurant gave way to a trendy Japanese-accented Art Nouveau pastiche. No more tablecloths; now there are simply shifting lights that throw into relief the white-on-white furnishings. No more paintings; only suspended glass partitions with nearly transparent Zen-like motifs. The decor is straight out of a trendy 1980s film, or an Eastern European take on "Paris chic." I'm surprised. Senderens is considered the most cultivated and intelligent of chefs, one of the few who genuinely loves wine (most chefs consider it a distraction, in gastronomic and status terms, from their own glory).

We are ushered upstairs into a small dining room featuring a large, white oval table to await the master of the premises. A young sommelier, Alexandre, appears not long after. He tells us, "Monsieur Senderens is on his way"—but when exactly he will arrive, he can't say. He offers me a look at the wine list. I'm pleased to see on the first page that there are six white wines and six reds of quality at less than €23 per bottle. Given that the average price per person for the food is €150, this seems like a felicitous inversion of the Robuchon principal of wine as punishment. I ask the open-faced young sommelier what the concept is. Solemnly he informs us that "We classify our wines at ten-euro intervals. We're no longer a three-star restaurant, so we can offer reasonable prices. That allows people to go immediately to the price point they were expecting." I ask him if it isn't dangerous to create a wine classification based on a comparatively invented relation to money. He responds that "We've had the list based on price points in place for the last two months, and the customers seem satisfied." "Of course they're satisfied," I think, "since the entire culture is predicated on money as the benchmark value." Alexandre continues: "If you look further you'll see that the first half of the list is based on price and then there's another more classical part, which is classified according to region." A canny strategy to satisfy old-time aesthetes as well as the (more than comfortable) masses.

But this list is radically different in all respects from Robuchon. There's a bottle of the rare and aged 1991 Domaine Weinbach Gewurztraminer for only €54 and a 1993 Domaine Huet Vouvray sec for €32. I compliment Alexandre, who, along with the other two sommeliers and Senderens, is responsible for the list: "This is the kind of price-quality ratio that wine lovers the world over dream of." He smiles discreetly: "Yes, but it's very rare for a client to order the latter wine spontaneously. It's up to us to sell it, to encourage the discovery of it. We try to make wine accessible and to work with as many organic winemakers as possible, like Huet and Weinbach, winemakers who have an ecological conscience and preserve the specificity of a *terroir*." Despite his formal manner (the effect, perhaps, of a restaurant that appears very uptight despite the advertised democratization), he seems passionate, informed, and frank. But after twenty minutes I wonder if Senderens is actually going to show up. Trying to loosen up this sympathetic young man, I ask, "Do you have fun with wine here or is it strictly a serious business?" "Oh no. We play around with wine as much as possible. Whenever the opportunity arises to 'have fun,' as you suggested, sir," he responds with a touching earnestness.

Finally Godot arrives. Alain Senderens, in his sixties and groomed like an ageing movie star, exudes a kind of gilded chic. He begins speaking as he walks in the room. The young sommelier vanishes. "I'm pleased to meet you. I liked your film. Even if it's a little Manichaean:

good guys and bad guys," he says with the blunt self-assurance of a man of unquestioned power. "What I liked was that American, the New Yorker, the . . ." He fumbles for the next word. Is he going to say "Jew," I wonder, or am I paranoid (a redundancy, of course, for a Jew, Philip Roth or Woody Allen would say)? "The . . . guy from New York who defends French wines so admirably. Excellent."

I smile. "Funny that you mention Neal Rosenthal, the American wine importer. Because he actually gives the lie to any Manichaean cliché. After all, how paradoxical that a Brooklyn Jew, son of a malted-milk-dispensing pharmacist, should end up being such an inspired and talented spokesman for the value of French *terroirs*. On the other hand, a *terroir*, he believes, doesn't belong to anyone in particular but in fact to us all. Otherwise it's not a *terroir* but a reactionary form of chauvinism. His views surely correspond to your own, no?" He responds with a kind of papal inscrutability: "A *terroir* belongs to a place, a climate, an ensemble of factors that produce a whole. Some places are more blessed than others." Does Senderens not understand what I've just said or was he not listening or is this a calculated evasion?

"But you agree that the value of a *terroir* is universal?"

"Oh, sure. There are wonderful *terroirs* everywhere, even in Australia."

"I meant, do you think that the specificity of a French *terroir* belongs only to the French. Or if—"

He cuts me off: "No. It belongs to all of Europe. Right now the fashion is for *Spanish* wine. I won't tell you that they're all wonderful, but there are *terroirs* like Priorat or Vega Sicilia where they succeed in making fabulous wines."

I try to resist—or embrace (I'm no longer sure which) the enveloping ambience: half Mad Hatter's tea party, half *Krapp's Last Tape*.

"I'm only fifty percent in agreement with you—given that I'm fifty percent Manichaean . . . but what I wanted to say was—"

He cuts me off again. "Would you like to drink something?" he says, waving his exquisitely manicured hand with noblesse oblige.

I nod my head, waiting for the March Hare in fact to pass the tea.

He half grins (or is it a disguised scowl?) and asks, "What *kind* of wine would you like. French or foreign?"

"I'd like to know your palate," I answer. "What kind of wine provokes a deep emotion for you?"

"For me? What moves *me* in a wine is elegance. Elegance comes from a *terroir*, a climate. The hand of man, of course. That's undeniable." He turns toward the half-open door and an unseen attendant: "Call Philippe at once, please!" He turns his gaze back to me: "I'm moved by elegance. I'm not a fan of heavy, overripe wines. I find them . . . indigestible." He looks nervously at me as if I might use this apparently contentious phrase against him and quickly backtracks. "Of course I'm not saying they're not good wines, but it's not my *taste*."

"So you're not fan of Michel Rolland's style of wine?"

"Not necessarily, but I'm a little bothered to say it because you really roughed him up in your film. He's a friend."

Just then a girthful chef in full uniform passes by the door. Senderens calls him in. "This is my chef," he announces, though he doesn't offer a name. He looks at me over the rim of his pencil-thin glasses, but addresses the chef: "*This* is the man who made *Mondovino*, the film about wine. I asked for Philippe, but if he's not here, send in Alexandre." He turns back to me, the Grand Inquisitor now unleashed, but because of that, more revealing of his real beliefs: "I was disturbed by that aspect of the film, because Michel is a man of wine, someone I like. And let's take Parker. I mean, in the end, Parker isn't responsible if the people in Bordeaux are chumps. To please Parker, to get good scores from him, they sold the soul of Bordeaux wines. And I'll never forgive them for that. Especially given how much I used to be a partisan of Bordeaux. And it's a loser's game, because the American winemakers and other hot-climate countries will always beat them in the ripe and sweet sweepstakes. I sold half of my wine cellar from Lucas Carton to pay for the renovation here. I got rid of a lot of Bordeaux."

I ask him if the menu and list have changed radically.

"Oh, for sure. Before, an average check was three hundred and sixty to four hundred euros per person, depending on whether or not truffles were in season. But I thought it was a mistake. Prices kept on spiraling upward." Alexandre, the young sommelier, returns. "Are you red or white?" he asks me. "Alexandre, this is the man who made *Mondovino*," Senderens says. Alexandre nods respectfully as if he hadn't been with us previously.

"Hi, again," I say to Alexandre and then turn back to Senderens. "I'd like to drink something with you that will give you pleasure. I'd like to know your palate, what provokes emotion for you," I repeat.

"Well, I'm a man for whites. In fact, I've been reproached for that. What do you have for us, Alexandre?"

Unhesitatingly, as if responding in an oral exam, he murmurs: "Emotion would be a Beaucastel white. You like that wine."

"Beaucastel? Do we have bottles left?"

"We could go for a 1990." My heart beats. Beaucastel makes beautiful whites, richer and rarer than its neighbor Château Fonsalette. Nineteen ninety is a legendary year, one of the most balanced vintages of the twentieth century throughout Europe.

"Yesterday I drank a magnum that was extraordinary," says Senderens, but he seems to make a subtle sign with his hand to the young sommelier as he says this.

"I'm afraid we're probably all out of the 1990. I'd have to check the cellar," Alexandre suddenly blurts out.

"What else do you have?" asks the maître.

"Old vines Beaucastel from '94, '91, and '92."

"Beaucastel isn't the best wine to drink on its own." (I happen to agree with him.) "How about some Dominique Lafon Meursault?"

"Or Anne-Claude Leflaive in Puligny. A bright 2001 Puligny from her, with their toasty notes. Or Coche-Dury. You find emotion in his 2000." I feel like asking where the emotion went in 1999 or 2001.

"So, what will you bring up for us?" Senderens asks with a flash of impatience.

"Do you know Jean-François Coche-Dury?" Alexandre asks rhetorically, since Coche-Dury is a legendary cult producer of Meursault wines. Senderens nods imperceptibly. Though not so imperceptibly that

Alexandre doesn't immediately declare, "We'll do a Meursault village wine from 2001."

"Two thousand one. Without emotion, then?" I wonder to myself.

"Just a village wine," Senderens asks petulantly, as if we were both let down by Alexandre in his failure to offer us the superior *premier cru* Meursaults. But then he adds: "Make it well chilled. And bring up a glass for yourself as well. So it will be a bottle of elegance and refinement, the way I like it. I often find that whites provide that better than reds. It must be my feminine side. I like to concoct special recipes that will work with whites."

Nonplussed that he left the opportunity to express a personal taste up to his junior sommelier—out of indifference to his guest or indifference to the notion itself?—I ask Senderens to discuss the place of wine in gastronomy, mindful that most winemakers I respect hold his views on the subject as important.

"I have to go back to my beginnings if you're to understand me," he says. "At the start of Nouvelle Cuisine, nobody could explain what it was. We did it instinctively. At the time, in 1970, I hadn't yet been to Japan. It was only afterward that we all realized that the dishes I wanted to create had an unconscious Japanese inspiration: less sauce, shorter cooking time, a more aesthetic presentation. When I finally did go to Japan, I understood that it was Nouvelle Cuisine. At the same time, there was a parallel movement of diet food, but we were creating an involuntary form of diet cuisine. Well, today I can tell you, my inspiration is China. Because tomorrow the whole world will look to China for inspiration. My latest creation is a deboned pigeon stuffed with crab, soya, and spices. Now, you're going to hit the roof when I tell you what I serve with it." He looks at me keenly. "Tea!" He pauses for effect. "For that reason, I consulted with a Chinese woman who owns thousand-year-old tea plantations that produce only two hundred kilos of tea. Since my customers often complain that they don't wish to drink alcohol at lunch . . . well, alcohol, you know . . ." And his voice trails off abstractedly.

"There was really no wine to match with the dish?" I ask.

"I looked hard. My technique is the following: I taste ten to fifteen bottles every day. When I find a wine I like, I need to create a dish for it. Sometimes I'm successful. Sometimes, not.

"With the pigeon, I started instead with the recipe and then searched in vain for a red. Then I realized I'd been the king of fools for not thinking of tea. And so I discovered the world of tea. I'm not saying tea is going to entirely replace wine, but now and then on a menu, why not? I'm telling you the people who eat my pigeon and drink the tea with it are astonished by their ability to go back to work after lunch!"

As I contemplate the long arm of the law of efficiency, Alexandre serves the wine with impeccable discretion. You can feel in the precision of his gestures that his love of the craft of wine service is true. "The wine is already out of its shell, open and waiting for us," he says encouragingly. Despite my growing affection for him, why do I think of a barker outside a Bangkok whorehouse? "The nose is very expressive: citrus, grapefruit, lime, linden—"

The chef cuts him off: "Now, here's the style of wine I love. It's about purity."

"It's not easy to talk about wine is it? "I ask mildly.

"The most important thing to remember is that people are ignorant about wine, ignorant about questions of taste," Senderens shoots back. "They don't have *the words*. And nothing exists until it is verbalized. If it's badly verbalized, it continues not to exist."

A secretary comes in, interrupting the conversation. It seems that a journalist from the AFP (the French version of the AP wire service) who was supposed to have come before us but has only now shown up is waiting for an interview with Senderens.

"How much time do you have?" he asks, already with his gaze out the door.

"Until four thirty. It was your secretary who determined the precise parameters of our meeting. And so we built our schedule around that," says Laure.

Senderens is visibly uncomfortable. "I'd really rather go and then come back later." He tries to change the conversation to avoid the sudden problem, but without enthusiasm: "What would you eat with this wine we're drinking?"

Laure and I, already dumbstruck by the way things are going, barely fumble the beginning of a response before we realize he's not paying any attention. Although the décor feels like a trendily kitsch Ridley Scott film from the 1980s, the encounter puts me more in mind of the '70s Arthur Penn masterpiece of noirish existential anxiety, *Night Moves*.

Senderens is already up and nearly away. "I'm sorry about this unfortunate little mix-up, but as you heard, someone is waiting for me. I'll leave you with Alexandre." He casts a furtive backward glance at Alexandre: "Don't say anything to silly to him, okay, Alexandre?" And Godot is gone again.

We leave Senderens, née Lucas Carton, a few minutes later. What just happened, we wondered. What was he so afraid of? Is there something in the new democratic luxury experience as practiced by Robuchon, Senderens, and Co. that leads to mistrust? Or did his pal Rolland warn him of the interloper and his nefarious ways? To each his own fears and insecurities. Certainly a man of taste—and it was that man that various winemakers had urged me to seek out—he behaved in front of me, alas, strictly as a man of power (fear being the principal agent of power).

7

LE DÔME

Miss Rampling

A few days later I recross the Seine (halfway, that is, to one of the islands in the middle). I've asked the British actress Charlotte Rampling (a Parisian for the last thirty years) to meet me for dinner at a restaurant with a growing reputation on the rue de l'Ile Saint-Louis. But when I get there ahead of time I see immediately that it's impossible, in the style of 80 percent of Paris's restaurants. Diners are already packed in like sardines, one table abutting the next. There's no chance for an intimate conversation of any kind. I mumble apologies and leap into Charlotte's taxi when it pulls up at the door.

The pleasure of dining with Charlotte Rampling has as much to do with the pleasure she herself takes in eating and drinking, as with the biting intelligence and goofily elegant charm of her company. We haven't seen each other since I moved from Paris to Brazil the year before and I look forward to catching up on the singular kind of gossip that emerges from a friendship forged in the heat of making a film together (a form of doing battle) and burnished more coolly for years thereafter. I also look forward to beginning the dialogue with her on a new film project that I'm planning in Rio, a fiction film that will seek to build on the spontaneous comedic joy I discovered was possible while making *Mondovino*.

On *Signs & Wonders*, the film I made with Charlotte and the superb (wine-loving, swashbuckling) Swedish actor Stellan Skarsgard, we were able to build a deep friendship, all three of us, in part because the circumstances of shooting this particular film in Athens were so brutal. Every day, every shot, required steeling your nerves against the chaos and tension that come from a huge multinational crew of Greeks, French, English, and Americans at war with one another in the already tense and brutalizing streets of a city where European conceit collides with Middle Eastern anarchy. Because of that, our friendship and certain wine memories remain indelible, like the restorative 1959 Château Beychevelle (a Bordeaux from the time before they lost their soul). I drank this refined nectar one night with Stellan, his wife, their six children, and his mother, after a fourteen-hour shoot in the labyrinthine and medieval meat market. Stellan compared drinking this wine to lapping up a few drops of civilization while the shells explode around you.

But for the upcoming film, Charlotte and a number of other actor friends and I are planning a comedy to be shot in Rio under more dulcet and joyful circumstances. And instead of the formality of a large crew and the economic restrictions of a large production, as we had in Greece, we're eager to reproduce the conditions of simplicity and spontaneity that made the shooting of *Mondovino* so profoundly pleasurable and stimulating. (Charlotte and her son David—who will play mother and son in my new film—participated, in fact, in one of the episodes of the series version, a delirious dinner with Yvonne Hégoburu, whose dream it was to meet the legendary actress.) Since we need to find the character for each actor, this will require complicated—wine-soaked—discussions over the next years.

In the cab, I tell Charlotte that this will not be the place to hash out our new story. "Where can we go nearby to have a nice chat and a jolly bottle?" she asks me. I look to the fourth arrondissement, across the Seine on my right, and then to my left, across the other side of the river toward the sixth. At this stage in my trip, it feels appropriate to be on an island in the middle of the two banks. "Fish," I say. Charlotte looks at me oddly. "Let's go to Fish: La Boissonnerie . . . the restaurant attached to the very good cave La Dernière Goutte. It's relaxed, modern, lively, but on a Tuesday night it shouldn't be crowded."

The taxi cuts left back to the sixth, crossing Notre Dame. I jump out of the cab on the rue de Seine and duck inside Fish. Fabulous bottles of reasonably priced wine litter the room. A half-finished bottle of Zind-Humbrecht Tokay lies on a table within a meter of me, its distinctive Alsatian perfume beckoning. This is a place, owned by a Cuban American expatriate, where people drink the list. It's not there for show. Alas, this is unusual enough in Paris that even on this Tuesday night, it makes Fish packed to the gills. The line is ten deep (with a youngish crowd) for the next table.

"Where to next?" asks Charlotte with her indefatigable cheerfulness, a quality known to her friends, giving the lie to her public persona as a melancholy femme fatale. "Not so easy on the Left Bank to find a good bottle, a nice bite, and a quiet place to talk, eh?"

"My family used to go to La Coupole nearly every Sunday, in the 1960s. Pity it's become part of the FLO Brasseries restaurant chain and been turned into a tourist trap. Hang on. Why not fish?"

"But we just tried and failed there."

"No, fish, as in eating fish . . . *the* fish restaurant. Le Dôme."

On the Boulevard de Montparnasse, a few hundred meters from La Coupole, it's still possible to find a remnant of the Paris of the 1930s, albeit at a steep price. Le Dôme is only a quarter the size of La Coupole and, unlike its giant neighbor, specializes in the neatest, simplest, but purest fish preparations. But it shares a common raffish, bourgeois-bohemian past. Like La Coupole, it was also a hangout for the Picasso crowd before the war. Today, it alone in the neighborhood remains a haven for film people, artists (with deepish pockets), and visiting vignerons of means. Wine producers, conscientious craftsmen that they are, in particular appreciate the simplicity of the preparations, the precision of the "cuisson" (the sacred cooking time), and the purity and freshness of the fish. Eating oysters on the covered terrace is also one of Le Dôme's attractions. But aficionados adore above all the simplicity and justness of the wine list. Charlotte and I are quietly brought over to a cozy booth, one of several dozen that line the cheery, elegant rabbit-warren interior. The restaurant has the buzz of activity of happily communal space. The noise level is just enough to mask our conversation from our (adequately distanced) neighbors, but not so high that we can't speak in normal voices. If the ideal restaurant allows for a table to construct their own sense of privacy and intimacy within the circuslike pleasure of a public gallery, then Le Dôme has to rank among the greater successes.

Charlotte, knowing me well (and being thirsty), asks the waiter immediately for the wine list. It appears almost instantly. The object, the list itself, is already a pleasure; semi-hardcover, tall and wide, it opens up to a single, comprehensive view: a page with all the whites on the left and all the reds on the right. Open it and everything is before you, simple and frank. No heavy books or turning of pages or complicated texts. Just the wines themselves, fifty whites, fifty reds. The selection is far from the best in Paris. There's nothing penetrating, surprising, or profound about it. I'd even say that I wouldn't drink more than half the wines on the list, and there are dozens of vignerons I think are distinctly mediocre. But I don't expect the list here to be the best or the hippest. I accept that for the sake of Le Dôme's regular (gastronomically conservative) clientele, half the red list is made up of Bordeaux, even though these are the least appropriate fish wines imaginable (because the pronounced tannins in Bordeaux—a form of tongue-drying acidity that gives structure to red wine—produce an unpleasant metallic taste in reaction to white-fleshed fish). I accept that 80 percent of the Burgundies are from mediocre producers, not the worst but far from the best. But the simplicity and sobriety of this list overall and the presence of some spectacular bottles at extremely reasonable prices and perfectly gauged for the style of the food make this list true to itself and therefore, for my taste, admirable.

Just the fact that seventeen of the fifty whites are available in half bottles—that pint-size token of true wine love—tells me that this restaurant is concerned above all with encouraging guests to choose what each considers the right wine with the right dish with maximum flexibility. In fact, the percentage of half bottles is probably the highest of any place I can think of. This is respect for the food and wine lover: €17 for a half bottle of the excellently crisp Menetou-Salon from Clément, €15 for an equally zingy Loire Quincy from Mardon—both Sancerre neighbors—or €28 for the Faller mother and daughters' pungent '04 Riesling "Cuvée Theo." (Theo is the deceased husband-father.) The shortcomings of the list are equally forgiven by the presence of a dozen fine full bottles of white from €29 to €139 (the latter, the Chave Hermitage white '01 from the Rhône, is one of the most profound and complex white wines of France). Each bottle is fairly priced according to the quality and rarity. Most important, these wines, like the mineral, acid Huet Vouvray Sec (€38) or the classic Serge Dagueneau Pouilly-Fumé (less showoff, more food friendly, and a quarter the price of his international superstar cousin Didier Dagueneau) are all vivid, attentive companions for the meal.

But tonight, I give the list only a quick scan and immediately spot two names from Burgundy that promise the magic worthy of the company, René and Vincent Dauvissat in Chablis and Colette Ferret in Pouilly-Fuissé. I order the Chablis (even though it's from the grape-scorched *canicule* summer of 2003). I'm grateful for the simplicity of the wine list's layout, which allows me to make a quick, happy choice and turn my attention to my cherished—and patiently waiting—guest.

Charlotte, who is always surprising, fixes me with her beguilingly aqueous gaze. I brace myself for one of her devastatingly probing questions about either the true state of my personal life or the deeper search of the film we will do together.

"So, Jonathan. Tell me about the wine list. How does it rate?"

8

LA CAGOUILLE

More Fish Tales

Le Dôme may represent the idea of a certain bourgeois charm (an essential quality in every artist and rebel's search for pleasure), but it's not the only place in the fourteenth arrondissement that rigorously marries fish of the highest quality with well-chosen wines. The only time I'd been to La Cagouille was with Hubert and Christiane de Montille, Aubert de Villaine, and about thirty vignerons from the "Family Domains of Burgundy," an association of producers of the highest quality. I was surprised that these discerning gourmands would hold their dinner in a concrete no-man's-land behind the Tour Montparnasse, the lone skyscraper that hideously disfigures the landscape of southern Paris. But the conviviality of my companions soon made me forget the desultory neighborhood. I was intrigued by the fact that Jacques Dupont had also chosen La Cagouille for our lunch today. A wine critic for the conservative weekly news magazine *Le Point*, he is considered the most pioneering wine journalist in France. An erudite wine historian and former political commentator, he's the rare critic respected by most of his competitors. Given how dispirited most of his wine scribe colleagues leave me, I wondered if Dupont was capable of taking and imparting any pleasure from talking about and drinking wine. Is he so well regarded because of the weight of his convictions or because of political savviness?

The taxi passes Le Dôme and its equally laudable offshoot (at a reduced menu and price), Le Bistro du Dôme. A minute later we're in front of La Cagouille, in the Place Constantin Brancusi. In this involuntary Alphaville, there is no Brancusi—and a lot of Alphaville. I don't see a "place." Only concrete and anonymity. I nearly run from the cab into the restaurant, anxious for some sign of life behind the façade of moribund 1970s urbanization. I don't seem to be in luck. The interior of the glass-and-steel box seems as charmless as the exterior. But after a few seconds the human intensity of its clientele, an evident joie de vivre from the adjoining rooms filled with people talking and laughing over glistening shellfish, oysters, and other delights of the sea, changes my perception. A bottle of 1990 Pommard Rugiens from Montille over the bar also tells me that we're in a place as serious about drinking as eating and talking, a quality as paradoxically rare as finding truly fresh fish at a Parisian restaurant.

Dupont, open faced, youthful in his fifties, welcomes me with a warm smile as if we are at his home. André Robert, the restaurant's proprietor, who will escort us for the duration of this long, bottle-studded lunch, also greets me with the twinkling eyes of a happily lapsed friar. I ask Laure to take out the voice recorder at once as I explain that "I don't really know where I'm going with this book, so I want to tape everything that's said at each encounter."

"That's not a stupid idea. But you're not the first person to exploit my words," Dupont says, laughing. "The number of times my colleagues have plagiarized my work! And often a year after I've done the initial reporting."

André asks us, "What do you want to drink? How about some wine?"

"Red, white. I drink it all," Dupont says, laughing.

"How about a René and Vincent Dauvissat Chablis *premier cru* La Fôret 2002?" André suggests.

"What about the 2001?"

"Very acid. Very mineral. Even more so with shellfish."

I tell them that I'd ordered the same wine the night before at Le Dôme, but from the 2003 vintage. I was disappointed. Dauvissat is one of my favorite producers in the northern Burgundy appellation of Chablis, but the softness and alcohol of the vintage dominated the hand of the producer. It's one of the rare instances where a problem vintage seemed to overwhelm the talent of a great vigneron. In general, in mean, rainy years, when average producers are stuck with bitter, diluted grapes, talented and rigorous producers manage to extract sufficient balance and maturity to produce lean but tensile wines. But in 2003, the problem was inverted because of the crushing heat wave that killed thousands in France and scorched the grapes into an excess ripeness, producing wines that were fat and alcoholic. Not even one of the greatest producers of the world's most fine-boned wines could escape the effects of the hottest and earliest vintage in 150 years, a vintage that will likely be duplicated with increasing frequency in the coming years because of global warming. But for the time being, many wine commentators and merchants are happy to have sweet, overripe wines to sell to an infantilized world. Dupont agrees: "I'm not a fan of 2003, even though a lot of critics all over the world are infatuated by its richness. With Bordeaux 2003s, I get the feeling that I'm drinking a heady wine from the south of France. Which is not a reason to drink Bordeaux."

We order the 2001, finding common ground in a notoriously acidic year, the polar opposite of the 2003. For me, acidity is to wine what light is to a film. It's the critical element that gives life to an image, that animates a person. A precisely gauged light provides the soul of any film. Even the greatest actors and sharpest dialogue fall flat in an over-lit, bland light. Conversely, an overwrought, unjustifiably self-conscious light can become an impenetrable barrier between the spectator and the emotional life of an actor and his physical context. Historically most wine was excessively acidic because grapes were harvested early out of fear of an untimely rain, frost, or disease attacking the vine. But for the past twenty-five years, thanks to innovations in technology and cellar hygiene, and also because of global warming, it's been possible to harvest riper grapes at either earlier (thanks to warming) *or* later (thanks to technology) dates, depending on the needs and region throughout the world. Today we're faced with the opposite problem in fact: a deluge of wines that are overrich, sweet, and alcoholic and lacking in sufficient acidity to maintain vitality. The great English wine historian Hugh Johnson has written that he's less interested in wines that make statements than in those that ask questions. Acidity is the key agent in provoking our palate to ask questions of our taste buds.

We taste the 2001 La Forêt Dauvissat Chablis. At €40 a bottle, its markup is less than even the 250 percent restaurant mean, evidence that wine at La Cagouille is for sharing. The deep straw-colored liquid, shot through with green highlights, is crystalline and precise in the mouth, lively, mineral, and sharp in its flavors. Its acidity wakes up the taste buds. By the time the oysters arrive (only a few minutes later), the four of us have knocked off the bottle. André explains that his oysterman is the cult figure David Hervet, considered "the Dauvissat" of the Marennes salt marshes in Brittany. To do justice to this pedigree, we decide to open a bottle by the other grand master of Chablis, Jean-Marie Raveneau, a *premier cru* Vaillons, also from 2001. Raveneau is legendary for refusing customers—either importers and restaurateurs who call or would-be clients who show up at his door in the Yonne. He's the artisan's artisan, and his limited output commands a waiting list that's rumored to have a ten-year backlog. It's not surprising that the lucky few in the trade who know him are able to demand stratospheric prices for his wines. In most Paris restaurants where his wines surface, the price varies between €120 and €300 a bottle. But the €45 that La Cagouille asks of its customers is in fact reflective not just of the restaurant's ethics but also of the remarkably modest prices that Raveneau himself sets, and a fair indicator, of course, of the unscrupulous speculation that often betrays a vigneron's intentions. The Raveneau is

so subtle that many wine drinkers accustomed to a conventional Burgundy, let alone a New World Chardonnay (the same grape as Chablis
and other white Burgundies), might miss what all the fuss is about. The
grain of the wine is so fine that it seems to barely land on the tongue
and touch the insides of the mouth before it's already evanesced. For
the drinker who listens patiently and intently for the echo of the flavors
and the textures, for its princely assertion of palate memory, the savory,
mineral pleasures are infinite. But in a wine world so completely dominated by the otherwise unobjectionable AC/DC, it's hard for aficionados to hear a Bach piano partita.

I ask André if he thinks the wine is too delicate and refined for the
saline intensity of the oysters. "You could definitely make that argument." He eyes me suspiciously but decides to continue anyway: "It's so
subjective. I've been in this field for more than fifteen years. I'm doing
what I love, even if what I do doesn't fit neatly into other people's ideas.
I never try to make wines match food. For me that's a fantasy. It's an
intellectual construction more than a sensory reality."

I appreciate his skepticism about the imposition of wine/food
orthodoxies, but I don't agree that it's purely mental. Jacques and I ask
him for a Muscadet, a light, crisp, simple wine, which might be a better
match for these sublime but powerfully textured and flavored oysters.
He comes back two minutes later with a 2004 Château de la Preuille.
After tasting it with the oysters, Jacques and I still aren't convinced by
the pairing; this particular Muscadet isn't acidic enough to cut through
the plump flesh of the oysters—a true flaw in an appellation distinguished, in principle, by its razor-sharp acidity. The oysters continue to
surprise us with their complexity, even if the right wine eludes us.

The Salinity of Power

More dishes arrive: Oléron clams, octopus "à la galicienne," and tender
scallops from Normandy. This marine combination is so bracing that
the table pulses with saline pleasure. It occurs to me that the childlike
delight we're taking is in flavors and textures that are resolutely adult:

saltiness, minerality, briny acidity. Dupont agrees that these qualities have been disparaged with pseudo-adult seriousness by the wine world's great demagogic infantilizers, who have indefatigably promoted the tsunami of sweet, alcohol-heavy, and acid-deficient wines characteristic of much of the United States, Australia, South Africa, and Argentina. It's a style of wine that has overwhelmed those previously admirable wine-producing cultures and the entire global marketplace itself in the past twenty years.

Robert Parker is considered the single most influential critic not just within the world of wine but in relation to any given field. The "emperor of wine" as his gossipy but admiring biographer, Ellen McCoy, has dubbed him, he has pursued his taste for sweet, fat, and rich wines with a missionary's zeal. Through the effect of his opinions on the world marketplace, he has become a principal agent in the dissemination of this new vinous world order. When I spent the day filming with him at his blandly kitschy suburban home in rural Maryland for *Mondovino* in 2002, he was at the height of his powers, not coincidentally, like George W. Bush. Parker's virulent righteousness, also like the former president's, was disarming in its bonhomie and apparent conviction. I found him genial in the immediate sense, even as his opinions horrified me, especially his dismissal of *terroir* as an elaborate European marketing hoax. Like Bush, his enemies—real and imagined—are agents of irreconcilable otherness. This is why the notion of *terroir* for him is anathema. *Terroir*, after all, is an expression of the "other" rather than the "self" in a state of permanent renewal and requestioning. Robert Parker's rather primitive proclamation of the self, himself in fact, as the fulcrum of taste judgments and his demagogic belief that the proclamation of his own personal taste is of intrinsically universal value is one of the factors that has led to his astonishing global success.

Dupont points out that when Parker began his career as an autodidact wine critic in the late 1970s, he accurately gauged the extent of hypocrisy in Bordeaux, among many of the more powerful châteaux, especially their use of the 1855 classification as a screen to mask a widespread lack of rigor. Seeing himself as a Naderite consumer advocate,

Parker attacked the Bordeaux status quo. But with the help of his friend the Bordeaux enological consultant Michel Rolland, he acquired such power himself over the next decades, determining the new style of Bordeaux wines that would appeal to the American and Asian consumer, that he simply replaced the old power and its abuses with his own.

Dupont laughs, commenting that food and wine critics and their power machinations are an old story. "After the war, most of the gastronomic critics in France were ex–Nazi collaborators. Why? Because it was the one place that newspapers and magazines thought they could dump these journalists without causing distress. It's always been a dumping ground for oddballs." So naturally I ask him how he got involved in the game.

"A funny place for the guy who writes for *Le Point* [a right-leaning weekly news magazine]. I was a radical in '68, working for the counterculture radio stations. I became a journalist by conviction after studying history at university. I still believe in what I'm doing, despite everything that I've seen. The one thing I'm sure of is that a critic should be the opposite of a guru. A critic, whether it's of wine or cinema, should never wish for anybody to follow his lead. His job is to provoke you to think about your own convictions and predilections. By the way, what should we drink?"

André brings us a bottle of Beaujolais from Pierre Chermette, one of a new breed of fiercely organic producers of Beaujolais wines of amazing purity and vibrancy. The lack of tannin and exuberant fruitiness (but not sweetness!) of the red makes it a cheerful companion (if not the perfect life partner) to the roasted sea bass. I ask André where he's from.

"Brittany, the Côtes-d'Armor."

"So that explains your relationship to the oysters and shellfish. It's a question of *terroir*—"

André interrupts me at once: "My *terroir* is nothing. I'm a citizen of the world. As much as you. Those guys who tell you that *terroir* is the answer to everything are a bunch of fascists. As soon as someone mentions the word *terroir*, I reach for my gun."

Everyone laughs. With so much good wine and food flowing, it's impossible for anybody to be taken too seriously. He adds: "People confuse *terroir* with truth. No. *Terroir* isn't truth. It's *a* truth. Of the moment. Any given moment."

Jacques rises to the bait: "There is a notion of tolerance and diversity at the heart of *terroir*. That's what André really wants to say, right?" André shakes his head no, but Jacques continues: "But you have to re-situate it in the historical context of French *terroirs*. Instead of saying 'Burgundy, the land blessed by the gods,' what we should be saying is, 'The discovery of great *terroirs* is not just nature but *also* politics.' For example, the diocese of Autun [ancient Roman capital of Burgundy] needed to expand, but the rival diocese of Mâcon blocked the flow of commerce. Take this bottle of Beaujolais on the table. Why is Beaujolais a recent invention? Because it was grazing land that had access neither to Lyon, because it was blocked by the bishop of Autun, nor to Paris, because you couldn't go upriver until the creation of the Briare Canal in 1770. It was then in fact that Beaujolais wine was created, when they could use a river route to Paris via Roanne and the Loire, and so open up a market for their wine. So Beaujolais exists because of nature's unique genius but also because of historical accidents."

Dupont explains that the appellation of Mercurey, which is in Burgundy but not part of the famous, and lucrative, Côte-d'Or designation, has soils and microclimates identical to its neighboring village of Santenay, which is the last village in the Côte-d'Or. But Santenay is also the village that marks the historical limit of the diocese of Autun, so Mercurey, through purely political jockeying, was banished to the less prestigious appellation of the Côte Chalonnaise.

The banquet feels Socratic in the sense that every apparent truth is being challenged by a competing one. It's also a pleasure to sit at table with a critic who clearly enjoys draining the bottles—I've lost count of how many—and whose opinions are formed by a close reading of the historical record, reinforcing the notion that most expressions of taste are rooted historically in matters of power. And yet if a taste persists, as in Burgundy, it's the taste itself and not the gesture of power at its origin that becomes the power in the end. And it is also for this reason that I'm convinced that taste needs time to evolve. There is no such thing as instantaneous taste, even for a critic like Jacques, who inexplicably accepts such counterproductive professional engagements as tasting 231 different Beaujolais in the same day.

We stagger out of La Cagouille as night falls, unquestionably drunk. And happy. After all the discussions about acidity and sweetness, food and wine pairings, and the judgment of judgments, one simple reality reasserts itself. No drink, no gastronomic pleasure, can exist as an end in itself. Wine is a vector of exchange between human beings. And despite the pressures of our society, the opposite cannot be true; no wine is a fixed object with a determined value—a product—before which people must subserve their judgment. Yet even this notion has been called into question throughout the course of the lunch. *Terroir*, the quality that allows wine to be fully realized, can easily be employed as an agent of exclusion and intolerance. For any particular identity to flourish, it needs to find a balance between the affirmation of its past and openness to the future.

9

CHEZ PANTAGRUEL

The Elitist Tastes (of the Democrat)

Wine shops for me have always been magical places, dens of untold (and sometimes untellable) pleasures and delights. After the rush of restaurant experiences, I started to think about the differences between Lavinia, Legrand, the spartan but beautifully selected Bacchus and Ariane in the sixth, or its funky neighbor, La Dernière Goutte, a classic Parisian neighborhood wine shop—run by an ebullient Cuban American. I thought also about my personal favorite, Les Caprices de L'Instant, tucked behind the Bastille on the rue Jacques Coeur, and its mad, quixotic owner, Raphael, irrepressible Argentine Swiss defender of French *terroir* integrity and of the vigneron's original pricing scale. Not far away, in the second arrondissement, is Wine and Bubbles, a sleek and trendy gathering place for young people—owned by two kids in their twenties. Though a little too yuppstery for my taste, this combined wine shop and bar is filled with bottles from the recent quality revolution in Champagne, where talented artisans such as Vilmart, René Geoffroy, Gaston Chiquet, and Pierre Peters are displacing the famous (and infinitely cynical) industrial *négociant* houses such as Moët, Piper-Heidsieck, and Veuve Clicquot. I imagined what was awaiting me at other favorite Paris haunts: Pantagruel, Cave du Panthéon, Lafayette Gourmet, Les Caves Augé, Les Caves de la Madeleine, and Le Verre Volé, champion of natural and organic wines.

But as I mulled over all these different places in my head, what struck me most was what they have in common. That is, while they are radically variable in size and ambition, each one represents a determinedly idiosyncratic response to wine. Through personal expressions of taste—most of which I don't share—they create the essential lifeline between the will of the vigneron to express his individuality and the distinctiveness of his vineyard and the will of the customer, who—in principle—is seeking that singularity every time he buys a bottle of wine. This places wine buying firmly in the realm of the acquisition of unique commodities, like paintings. And makes it equally subject to acts of bad faith and fraud.

With wine, as with an original work of art, there is something inherently beautiful simply in the notion of its uniqueness. And it should be noted that even in a case with twelve bottles of the same wine from the same producer and vintage, subtle bottle variation is not a flaw but a testament to the living, reactive nature of the liquid. Imagine a house with twinned pairs of sextuplets. All biologically issued from the same parents and, presumably, brought up in similar fashion. And yet, as the father of twin girls, I've witnessed how nature (and happenstance, when happenstance is *allowed* to occur) imbues what is truly alive with its own path for asserting its individuality, independent of provenance and upbringing.

In fact, the situation of champagne is instructive in this regard. The big merchant houses like Veuve Clicquot and Moët produce millions of bottles of champagne each year with one clear directive from their multinational corporate owners, maintain product uniformity as much as technically possible, including the significant use of fertilizers, pesticides, and other chemical-stabilizing agents that will create as little bottle variation as possible, thereby creating an unalterable brand and taste, as efficient a chain of industrial output as possible. The new breed of small artisanal producers, on the other hand, inspired by the example of Burgundian resistance to homogenization and by local biodynamic pioneers like Jacques Selosse, have sought to claim (and in some cases reclaim) the notion of *terroir* in Champagne, emphasizing organic farming, the distinctiveness of individual parcels of land, and therefore individual bottlings of limited (but still statistically important) quantities in the two- to ten-thousand-bottle range. The joy of fully living champagne, variable, unpredictable, but always vital and healthy because of the commitment to organic practices, can be found in these profound expressions of the Champagne region.

Wine under these circumstances is alone among products of nature in approaching the human as a sacred vessel of what is most supremely individual. When we drink a bottle of true *terroir* wine, we share in the particular beauty of one expression of nature and then trust in man—many men and women, in fact—to bring that living expression of uniqueness to us. We often underestimate the importance of the chain that stretches from the vineyard through the vigneron to the distributor or importer and on, finally, to the restaurant or shop. Actually, the final link in the chain isn't the place of purchase. It's the place of service. We trust in the restaurant, our host, our wife, our friend, that the bottle has been cared for (whether it's a five-euro Aligoté or a fifty-euro Puligny), that its living contents have been respected.

Even if there are twelve thousand bottles from the same vineyard in the same vintage from the same vigneron bottled at the same time, it's not just the vigneron's intention that creates singularity, that ensures that not a single one is the same, but also the journey of every bottle. Because wine is alive and responds to all stimuli—light, temperature, vibration, smell (and many would say the gravitational pull of the moon)—it remains reactive up through the moment it passes your lips. One of the problems with wines that are overly heavy and overconcentrated in fruit and alcohol is that they are literally so dense that, like a mind or a body with thick walls of resistance (or fat), very little energy gets through to keep them vital and alive.

This singularity leads to a corollary notion: *terroir* extends through the consumption of the bottle. Drinking a wine in the semitropical atmosphere of Rio, where I now live, is radically different from drinking the same wine in a cool, temperate climate. Fully sentient and reactive, wine is like an ideal traveler. While never losing its own identity, it does shift—sometimes subtly, always decisively—in response to sustained motion, shifts in weather, barometric pressure, local customs, and particularly in relation to food. The relation of food to wine takes into account the time of day a meal is served as well as the traditional local rhythms of service and of what is normally drunk during mealtime. It should be no wonder that in traditionally non-wine-drinking cultures, where sweet drinks and hard alcohol are consumed (the United States with soft drinks and whisky and Brazil with fruit juices and Cachaça, for example), when people turn to wine they are easily seduced—fooled, even—by sweet, overrich, and sticky wines. If they're gradually able to progress to more balanced, subtle, and complex expressions, then these wines are perfectly innocuous as a stepping-stone. But as the market becomes more and more saturated by these wines and the relentless marketing of them, from the most industrial Australian confection to the newest luxury release from Spain or California or Tuscany or back to Australia, from multinationals to the faux artisanal operations of wealthy individuals, it becomes harder and harder for the general public, particularly in places like Brazil, the United States, or England, but increasingly in France and Italy also, to become exposed and develop a taste for wines of subtlety, complexity, and the specificity of place. Just as generations of film students are not getting exposed to Fellini, Bresson, Wilder, Sturges, or Fassbinder (including in film schools in Italy, France, the United States, and Germany), and so will gradually lose any appreciation for or natural relation to them, wine drinkers today are increasingly without any historical reference for their palates.

The intention of the author-vigneron is essential for unleashing the chain of meaning for a *terroir*. The *terroir* of origin, along with the vigneron's intention, are obviously the most essential qualities in determining the global expression of *terroir*. But after the bottle leaves the winery, how and by whom that bottle is handled and where and how it ends up are also critical for determining our experience of that wine. If the *terroir* of origin is without merit, then no one can ever restore merit later. However, no matter how great the *terroir* of origin, if there isn't a sufficient relay of respect from the vineyard to the city, then there's no guarantee the wine drinker will participate in that greatness.

I suppose my sympathy for courageously idiosyncratic American importers such as Neal Rosenthal, Terry Theise, Michael Skurnik, Marc de Grazia, Louis Dressner, and Kermit Lynch, and for wine shop owners everywhere, has much to do with this. They are committed keepers of the flame. Like priests, they are fallible. And as we know, betrayal by men of the cloth is always felt more bitterly. But by the same token, those who defend wine on principle and for questions of taste fill me with deep admiration. Imagine the terrible additional pressures on a parish priest if he had to make his work of the spirit economically viable. With these things in mind, I went to visit a young caviste who reminded me of the lead in the Robert Bresson masterpiece *Diary of a Country Priest*.

Terroir Is a State of Mind

Nestled in a pleasant if nondescript street of small businesses, the wine shop Chez Pantagruel, on the rue Berthollet in the fifth arrondissement, doesn't draw much attention. Through the window I see a small, clean, well-lit space with shelves that are well organized but contain surprisingly very few wines. I know that Laurent Foubert, the owner of Pantagruel, has been struggling since he recently opened his business. A graduate of the immensely prestigious Ecole Normale Supérieure (a kind of Harvard-Yale-Princeton-Dartmouth condensed into one insanely daunting school of five hundred students) and a former professor of French, Laurent greets me with his Colombian wife, Valentina Tabares. The shop has room to display hundreds of different bottles, but there can't be more than forty visible. "No wonder his business is struggling," I think as I walk in.

Laurent launches immediately into an impassioned discourse: "In today's society, we inculcate in people what they should like. We explain to them why they should love this wine and not another. It's infantilizing. And a form of repression. In this way, we permanently close the doors of discovery, shut off curiosity. This is the definition of marketing. It's horrific. It eliminates people's capacity to exert a critical judgment in the political, ethical, and economic sense. We accustom people to assimilate not just slogans but notions that are empty and theoretical, behind which lie identical products. Only the packaging changes."

He explains that his response is to try to meet these forces head on. He considers each choice of producer to sell in the shop an ethical act, by which he means that the vignerons he represents need not only to make wines of quality but also to respect as restrained a price scale as possible. Pricing for Foubert and his wife is the clearest gauge of the vigneron's sense of responsibility. When a vigneron begins to speculate with the prices of his wine, according to Foubert, this is when he ceases to be a vigneron and becomes a financier.

I ask if he believes that a vigneron shouldn't have the right to earn what he can, and if his discourse isn't essentially Marxist.

"No, not in the least. I'm neither a pure egalitarian nor would I condemn someone for making money," he answers.

"Elitist, then?"

He and his wife, Valentina, look startled. She asks me: "How could you even view us remotely as elitists?"

"Does that bother you?" I ask.

"Yes," Valentina says, but Laurent cuts in.

"Actually, I'm in favor of a certain elitism. Our starting point here at the shop has a parallel in education. We don't accept the notion that children can't grasp complicated concepts. We want people to understand they don't have to go to the supermarket (where ninety percent of the French buy their wines) and spend seven euros on a wine that is identical to the other one hundred and sixty wines on the shelves. Here they can spend six euros and buy a wine that is unique. The paradox here is that makes us both elitist and antielitist."

I smile and explain that that's exactly what I was getting at. By imposing a selection of his own taste, selling those expressions at unequal prices, he automatically confronts the conundrum of taste and power. How to reconcile democracy with elitism, where elitism is understood as a carefully considered expression of taste that seeks to be distinguished from others? It is intrinsically elitist to bring a critical judgment, make distinctions. What seems crucial is to recognize that there is an ethical engagement at the heart of this elitist activity. If one employs one's elitism to denigrate others, then it's reprehensible and renders a notion like *terroir* in wine unspeakably chauvinist and anti-democratic. Where elitism acquires nobility is in the suggestion that we're not all the same and that a distinction is being made in order to affirm the potential singularity of us all.

Laurent laughs. "It's funny that you bring this up. Last Saturday a customer blew up in the store, shouting that we were nearly fascists and certainly elitists. 'How can you not have any wine at three euros?' he screamed! Given that the median price in most Paris wine shops is twenty-five euros while ours is closer to twelve, this is pretty funny."

We walk around the shop, where he and Valentina have left room for people to sit at tables and sample many of the wines with a snack. The atmosphere is airy, bright, inviting, but somehow also a little austere. It's odd to see so much shelf space unused, a business decision that is consciously counterproductive. But Foubert has taken great pains with the limited number of wines he has to sell. A paragraph description of the *terroir* and the producer, written in a French that is as crisp and impassioned as his speech, accompanies every bottle. At a glance I can see that half of his selection includes wines I'm not enthusiastic about or don't know well. I'm pleased. This is proof that someone so sympathetic can hold contrary tastes. Still, that half of the wines in the shop are bottles that I know and love is equally meaningful to me. I see a delicious "Bourgogne rouge" from Régis Forey in the village of Vosne-

Romanée. It's only eleven euros, an achievement on the part of the grower and seller for a Burgundy of even the most modest designation. Next to it is a princely wine, a 2002 Chambolle-Musigny from Amiot-Servelle. At thirty-two euros, it's also a comparative bargain. Farther along the shelf is a rugged Madiran from the southwest of France, from Denis Barréjat. It's only ten euros for a wine that comes exclusively from the gnarled one-hundred-year-old vines that I once cradled in my arms with the same astonishment that I could imagine if engaged in a fully lucid conversation with a one-hundred-year-old man.

Laurent picks up a bottle of one his favorites, a fiercely strange and beguiling wine from the Jura Mountains known as *vin jaune,* or "yellow wine." "It's from the Château D'Arlay, whose proprietor is the Marquis de Laguiche, a relative of the princes of Orange. They've been making *vin jaune* for at least five centuries at their castle. It's hard to imagine a more aristocratic situation. But paradoxically, both Laguiche and the wine are completely peasantlike, rustic, untamed, and down-to-earth. Yellow wine is so earthy and dirty that when you explain to most people how it's made, they turn away in horror." Unlike with other wines, where it's essential to prevent air from turning everything to vinegar, producers of this golden yellow wine leave the barrel partly open for six years, so bacteria in the air can attack the wine. But a natural miracle occurs in the cool and rarefied air of the mountains bordering Switzerland, a mirror of the process on the sun-baked plains of Andalusia with dry sherry. Instead of turning the wine into vinegar—the normal result of such a practice—the bacteria form a film of yeast on the surface that protects the wine from spoiling and imparts a savagely haunting and bitter character. But this phenomenon doesn't always occur, since the microbial balance that ensures life instead of vinous death is delicate. Perhaps four vintages a decade on average produce a *vin jaune* for a given producer of quality. But, like many creatures that begin life precariously, the wine becomes nearly invincible if it reaches maturity. I've left half-consumed bottles of *vin jaune* open for weeks in a cupboard and the wine didn't deteriorate in any way.

Laurent says, "This is one of the greatest dry whites in the world, absolutely unique and at a comparatively reasonable price. It's exactly the sort of exceptional experience I'd like to offer to my clients. People ask me if I drink a ten-euro wine every day, but I tell them that I don't even necessarily drink every day. What does preoccupy me is that any given drinking experience be singular, that it allows me to take advantage of the particular personality of the wine in a way that brings me and others pleasure. In the case of the *vin jaune,* this is the summa of a singular experience and at thirty-nine euros for a bottle that can last for months, I think the price is very ethical." (It also yields twelve to fourteen glasses instead of the seven to eight glasses of a normal wine. Because of its intensity, it's traditionally sipped in smaller quantities.) "Given the immoderate speculation that takes place with fabled white burgundies," he continues, "the price becomes risible if you calculate its complexity, uniqueness, and rarity."

Laurent grabs another bottle from the opposite wall, a red wine from the Loire region, a 1990 Bourgueil from Druet. "I chose it because I'm very insistent about the idea of ageing wine. A lot of people think a '90 Bourgueil is dead and buried after all this time. Well, we'll see about that. And forty-one euros for a nearly twenty-year-old wine. When I tasted it six months ago, it was astonishing because it was 'Pinot-ing.' There's some jargon for you."

"You mean it tasted like Pinot Noir?" I ask.

"It tasted like the old Beaunes, the old Volnays from Burgundy, with that sort of earthiness, that cherry flavor, that gaminess."

I look at him carefully. Is he going to erupt in a flow of sylvan metaphors? Then he frowns as we both taste the wine.

"It's completely different. There's none of the racy acidity and openness. This bottle is closed, with aromas of licorice, smoke, rubber . . ."

This time I stop him. "I'm sorry, but if you wanted to convey to me that the wine you drank six months ago was riper and more sweetly mature than this one, I can stay with you. But the hackneyed list of flavor associations is beyond my grasp."

"You're right." He smiles wryly. "These kind of metaphors are shop-worn."

"We need to find other forms of language that are more open and inclusive and yet that are precise," I add.

Valentina looks up from her glass: "The word that occurred to me as this bottle opens up—and it is opening up and changing, no?" Laurent nods. After only fifteen minutes it's evolving in a surprisingly positive way. She continues: "The word that came to me was *savage.*"

"Perfect," I say. "*Savage* signifies something concrete for me. It says that we're in front of the living. And what's lacking in wine, wine lan-guage—hell, even in cinema and politics—is an appreciation of the vital, the animal. Gracefully, not brutally savage, of course."

"That's why even this bottle of Bourgueil is so magical. There's an uncontrolled intensity that gives it emotion. You may not even like it—and I can remember a much better bottle of it—but you can't deny its life force."

Valentina sees my look of contentment as I sip the wine, and adds: "We try to make money because we need to earn a living, but our pur-pose is the exchange of pleasure."

Though Laurent says that the shop survives despite the lack of foot traffic, he insists that conviviality is its raison d'être. And that is why they chose the name of Rabelais's Pantagruel. Interestingly Laurent has foregone the wines of Charles Joguet, the most famous producer from Chinon, the ribald Renaissance author's hometown, "because I knew the wine in its greatness, when Joguet made it himself. It's not his wine anymore, half of it comes from the sandy plains, and it's much more expensive. Why would I put a faceless brand wine in this shop?"

Before I go, Valentina explains the heart of the store's philosophy. It lies in something they've dubbed "vinorazzia." It's a scheme to expand and share the purchasing power of individuals through the Fouberts' Internet site. The more wine lovers, anonymous to each other, who agree to buy the same wine together, the lower the price goes. The final price is determined at the end of a fixed period. Valentina says, "It allows us to compete with the crushing economies of scale of a super-market chain by using the same weapons, but with decidedly different products and intentions. It's our little revenge against the chain stores and their steamrolling of wine production and consumption." She knocks back another draft of the still-changing, and ever more deli-cious, 1990 Bourgueil and looks at Laurent. They laugh like naughty children who believe they can—and should—burn down the school. And then they pour me another glass.

10

(URBAN) WINESPEAK

Ex Nihilo, pro Nihilo

Wine has always been an expression of power, at least since the Greek and Roman empires. The ancient Greeks planted the vine in their new colonies in Sicily and elsewhere as a sign of Greek civilization and empire. The Romans were even more explicit in the use of wine as an imperial prop, staking out new territory by establishing the vine as a symbol of the colonists' Romanization. But there's something particular about the use of wine in our time as an agent of power. I suppose it's actually no surprise that in the absence of a clear imperial power in nationalist terms (however much the United States may kick and shout), it is the force of transnational economic empire that determines wine's symbolic status. Today we demand that wine be seen as an inert object, devoid not only of its historical and agricultural dimension, but even of its function as an agent of pleasure. Wine in the contemporary urban *agon* has become a socioeconomic trophy in itself. From the critics and their attempts to impose a spurious scientificity on the art of tasting, to the ambitious restaurateurs who make their fortune on inflated wine pricing, to supermarkets and multinational distributors who simply demand that wine fulfill its purpose in their food chain (greater efficiency, marketability, and uniformity), it's a miracle that living wine survives at all. In fact, any vigneron, importer, wine shop, or restaurateur who labors to offer us wine as a link to nature and history deserves at the least the Légion d'Honneur or Congressional Medal of Honor (though they might argue more for a purple—or crimson—heart).

"Off with Their Heads"

What are those who struggle to defend this notion up against? Consider, for example the jargon employed by the dominant critics and so-called experts, from Paris to San Francisco. The most ludicrous offender is surely Robert Parker, who also happens to be the most influential. The evening following my visit to Pantagruel, I opened his Bordeaux wine guide at random at a friend's house. In the 1991 edition, I read this about the 1982 Château Lynch Bages (an innocent bottle before this judgment was rendered): "Lynch Bages is a massive, huge, densely colored wine, with an intense bouquet of ripe cassis fruit intermingled with scents of hot tar, soy sauce, and vanillin oakiness. Viscous, rich, very full and concentrated on the palate, with plenty of soft tannins, this big-framed, extroverted, decadently intense Lynch Bages . . ." The Gryphon and the Mock Turtle would be proud . . . especially if you played a Wonderland trick of opening Parker's *Wine Buyer's Guide* (2002 edition) at random, one page after another (which I did on my return to Rio):

On page 1,563, in the Australian section, you could try a wine that "offers a big, sweet, peppery, earthy, creosote, blackberry and cassis-scented bouquet and flavor. Fat and chewy, with low acidity, this plump shiraz should drink well for a decade . . ." And then, on page 376, back in Bordeaux (but surely through the looking glass), he has this to say about a dry red wine: "An explosive, hedonistic, seductive, sexy fruit bomb . . . a dramatic, flamboyant, head spinning nose of melted fudge, coffee, tobacco, kirsch and cassis backed by smoke and scorched earth

[Sherman strikes again] soars from the glass." To think that Bordeaux was once considered the supreme adult drink.

But since his one-hundred-point scoring system has been the key to his success, merchants, especially in the United States, have mercilessly recycled his scores in advertising and marketing campaigns for the last twenty-five years. As the scores are the principal source of interest for his followers, perhaps he never intended anyone actually to attempt to read this ludicrously overwrought, nonsensical, frequently ungrammatical prose. Every wine is scored from fifty to one hundred, with the notation prominently displayed before anyone need glance (blanch) at the thick, gooey, fudge-covered gobs of text. Indeed it's not inconceivable that the text is actually a code to specifically deny access to the uninitiated, non-Masonic brethren.

But Parker is not alone. Modern wine gibberish (and the desperate attempts of winemakers to make wines that correspond to that gibberish) is a global product. The Masonic-mafioso urge to encode and exclude has universal brethren. In France, the leading wine magazine, *La Revue des Vins de France*, notorious for its cozy relationship with its chief advertisers and the resulting coverage they enjoy on the editorial side (a practice repeated by 95 percent of the world's wine publications), had this to say in 2009 about a wine from the Rhône valley, a Cornas from Thierry Allemand: "A nose of smoked meats, various fruits, and black tea. A puckery mouth, inflamed with spices, with a wholesome texture and dense but fine tannins. In the mouth, it leaves persisent notes of bacon strips."

In Italy, the dominant wine guide, *Gambero Rosso*, treats us to descriptions like this: "But let us offer you a number of superlatives for the 1998 Ornellaia, another great wine [supervised by our globetrotting Michel Rolland]. The nose yields up a complexity worthy of a *premier cru* Bordeaux: blackberry, black currant, lead, cedar, mint and oriental spices. In the mouth, for its part, no power is lost, unsheathing a thick and flawlessly erect structure with sumptuous tannins."

In Brazil, you can discover the dubious joys of Chilean wine by reading Saul Galvão in the otherwise sober, conservative newspaper

Estadão. For a wine designed for an estate/brand that belongs to one of South America's largest investment funds, Galvão had this to say in May 2007: "The Limited Edition Morandé Carignan 2003 is a quasi legendary wine [quasi?]. The 20 months in entirely new American oak have marked it deeply and truly. The intense concentration of the wine matches the heavy effect of the oak. There's a medicinal note, with floral touches, licorice, and roasted coffee beans. Impressively, deliciously concentrated, powerful and hot but not alcoholic at an alcohol level [remarkably high] of 14.8 percent (93/100 points)." I wondered if the ever-affable Saul Galvão had accepted this time, as his colleagues in Brazil and everywhere else in the world do regularly with glee, an invitation to travel to Chile to review this and other wineries' products at the expense of the wineries themselves.

The Different Branches of Arithmetic
(AMBITION, DISTRACTION, UGLIFICATION, AND DERISION)

Of course one has to distinguish between classifying wines—expressing hierarchies of preference—and scoring them. There is a profound difference between the admirably restrained critic Michael Broadbent's purposefully malleable five-star rating and a pseudo-precise one-hundred-point scoring system. Broadbent, without a doubt the world's most experienced wine taster, adds stars at the end of his short descriptions of each wine. These stars are explicitly variable and general, and he insists that the expression of preference is dependent on the precise circumstances that the wine was tasted in. And he often shifts the starring with each subsequent retasting of the wine. Not surprisingly his prose is also modest, straightforward, and coherent. Whereas Parker rhapsodizes about the 1983 Rausan-Ségla like this: "Fully mature, this seductively rich wine offers a knock-out nose of spring flowers, black fruits, smoke, and roasted herbs. Expansive and round with a velvety texture, real opulence, and low acidity, this concentrated . . ." And on it goes, whereas Broadbent dryly notes: "Firm flesh, stylish. Gentle fragrance. Good flavor and grip."

The numerical point system inherently implies a mathematical certainty, whether out of twenty or one hundred points. However absurd, this ersatz scientificity is perfectly suited to a culture uneasy with the notion of informed critical judgment coexisting with ambiguity and complexity. This culture prefers specious absolutes, an infantile and incomprehensible language for which no real engagement is required and a falsely pedaled sense of democracy, the fatuous reassurance of pseudo facts and factoids. This has been true from the dominant political discourse since Reagan, across the globe's television screens, right into the computers of the self-appointed custodians of our wine culture.

Consumers all over the world have now become accustomed to seek out "Parker 95 wines" or "*Wine Spectator* 90s," no longer sure of, or necessarily interested in, the wines' origins, makers, or contexts. Parker, the *Wine Spectator*, and other "serial scorers" reassure people who are insecure about wine but who want to be "winners." Anything above ninety points is a winner. A ninety-five-point wine is a real "winner." Hence there is a gradual inflation of ninety-point wines, as the Christie's director said about the contemporary art world, to increase the supply of winners and keep everybody in on the game remunerated. Imagine: "Matisse 95 points! Chagall 99 points! Jeff Koons 100 points!" Or: "Chagall is explosive on the eyes, bursting with color and flavor." But poor old dirty, messy, edgy Georges Rouault wouldn't get above a 75. To assign numbers to a wine, given that a wine is fully living and infinitely mutable, is almost as repugnant to me as assigning numerical worth to humans.

The Drawling Masters

Across the globe, many—but not all—critics are helping to kill the *culture* of wine (however much their collusive practices may be stimulating sales). They are removing it from its human context. They have created an artificial world of childish incantations and certainties. It's also the case that the vast majority are self-taught, have no enological training, and would be incompetent even to prune the vine that produces the liquid that guarantees their livelihood. All can (and do) play the game (as Hugh Johnson has dryly observed). This is not to say, of course, that all wine critics are assassins. To cite just a few of the numerous (largely freelance) exceptions writing in English: Michael Broadbent, Hugh Johnson, Oz Clarke, and Stephen Brook are all highly trained and skillful observers of the inner workings of the wine world who have labored tirelessly for decades (and in generally stylish prose) for the benefit of those on the outside. Matt Kramer's primer *Making Sense of Wine* is essential reading for the neophyte (despite my misgivings about him, noted in chapter 2). Burton Anderson's *Wine Atlas of Italy* is as indispensable a reference for Italian wine lovers as Remington Norman's book about Burgundy is for fans of that region. David Rosengarten has written valuably and intelligibly about wine in its relation to food, and Gerry Dawes is a rare voice of sobriety and independence in the field of Spanish wine.

But maybe, at the end of the day, we should be happy that most wine talk is so ridiculous. In a world that is oversaturated with overdetermined meaning, there's something decidedly cheering about this mischievous drink that resists plausible description. However ferocious the verbal assaults, the anarchic, resistant spirit of Bacchus lives. Reeling and writhing and fainting in coils.

11

TAN DINH

The Taste of Wine and the Words of Taste

I decided to gather several friends who are wine professionals to take part in a lunch tasting, to see if we could find a different way to talk about wine. Luckily, we've been invited to stage our get-together at the gracious Vietnamese restaurant Tan Dinh, tucked behind the Musée d'Orsay. The wine distributor Danièle Gérault is the first participant to walk through the doors. I met Danièle one summer evening at a dinner in the home of Robert Vifian, the chef and co-owner of Tan Dinh. Robert always has surprising friends, including Michel Rolland and Robert Parker. But he's one of those rare souls capable of maintaining friendships with the widest range of people without ever betraying any of them, always remaining true to his own scrupulous intelligence and his unrepentant adolescent passion for wine. Robert, who emigrated from Vietnam with his family in 1968, and his wife, Isabelle, generously receive whoever stops through their doors, either at their cat- and contemporary art–crammed loft in the fifth or in their sophisticated family-run restaurant on the rue de Verneuil, in the seventh arrondissement.

But nothing prepared me for my first encounter with Danièle. On arrival I was greeted by her husband, Maurice Rosy, a sly and refined octogenarian comic strip author. Then we heard Danièle's voice, an explosion of passionate, clashing sounds. With Danièle, I discovered, you never know if she's going to burst out laughing or dissolve in tears. This time, she emerged mirthfully, a glass of glistening off-dry Vouvray from her beloved Domaine Huet in her hand. Twenty-five years younger than Maurice, she's slim and elegant, her gray hair cut short, chic without being chi-chi, with eyes and a nose like a big exotic bird. If Robert's passion for wine is a steady flame, Danièle's is at perpetual full boil. She began her career in the arts, but quit at thirty-five to dedicate herself to wine. One of the rare women who works as a wine distributor in Paris, she created her own company in 1985 with "just one vigneron, Gaston Huet in Vouvray, and one client in Paris." This irrepressibly high-spirited battler in a very macho world navigates the city in her lilliputian Smart car, overflowing with as many gift bottles as samples (to the consternation of her male competitors). If I love Robert for his deep experience of wine and for the rigorously analytical way he approaches the subject, with Danièle, I came to discover a delightful counterbalance in the eno-universe, with her quest for the potential emotion in a bottle.

Bruno Quenioux is next to walk through the doors of the restaurant. He's weighted down with the bottles he's brought. The son of a very modest vigneron in the Loire, Bruno is an autodidact who manages to reconcile an apostolic belief in organic wines and artisanal winemaking with his position as head wine buyer for Lafayette Gourmet, the wine shop inside Galeries Lafayette, one of the most traditional of Paris's nineteenth-century bourgeois department stores. Isabelle and Robert seat us in the back of the restaurant dining room. Laure Gasparotto, my adjutant for this book and former wine writer for *Le Figaro* newspaper, is the last to join us.

The idea for this lunch was for each person to bring one or two bottles that might provoke an emotion, negative or positive. It occurred to me that if the wine market is dominated by impossibly dense and opaque wines that are constructed as a means of imposing some power (personal or industrial, it doesn't matter), then it's inevitable that the discussion about these creations should be as impenetrable as the liquid itself, regardless of whether it's pure marketing or marketing's covert form, the language of journalists dependent on this economy. But I wondered if it would be possible for six friends with intimate relationships to wine to avoid falling into the traps of jargon, snobbery, and the myriad other sins associated with winespeak today. At the very least I was sure that we'd have some pleasure thanks to Robert's sophisticated rendition of Vietnamese cuisine.

Tan Dinh has been a refuge for me in Paris for the last twenty years. It's where I splurged my limited income in my twenties before completing *Resident Alien*; where I was taken the day before the release of *Sunday* in France in my midthirties; where Stellan Skarsgard and Charlotte Rampling and I had our first lunch together before going to Greece a few years later for *Signs & Wonders* (and where we drained several bottles of twenty-five-year-old Raveneau Chablis); and where, in my forties, I took my assistant, Laurent, and Juan the night I finished the editing of *Mondovino*. Robert's wine list is simply one of the most amazing thick black books on the wine planet. Beginning in the early 1970s, when he and his brother Freddy were studying at university and helping their parents in the first version of Tan Dinh, they began to amass a staggering collection of wine—and gradually offered all of it at risible prices to their customers. The wine list today is still one of the most impressive in Paris, but alas, thanks to recidivist wine groupies like me, the old stocks are much depleted. And because the cost of maintaining their restaurant and the stock of high-end wines has itself become a strain, it's taken its toll on the pricing, which remains fair but no longer holds the same quantity of gift wines (an echo of Manducatis, in New York). At any rate, a near-Buddhist tranquillity reigns in the dining room of Tan Dinh, which allows wine and food lovers to find their pleasure at their own rhythm.

I've always been skeptical of blind tastings, in which the bottles are hidden from view so the drinker is forced to taste in the dark. It can be an amusing exercise but probably has no more lasting emotional value than kissing an anonymous person in a darkened room. Nonetheless, undertaken in such a convivial context, I'm hopeful that it can bring us some additional truths, even if not "the truth." I was curious to see if the most enlightened of professionals in a setting devoid of any personal stake could lead us back to a state of innocence as we tasted and talked. Even if I was far from certain that a state of innocence in relation to wine was at all desirable.

In the Shadow of the Cave

The first disguised bottle we open is mine. Bruno immediately offers an opinion: "It smells like linden trees, like verbena." Despite my affection and respect for Bruno, I can't help thinking we're getting off on the wrong foot. It's exactly this type of word association that terrifies us all. But I hold my tongue. Robert is already taking notes. Danièle speaks next: "I love harmonious wines. This one isn't harmonious, but it's got a different sort of pleasure. It's very vibrant. With a very pungent nose."

I sip the wine. The acidity is so extreme that it cuts into the mouth like a blade. This may be difficult to swallow on its own, but I'm banking on Robert's food preparations to reveal another expression for this wine. Isabelle pipes in: "I like it a lot; that's all I can say about it. I like its ferocious acidity." Robert laughs. He knows Isabelle and I are acidity hounds. "It's a quality that's disparaged today, Robert," I say. "People don't want to be provoked by acidity."

"True. It's less and less appreciated. Acidity and bitterness are often shunned in favor of alcohol and sweetness."

Bruno chimes back in: "It's a wine that brings energy and light. A wine is as capable of imparting that as a person."

Danièle considers the wine further, seeming to chew it in her mouth: "The complexity in the mouth is starting to emerge," she says. "It makes me think of a purely organic wine and therefore transparent, made in an atrocious year. It feels like the vigneron waited and waited, praying for the grapes to reach maturity despite terrible rains. But it didn't happen. I think the grape is the Chenin Blanc from the Loire and has been in bottle for a number of years. The person who made the wine spilled his guts to produce what we're drinking."

Bruno agrees: "This wine was brought into the world in circumstances of great suffering. The grapes actually reached a decent level of maturity, but the phenolic acid was blocked because the vegetative cycle was blocked."

This time I call Bruno out and tell him that I believe technical talk is as deadly for the sharing of a wine's pleasures as the infantile metaphor-and-simile game. He nods his head in agreement but explains that the reflexes are built in very deeply. I ask him if his father and brother (who's also a vigneron) speak in these terms when trying to communicate what's happening with their wine. No, he says. I am, however, pleased to see that nobody is pressing to have the label of the wine revealed. Although it's a blind tasting, the idea is not to let it descend to the level of a parlor guessing game. So I reveal the bottle even while we pour the second one. Danièle and Bruno had "understood" the wine, without feeling the need to guess exactly what the label said. It's a 1984 dry Vouvray from Philippe Foreau, a producer as committed to organic wines, from long before it became a fashion, as the other master of the natural chalk caves of Vouvray, Domaine Huet. At any rate, what's astonishing is that a simple, inexpensive dry white wine from one of the most disastrous vintages in memory can excite so much complex pleasure and curiosity after more than twenty years of ageing.

I chose the bottle because it embodies two qualities that I admire deeply. No matter how humble the origin and price of a wine and no matter how unhappy a vintage, or how long it has stayed in the bottle, it can nonetheless produce the most inspiring form of nobility: the survival of the humblest. It's also proof, to my palate, that even the meanest characters (and the '84 Vouvray must have been bitterly antisocial in its youth) can sometimes acquire a certain glory if given enough time to evolve. Robert points out that the beauty of this wine—which isn't necessarily in a style that he loves—comes from the fact that while nature didn't pamper the grapes, the person who received the troubled fruit gave them a care that less courageous or respectful people might not have, without trying to modify their scarred nature. I'm convinced that precisely *because* this bottle carries with it the undisguised traces of its suffering, like a Fassbinder film from the 1970s made under duress (say, *I Only Want You to Love Me*), it possesses a distinctive vitality and beauty.

The first dish arrives as we sip the next wine, also provided by Robert. "It couldn't be simpler," Robert says. "Shrimp with garlic bread-crumbs in a salt, lime, and pepper sauce, just slightly sweetened." Bruno digs eagerly into the shrimp, but seems less seduced by the second wine: "It's a style of white Burgundy that's been aged in significant new oak [a process that imparts a creamy, easily flattering vanilla-tinged aftertaste to any wine. Consider it the Botox remedy of current winemaking]." Danièle, who always seeks to bring people together, immediately says that the wine is to her taste just as much as the previous one.

"It's a *comfortable*, comforting wine," counters Bruno with a smile.

"It may be easy, but why spit on easy pleasure?" she asks.

Robert explains that it's a 1994 Burgundy, a year in which they had the opposite problem of 1984: insufficient acidity. Because of the excess natural grape sugar due to the high heat, some wines reached 15 percent (2 or 3 percent above the norm). In fact it's a 1994 Chassagne-Montrachet Clos-Saint-Jean from Michel Niellon, a very prestigious bottle from a complicated year. Robert and Danièle are delighted by its "butteriness." He admits that he chose it to challenge the palates of Isabelle, Bruno, and me. We all *chew* on the wine, to try to extract the maximum sensations throughout the palate. There's no doubt that it coats the mouth in an initially seductive fashion and is a wine of a certain charm, but for me the lack of acidity deprives it of the energy needed to refresh the mouth after a bite of the salty, spicy, sweet, and meaty shrimp. Danièle opens two wines that Robert immediately says are so delicious that there's no point in drinking them blind: a 2002

Huet dry Vouvray and a 2003 Pinot Gris from Zind-Humbrecht, both wines that meet with universal approval. Danièle's yen for generalized harmony expresses itself in all of her actions.

Robert serves us the second dish: Vietnamese ravioli filled with goose confit and mint in a black mushroom fish sauce. Isabelle prefers the two Vouvrays with the shrimp and the rich Pinot Gris with the ravioli. Robert, Danièle, and Laure go with the "comfort," as Bruno says, of the Chassagne. What's fascinating is that both the razor-sharp 1984 Vouvray and its polar opposite, the rich, soft, and meaty (but never vulgar) Burgundy, offer complementary pleasures with the food. With the first wine the acid cuts the richness of the dish while with the second, the depth of the dish is matched by the weight of the wine. Robert explains that for him "food and wine pairing is based on either what is complementary or what is analogous. Two people marry because they are opposites or because they are, heaven forbid, similar."

We taste several reds as we eat a mango and chicken breast salad and skewered veal steeped in cardamom. The experience continues cheerfully, but we're still far from cogent and engaging wine talk. I'm surprised by an admirably austere red Burgundy from a large *négociant* house, Jadot (a 1999 Gevrey Combe aux Moines), which goes against my a priori of not liking *négociant* Burgundy. It took several sips and a half hour for the wine to show its character, and Bruno says how often he has to upbraid young sommeliers who dismiss a wine after one sip or think they can taste fifty wines at a single tasting. "They're not testing cosmetics, dammit! As the poet Francis Ponge says, 'For he who wishes to know a wine, you have to let it settle in the deepest part of your being for it to reveal its truth.'"

Isabelle pipes in: "I'm glad you changed your mind, Jonathan, but it's not good to have a prioris." But I disagree. Because these a prioris constitute my taste. They're forged from years of personal experience. For instance, in this case, I can safely say that 90 percent of *négociant* wines that I've drunk over the last thirty years reveal little or nothing of the *terroir* and much of the instinct of a large merchant house to create an internationally saleable product. "They're dear to me, Isabelle, my a prioris. I won't abandon them brutally. That said, of course, I'm always ready to be proved wrong by experience, like right now."

We arrive at the final wine, brought by Bruno to make a point. Danièle immediately says that it's a "manufactured thoroughbred. Perfect harvest and perfect juice. It's a very sweet wine, like an Australian or Californian, but probably from the Languedoc." Bruno explains that "it's a modern wine. *Very* comfortable. Lots of immediate pleasure. Everything soft and easy in the mouth."

I ask, "But is this comfort and luxury from nature or from technology and manipulation? Frankly, it's undrinkable to me."

Bruno says that it's a Coteaux du Languedoc wine, "Truffiers," made from syrah grapes so concentrated that instead of harvesting sixty hectoliters, they've harvested only ten. It makes the wine as dense as jam. And almost as sweet. This sweetness, Bruno informs us, is redoubled because it was raised with not 100 percent new oak—considered the gold standard for vinous plastic surgery buffs—but 300 percent. Which is to say that the unfinished wine was removed every few months into unused oak to maximize the roundness and vanilla sweetness, effectively using so much Botox you arrive at a hyper-rigid version of a full facelift. Although Robert defends the wine as the summa of modernity, even the great conciliator Danièle can't stomach it. It's so rich, in fact, that it takes the place of food. It has been perfectly imagined to capture the attention of a critic taking a quick few sips of one hundred wines at a so-called professional tasting. Bruno says that for him "The wine is dead. A mummy. And overseen by Michel Rolland to appeal to Parker's palate, who always gives it a spectacular score. But I don't know what to do with this mummy. One of the wine's conceptual designers, Jeffrey Davis, showed up one day at the Galeries Lafayette and told me, 'Bruno, I have the latest vintage of Truffiers. Wait and see. You're going to love it.' Well, my brother and my father—who's the archetype of the old-school peasant—happened to be in the shop with me at that time. He took the glass in his hand, had one look at the impossibly dark and opaque color, and asked where it came from. 'The

Languedoc,' I told him. He looked at me and said, 'Those dumb bastards have gone back to making falsified, beefed-up wine from North Africa [a common practice before a quality revolution in the 1980s].' Jeffrey was terrified. I mean that's one hundred euros a bottle for that stuff."

Robert, with great delicacy, counters: "It's a contemporary wine for contemporary tastes. Made with a biblical simplicity. What do people want today? Deep color, strength, sucrosity, lots of alcohol, and the flavors and texture from new oak barrels."

I say, "But, Robert, if you want to make people feel—"

Danièle cuts me off: "You said, 'make people feel.' But you can't *make* anybody feel anything. How presumptuous. You can only set out some glasses, pour the wine, wait, and listen." Rightly chastised, I sense the blind tasting is coming to a close. What have we learned about how to communicate the mystery of wine? Nothing that makes me feel like we are even the proverbial one-eyed kings in the land of the blind (tasting). Before we take leave of one another, Robert, perhaps in an effort to soften the general unease, observes that his twin cultures, Buddhist Vietnamese and Cartesian French, have proved a balance for appreciating wine. Like the philosopher and mathematician Pascal, he says, he's hedging his bets on both sides.

"Because wine is ultimately unknowable?" I ask.

"Because wine, finally, is about inebriation. People hope to go beyond the immediately human."

Bruno adds: "For me pleasure is strictly sensorial, therefore profane. In the Latin sense, 'profanum,' which means 'in front of the temple.' I hear people speak too often about pleasure in discussing wine and not enough about emotion. Pleasure is only the threshold of emotion. These days, we base everything on the gustatory, on an analysis of what our palates can perceive. But emotion doesn't occur because of explanations."

A deeper and more uneasy silence settles on the table. In the corner, I notice that Danièle is crying discreetly. She wipes her face. "I discovered beauty very late in my life. I grew up in a housing project in a brutal industrial region. Only when I came to work in Paris did I realize everything that I'd been deprived of. There are so many people who have no access to things of beauty. When I do public tastings, I realize how profoundly wine allows people to exchange and experience beauty. But we treat too many people like shit. If only we were more generous in allowing them contact with beautiful things. What I'm unnerved by at this table today is that we're all behaving as if we were the chosen ones."

No one says anything. Danièle wipes her eyes. After six hours of a Rabelaisian feast, we thank Robert for his profound generosity and quietly make our way out. We sought to create an exchange of emotion and find a language worthy of that exchange. But we didn't begin to succeed. We tried to forge a novel approach, and fell flat on our faces with the first steps. Danièle pronounced the apt eulogy for the pileup of the six bodies at the path's entrance.

The next day I drive down with Laure on the Autoroute du Soleil (the "Highway of the Sun") toward Burgundy, the Grail of this tale's journey. I think back to the lunch tasting. "It should've been a celebration of emotion, and nothing happened." But why am I surprised? When I make films, every time I go *looking* for emotion, nothing happens. Bruno and Danièle are right. Emotion occurs on its own. It cannot be guided. I have the feeling that after several thousand years of wine writing, no one has found a successful way to describe it. Who can and should speak about wine? Who really has the authority?

Laure points out that monks arrogated that right for themselves in the Middle Ages, thereby extending the sacramental nature of wine, the blood of Christ. "We try today to humanize wine through our analytical powers, stripping it of its relation to the divine," she says. "The danger of critical judgments, of course, is that we become suffused with arrogance. To criticize wine, in effect we criticize God. Or at least we place ourselves next to him as equals among the elite. Are we necessarily the chosen ones because we decide we have the right to speak about wine? We shouldn't forget that wine is of the earth, historically a source of humility. According to the Burgundian monks, when we bend down to harvest the grapes, we turn toward the earth, not toward heaven."

PART III

All Roads Lead
to Burgundy

(In Search of the Holy Grail)

12

AT THE HOME OF
JEAN-MARC ROULOT

A Vignerons' Lunch

I had mistakenly imagined that a table of iconoclastic friends at Tan Dinh might discover a more transparent way to discuss wine. Now I wondered if instead the vignerons of Burgundy could find a means of communication as limpid as their wines. We are in the home of Jean-Marc Roulot and his wife, Alix de Montille, to find out. They've been joined by their friends Dominique Lafon and Christophe Roumier, creating a quartet of inspired vignerons, all of whom are themselves children of talented vigneron fathers. Though anchored in a sense of tradition, they have each one of them acquired international reputations as modernist pioneers. Indeed, because the opposition between tradition and modernity is as absurd in wine as it is in cinema, it's not surprising that the tradition within the Roulot, Montille, Lafon, and Roumier families is to assert a new ideal of progress in the expression of *terroir* with each generation.

Alix and Jean-Marc's home is in the small limestone village of

Meursault, where the Roulot and the Lafon domaines are both based, and where Alix makes her wine for her newly founded artisanal *négociant* business (that is, she doesn't own any vines herself but buys grapes from others, like a large merchant but on an artisanal scale). Christophe Roumier has come down from his family estate in Chambolle-Musigny, about twenty kilometers away. It's snowing outside as we sit around the upper-floor fireplace of a subtly reconverted seventeenth-century windmill with contemporary accents. For me it's like sitting down to lunch with a lineup of the greatest film directors, from the Japanese minimalist master Ozu (the infinitely subtle wines of Jean-Marc), to the uncompromising Catholic Jansenist Robert Bresson (the sometimes painfully rigorous wines of Alix), to the Italian renegade purist Pasolini (the captivatingly vital yet classical wines of Christophe), to the German American genius of comic delight Billy Wilder (the impeccably delicious wines of Dominique). It's a great privilege to sit down with this quartet, a privilege that I doubt could happen in the purely ego-driven world of the cinema. What they tell me about their craft should be included in the curriculum of film schools everywhere, revealing the underlying tension necessary for any art form: between the imposition of an artist's ego and the humble recognition of the fragility of any individual in the universe.

Jean-Marc and I hit it off from the first time we met, maybe because we shared a passion for cinema and wine in equal measures. He's not only one of the most respected vignerons in Burgundy, but also an actor of considerable talent and courage. I was to witness this firsthand when he would later play opposite Irène Jacob and in several scenes with Charlotte Rampling in my most recent film, *Rio Sex Comedy*. Especially admirable was the sangfroid of this otherwise extremely reserved and shy man as he pranced for two days of shooting through the crowded streets of Copacabana dressed in nothing but the skimpiest underwear. Jean-Marc's acting career has in fact been a bracing series of surprises from the outset. He shocked his father, a salt-of-the-earth peasant vigneron when he left the modest family estate of eighteen acres at the age of twenty to enter the national acting school in

Paris, the prestigious Conservatoire. Only the premature death of his father eventually brought him back to run the family domain, though after an interval of almost ten years. Since then, he's found a way to juggle his winemaking duties with spot roles in theater, television, and cinema. What distinguished him for me, from the start, both as a vigneron and as an artist, was his profound conviction that *his* convictions are not necessarily universal. Somehow this balance between the "I" and the "other" is present in his wines. To taste a Domaine Roulot wine is to taste a sense of deep rootedness, fine and crystalline, and yet somehow open. Although subtly powerful, the wine never imposes itself before the taster has time to form his own reactions (and hence often leaves professional tasters ambivalent, since they rarely take the time for this exchange). As with the films I most admire, his personal style is clear and firm but only to lead the drinker to an infinitely open-ended interpretation. For me, the subtlety and finesse of Jean-Marc's very feline wines fulfill the criteria for a legitimate work of art: conviction coexisting with freedom of access and interpretation. His feelings about *terroir* are complex, which also seems to me the most ethical way to engage with it.

We had agreed to play the same game as at Tan Dinh (despite the previous day's failure), with each one bringing a bottle he liked and one he disliked. Jean-Marc serves us a delicate if thin white as we warm up by the fireplace. Alix, more than ten years younger than her husband, and as fiery a woman as he is discreet, sips distractedly as their son Félicien runs amok in the living room. Christophe, slender and graceful, in his forties like the other men, cradles his glass like a Siamese cat. Dominique, brawnier, more extroverted (like his wines) and with a deeply craggy face framing penetrating blue eyes, knocks back a good draft, like the Asterix character that he sometimes resembles. He explains that "between us, we're very spontaneous about wine. We don't mystify it. We've always got a wine in front of us, often the great wines of friends, so there's usually an extra emotion attached. To explain that to a guy buying his wine in a restaurant or a store where price is such a factor for him . . . it's tough."

No one seems wowed by the wine. Jean-Marc shows us the bottle, a Chasselas from the Vaud in Switzerland. "Okay, it's not a great wine," says Jean-Marc, "but it comes from slopes that are difficult to cultivate, and the Chasselas grape is hardly extravagant. That's why there isn't much relief to the wine. It's a little flat. But I once visited the very sympathetic vigneron Ludovic Paschoud. It was a beautiful day, and the hillside that plunged down into the lake was spectacular. And the wine costs about five euros."

I laugh at such undisguised romanticism, the opposite of the fierce analytical judgment one could expect from a vigneron. But Christophe says that "for the same price I can find you a much more interesting Chasselas from the Vaud." After Dominique dismisses it and Alix's grimace tells her story, Jean-Marc adds: "I'm not saying this is a great wine. But I feel a lot of sympathy for it." I ask Jean-Marc how much personal feelings about the vigneron affect his judgment (knowing full well that I can't stomach films made by directors I know personally and dislike, no matter their talent). "I can't like a wine made by an asshole. There's a famous guru-vigneron in Alsace—whose name I won't mention—"

"Oh, come on," everyone chimes in. "Marcel Deiss, right?"

"Anyway, this guy, he's absolutely sure that everything he does is right. And the truth is, his methods are rigorous. But he insists that we should all follow him or go to hell. One day, when I went to his domain, I said I'd just come from seeing Marc Kreydenweiss [another reputable producer in Alsace]. He was angry with me for having visited another vigneron! I mean, there's room for everybody. People *should see* Dominique Lafon before—or after—they come here. I can't stand the attitude that there's one right way to express a *terroir*. Whether or not we have talent, it's odious to imagine that we alone exist."

"That's the whole point for us here. We want to share what we do and what we have. We get inspired by one another, even if the styles are different," says Christophe.

Jean-Marc adds: "A friend said to me, 'All my buddies make good wine.'"

"That's also dangerous," I tell him. "With my filmmaking friends we try to encourage one another's work. We even formed a loose association to foster more exchanges (both practical and creative) and called it Dependent Cinema. We started with me, Ira Sachs, Karim Aïnouz, and Oren Moverman [director of *The Messenger* and screenwriter for Todd Haynes and others], and soon added Laurent Cantet [director of *The Class* and *Time Out*], Caveh Zahedi [director of the nineties indie classic *A Little Stiff* and *I Am a Sex Addict*], Walter Salles, and others. Today I don't know (and probably wouldn't feel a great affinity for) more than half the people in Dependent Cinema. Thank god. That was the point in founding it almost ten years ago: interdependence with freedom of taste. And if I see a friend's film and I don't like it, I tell him. And expect the same in return."

Christophe shakes his head: "You can say it's not your taste, but you don't have the right to tear apart someone else's work. His creation is his personal interpretation, just as a vigneron translates a *terroir*. It's his way of seeing things. You can't demolish his interpretation, can you? Wine is a multifaceted creation. Its purpose is to be widely disseminated. Every time it's drunk, it's drunk in a different way, in different conditions."

I agree that in that way it resembles a film. But none of those considerations should prevent the application of a critical judgment. I ask Christophe how many of the thirty-odd producers who make and bottle wine in his village of Chambolle he likes?

"Not all of them," he responds, "but I know why I don't like the ones I don't like. I'm not going to trash what someone does just because he doesn't make wine according to my ethos. In our field, we're all free. Given the crippling administrative side of running an estate, a personal style is one of the few critical freedoms left to us. I can respect someone's work and criticize it at the same time." Jean-Marc is eager to explain further: "We proclaim the right to do as we wish. It's as much a question of style as *terroir*, isn't it? We talk a lot about resisting trends, but when I make the wines I make, I don't feel like I'm resisting anything. It's just my culture. I've seen it done since I was a kid, and I want to follow in that tradition, even if what I do today is different. I want to make the wines I like to drink. I don't want to make any concessions to the marketplace."

I ask him if the defense of *terroir* isn't an act of resistance.

"*Terroir* is a word that's too easily thrown about. Everyone today claims to make a *terroir* wine if it suits them. What does it mean, really? If you make *terroir* wine that's overextracted [i.e., with excess concentration] and disgusting, what value does it have? For me, *terroir* on its own doesn't mean much. It's not a guarantee of anything. I'm more drawn to the idea of a personal style. But that said, without *terroir*, we're nothing, nobody. The issue is complex."

Tradition Isn't What It Used to Be
(AND NEVER WAS)

A second white wine is poured; it's a German Riesling, a 2002 Mosel Wehlener Sonnenuhr from the glorious estate of Johannes Selbach. Alix, not known for her reticence, finally speaks up: "Now, here we have both *terroir* and emotion!"

Jean-Marc agrees: "I've only discovered these Mosel wines recently because France is so chauvinist, but I've developed a real passion for them."

Christophe observes: "It's only eight percent alcohol." (Most wines vary between twelve and thirteen, the difference in alcohol producing a body as different in type as a classical ballerina's from an eighties porn star's). "The acidity is at the same level as the sweetness. It's perfectly balanced. On a pin drop."

I'm pleased that they're enthusiastic about the Selbach Riesling. Twenty years ago in the United States only a few cognoscenti knew of the glories of German Rieslings. Most wine lovers associated German wine with treacly sweet teenage party fare like Liebfraumilch and Blue Nun. But thanks to the indefatigable proselytizing and business savvy of American wine importer Terry Theise, the German wine landscape in America (and therefore eventually elsewhere) has changed radically. There are few wine people in the United States today who would dispute the position of great German Rieslings from the Mosel, Rhein, Pfalz, Franken, and Nahe among the elite of the world's whites. And generally at hugely reasonable prices. In fact, the creation of the robust American market by Theise (and to a lesser extent by the talented if more stolid Rudi Wiest) has been a principal motor in the renaissance of German wines (much like American importers' effect in Burgundy). Theise, a self-proclaimed idiot savant (with a lot more savant than idiot) has been able to convey that the precision, depth, and complexity of German *terroirs* are among the few that are equal to the Burgundian. Working with Michael Skurnik as distributor (also Jean-Marc's U.S. distributor), he has brought the finesse and delicacy of German and Austrian Rieslings, as well as small-grower champagnes such as Vilmart, Pierre Peters, and Larmandier-Bernier to the attention of wine lovers across the continent. He's succeeded partly though his personal appearances—half revival meeting, half Groucho Marx improv—and partly through his brilliantly lucid (if playfully overwrought) commercial catalogue, as good a wine primer as anything published. (In that spirit, he's also written an upcoming book, *Reading Between the Wines*.)

I hear Jean-Marc delicately slurping his Riesling. He looks up beaming: "I love these wines, especially because of their low alcohol content. People write a lot of bullshit about wine, and whether, for example, people harvest too early or too late. When I really like a wine, I think, 'It's sippable and slurpable.'"

Dominique adds: "If you can sip a wine, it finds its true place; you can talk about something else. Sometimes people make too big a deal of wine. It should bring you pleasure, but it shouldn't be the be-all and end-all. I mean, it's just a drink!"

The Vignerons Taste Their Own Wines

Jean-Marc opens both a 2002 Bouchères Meursault and a 2004 Tillets Meursault from his estate, the Domaine Roulot. Jean-Marc and Dominique immediately say the Bouchères is corked. Alix laughs: "I didn't want to say anything . . ." She winks at me because she knows I'm thinking about an incident at Romanée-Conti a few years earlier, when she had the temerity to tell Aubert de Villaine at a lunch we were having in the estate's kitchen that the bottle of 1953 Grands-Echezaux he'd just opened—one of only five bottles remaining in the estate's cellar—was corked. More astonishing was Aubert's reaction. He sniffed the wine, said, "Merde," and then went down to the cellar to retrieve one of the last four bottles.

This time, with Jean-Marc's wine, Alix insists that it tastes corked only at the beginning and that the effect blows off quickly, but Jean-Marc obviously is miffed to serve even a subtly tainted version of his own wine. As I taste it, I feel sure that no more than a tiny fraction of potential drinkers would even be able to discern this level of corkiness, and even then would still enjoy drinking the wine. Of course a completely corked wine is undrinkable, the moldy cardboard scent and flavor overpowering anything else and rendering the mouth flat and lifeless. If it is half-corked, the complexity is compromised but the wine may be drinkable. When it is slightly corked, only the vigneron and a valiant few would notice anything . . . and the wine remains largely itself.

Jean-Marc explains that even if the Bouchères had shown better, his preference is for the Tillets. As Dominique points out, it's a *terroir* that's more representative of its author. "That's really what we expect from you," he says. "The Bouchères is bigger, rounder, easier. You have a bunch of other vineyards on the upper slope of the hillsides that make very biting, precise wines. Your palate was formed by those wines." Jean-Marc nods his head in agreement as Dominique continues: "And you have the Bouchères vines, lower on the slope, which mature more quickly and are fatter, riper. They're a definite part of the Meursault *terroir*, but I think they disturb you. I love rounder wines, even if I understand Jean-Marc's wines well. I think if I made a Tillets, its austerity would bother me." Alix adds: "Dominique makes wines that are more easily likeable. And I make wines that are more austere than any of yours." Dominique laughs as he opens the first of his two bottles: "Yeah, it's a well-known fact that you're a pain in the ass."

He immediately opens his second bottle and explains, "I brought a '97 Genevrières. The *terroir* is amazing, full of sensitivity and finesse. It's a real joy for me. I love the '97s because we had a wonderful harvest; it's got a lovely tautness, with a suave hint of the riper Meursault from the lower slopes. I see myself in this wine. And I brought a '98 Perrières, which can be very powerful, but is strange. I make fifteen hectoliters per hectare." This is a tiny yield considering that 48 hectoliters are permitted—a hectare equaling 2.47 acres—and he makes on average 40 hectoliters per hectare in his other vineyards. This is the difference between 5,500 bottles per hectare as opposed to about 1,300 bottles if the yield goes down to 15 hectoliters per hectare. It's worth noting that in a world that prizes intensity and concentration at any cost—including at the cost of balance and subtlety, most wine journalists would be delighted for Dominique that this vineyard yielded only fifteen hectoliters per hectare. "I only rarely understand what's happening in the Perrières vines or in the cellar after. The wine often lacks freshness. It's a vine that has a hard time producing. I'm in a state of constant doubt about it. Especially since your Perrières is so magnificent, Jean-Marc [and it's worth remembering that it is the identical grape, Chardonnay, in all these different vineyards]. So this bottle is an adventure for me. And bringing it to you is an adventure, too. I know people buy it for a lot of money, so it's ridiculous for me to be saying all this. But if you want to be rigorous, you have to take risks and embrace the unknown. You never know quite how to approach a great Burgundy. What you'll find when you open it. You may get fireworks or you may not perceive much at all. It depends on how you open it, with whom, with what. Burgundies are full of panache and as unpredictable as life."

Christophe observes both wines carefully: the brighter golden yellow of the '97 Genevrières and the more troubled, darker, honey tones of the '98 Perrières. He seems to draw his conclusion just from the colors. But I'm wrong. "Wines don't always behave the same way," he observes. "Burgundies, especially, can be moody. There's a very strong human element to them. They're not the product of enology or technology but of people. Sometimes the wine shows badly. It grumbles a

little. But the core of its personality is always there. There's a tremendous amount of work that goes into it, guided by your intentions. Then
you wait a long time after fermentation before bottling, and the wine
emerges. But it's not a finished product. Nor is it the result of your
intentions at the end. It remains open-ended. The romance and the
mystery of it is a factor for all of us."

Lunch (Liquid and Solid)

We drift from the living room through the spacious country kitchen to
the unadorned but homey dining room, anchored by a large fireplace.
Favorite empties from recent bacchanalia line its marble-topped man-
tle. It occurs to me that after more than an hour of tasting and discussion, everything that's been said about the wines describes a physical or
emotional quality. The conversation has had its feet firmly planted on
the ground or based in the heart. Christophe explains as we sit that "as
vignerons we can't remove ourselves from its nature as a substance. We
need its physicality. I mean, I don't know a thing about all those efforts
to identify specific aromas in a wine. What interests me is an overall
harmony. I look for the dominant factors. A wine consumer necessarily
has another view. And a Japanese person will see things differently from
an American. Everybody looks for different things, in fact, from the
same wine."

In the wine world, Christophe is one of the most renowned stars of
red wine and Dominique a celebrity of equal, perhaps even greater status for his whites. However, the good-humored spontaneity of the latter
and the elegance and humility of the former have already removed any
barriers that could easily occur between rivals. Christophe opens his
first red, a 2001 Chambolle-Musigny *premier cru* Les Amoureuses (in
English, "lovers" in the feminine). He explains that despite the vineyard's (justified) cult status, he doesn't like what he did in this vintage.
Its character, he says, is vegetal. Dominique agrees: "It almost tastes
soapy and it seems like there's a little prick of carbonic gas that didn't
disappear during the fermentation [when yeasts provoke a grape's fer-

mentation, the tanks are left open for the resulting gases to escape]. It's not a wine that's at ease. Though at the end, you can sense a certain delicacy and grace in the mouth."

Christophe explains that "this was the first time I'd ever had a blocked fermentation with any tank. It just stopped fermenting in mid-conversion [of the grape sugars to alcohol]. I tried everything: replunging the mass of solids back into the liquid, refunneling the wine. I couldn't believe this was happening to me. Then I had to do something I never do. I introduced artificial yeasts to restimulate the process." (Normally, he would rely on yeasts naturally present in the atmosphere to complete the job.)

Dominique sips the wine carefully again: "We could easily be surprised by this wine in ten years. You can see on the finish that the wine has breed." Alix serves a precisely sautéed steak from Limoges beef that Jean-Marc brought back from a visit to that region the day before. She adds, "It's a little severe, even for me. The nose isn't clean, either. You feel it's troubled. But maybe it will become more serene as it ages."

Dominique bites into the steak. "It's delicious, amazingly tender. But with this Chambolle and the other that Christophe brought, the '95 *grand cru* Bonnes Mares, you could imagine that a dish like a *ris de veau* would marry better with the delicacy of the wines. But it's amazing with the wine that you stayed with the natural process as long as possible before using the foreign yeasts. We're often gamblers in this profession, and often to the brink of losing everything. We don't usually think about the economic implications of our decisions . . . how much money is at stake. I think about my Meursaults, trying to keep them as pure as possible."

"And yet your wines are sold for ninety to two hundred and fifty euros a bottle," I say.

"That's pure speculation," responds Dominique. "I sell them to the middlemen for thirty to forty."

"Even though you could easily demand a hundred."

"That's true. But I don't."

Christophe quickly adds: "It's a question of ethics."

"We're very lucky here, too. Our domains aren't doing badly at all. We could ask more and don't, but we also aren't in trouble economically. So why be exploitive?" asks Jean-Marc.

Christophe elaborates: "We're the first generation of Burgundians who've traveled extensively abroad, from the United States to Singapore. This has changed our mentality, made us much more open and receptive, even as it also makes us appreciate where we come from in a way maybe our parents couldn't. And we could've adopted another method in Burgundy, but we have always opted for a single grape. And we have fun with that, distinguishing special parcels within a given vineyard and pursuing those subtle differences through the lens of the single grape. The richness of Burgundy is precisely in this decision not to pursue a cultural fusion but a culture based on the exploration of details. This is why Burgundies are in such profound sync with the Japanese. Plus, they appreciate acidity more than the vigor of tannin, which our Pinot Noir also favors. And they're more drawn to the lightness of the aromatic rather than to the weight of sugar."

I look around. Both bottles from Christophe are already empty: the only gauge of a wine's quality that matters to vignerons. Dominique takes a last sip and says: "I love the Amoureuses in the end. It's so sensual, like the more profound Bonnes Mares. But you can also feel the profundity and sensuality are expressed with modesty. Nothing demonstrative, because everything with Christophe is done with a light touch. There's an intensity of flavor without force or pressure. Like magic. In the Côte-de-Beaune [this is a region known more for its whites] I make a red among all my whites, a Volnay-Santenots. You can try to make it as fine and elegant as you want, but the almost rustic density is always there. But with these wines from Chambolle, in the Côte-de-Nuits [home of the most prestigious reds], they're simply evanescent. Fabulously delicate. Maybe I'm simplifying, but the most beautiful wines are those that are full of flavor but never because of their power. A taste-filled evanescence!"

Christophe laughs. "I agree with you even if I wouldn't use such hoity-toity words. The great wines above all need to privilege elegance over power."

Fathers and Sons

The lunch winds downs. Laure, thinking about Danièle's comments the previous day, asks them if they feel like they are the elite of the wine world. Dominique bristles: "We're not an elite. But we are appreciative of our positions of privilege." A Cheshire cat smile forms around Christophe's mouth: "Sometimes we could be viewed as spoiled children. I could have been born into a winemaking family anywhere. But I happened to be born here. I couldn't dream of anything better than Les Amoureuses and Bonnes Mares. I have a father who showed me how to work and a grandfather who left behind a bunch of wines in the cellar that I can still taste today."

Dominique nods: "Your father, Jean-Marie, taught me so much about reds. I often think about that with a lot of emotion. I was devastated the day of his funeral in 2002, and I still am. He was a gentleman of wine. And you, Christophe, you've gone so far beyond what your father did."

Alix has disappeared into the kitchen. It's dark outside. The mood has grown more contemplative. Jean-Marc looks at me and then at Christophe: "I lost my father in 1978. I was twenty-four years old. Christophe, you went to see him before he died."

"Your father told me he wanted to exchange some wine with me. I was touched," Christophe answers. "My father, unfortunately, was ill and wasn't himself for the last few years of his life. But I think he knew how to cede his power intelligently, little by little. That's not easy to do in our field."

"Wow. That's a huge theme in Burgundy," says Jean-Marc. "There's a terrifying number of people our age whose fathers didn't want to turn things over to them. Whole generations are wasted that way."

We are fully immersed in the complexity of transmission, at a personal level and also a cultural one. It's been dark for hours. I want to ask one last question before we head to the kitchen for coffee. Do they see themselves as innovators?

Alix answers. "No, I don't innovate."

"Do you feel like you're frozen in time, then, just imitating the gestures of your parents?"

"No. I feel like I'm progressing at my own speed. Every year I advance. We have the culture of *terroir*, but rather than being imprisoned by it, it frees me."

And with that we go into the kitchen, with Jean-Marc already on the boil: "The other day some hotshot owner of a Côte-de-Nuits estate said that Burgundy is too confusing for the consumer today, with all of its classifications and subclassifications. 'We can hang on to the designations of *grand cru* and *premier cru*, but everything else should be eliminated to simplify sales,' he said. Well, in Meursault there are no *grand cru*, but we do have a number of *premier cru*, as you know, of which I share a part of several. But I'm as attached to my village vineyard designations as the *premier cru*. The day I can't bottle my Tillets, Meix Chavaux, and Tessons separately is the day I'll leave any system of official designation. I'm going to continue to put these ancestral references on my labels. If there's anywhere where this attention to detail needs to be respected it's in Burgundy. Especially as most of the world moves in the opposite direction. We need to continue to work to understand the individual identities of each parcel of vines, whether it's at the village, *premier cru*, or *grand cru* level."

Dominique shakes his head vigorously: "This pressure comes from the outside world in general. They want us to believe that our system is shit and that we should make brand name wines based on varietals like the others. The AOC [*Appellation d'origine contrôlée*, or "official designation of origin," which determines what vines can be cultivated where and what historically are the guidelines for the resulting wine] is far from perfect, but at least it places the emphasis on a sense of place and on the human element in that given place rather than on industry and technology and marketing. It's a system that protects human values. It doesn't matter at all whether it's a *grand cru, premier cru,* village wine, or even a generic 'Burgundy.' What counts is the authenticity of an origin, a history. That's where the emotion is. It's the reality of lived lives. And who gives a damn if we're talking about five-, ten-, or fifty-euro wines? Above all the important element in wine is its historical agricultural sense."

I ask them if there aren't restrictions that the AOC system imposes against which they chafe. Christophe shrugs his shoulders: "Oh sure, why not put a little Syrah [a hefty, fruity grape from the Rhône Valley] in my Bonnes Mares," he says with a naughty grin. "In the U.S., they're allowed to sell a 'Pinot Noir' with up to twenty percent of any other grapes they want. Is that cheating the customer? I don't know. But it means that even the notion of varietal wine is suspect. We've determined certain rules which we believe best allows the land to express itself. Wine is not a purely constructed product. It needs to respect an origin larger than itself."

"To respect the culture, the history of the place," Dominique emphasizes.

"Those guys in Santa Barbara who throw in twenty percent Syrah to beef up their Pinot Noirs are in search of a different ideal for the grape. Something massive, sweet, and powerful," says Jean-Marc. "Whereas when Christophe talks about why he doesn't like his 2001 Amoureuses, it's in relation to what his conception of that vineyard should be. The *terroir* for us is the screenplay. Our intervention in the winemaking process is very different from the guys in Santa Barbara. They're closer to Hollywood: varietal stars and special effects wines. It's not better or worse. It's just a different pursuit of pleasure. Here everything passes through the vector of *terroir* and of the history that it contains."

Listening to these three very different men discussing their common rootedness in their family *terroirs* reminds me that I have no ancestral claim to a *terroir* of any kind and that I am, to some extent, rootless and stateless (beyond even my origins as a Jew). But in their wines, I receive the same sensations that I get before the thirteenth-century frescoes of Cimabue in Assisi. On the one hand, I'm compelled to accept an affirmation that the intrinsic value of, say, an Andy Warhol painting is equal to a Cimabue. This is a question of taste, as the old Latin saw goes, about which there can be no argument. But that which distinguishes a Cimabue from a Warhol goes beyond a notion of beauty or taste. The value of a Cimabue is determined, aside from its aesthetic factors, by the historical fact of its survival as a witness to a civilization. This also must be true for a *terroir* of comparable historical dimension. *This* intrinsic value cannot be replicated by talent, money, or power of any kind. And the survival of historical testaments becomes a question of a world patrimony, of a universal value. It goes far beyond the actions of the person responsible, the ephemeral agent of its expression, whether the artist or his buyer.

A wine—or a painting—of *terroir* encompasses an individual expression that can attain nobility only with the passage of time. *Terroir* is an expression of the liberty of the individual, but within a communal and historical context. And in that case, I'm a co-citizen of the *terroirs* of Jean-Marc, Christophe, Alix, and Dominique. The simple fact of drinking these wines *places* me in the world. I don't need to be the owner of the land. It's for that reason that *terroir* is as democratic a concept as any museum. It's never a question of ancestral ownership, of an inherent inequality. The opposite: it's the sharing of privilege with the world at large.

13

WITH CHRISTOPHE ROUMIER

I wanted to meet up with each of the lunch's protagonists individually. So the next day we drive the twenty-five kilometers that separate Meursault from Chambolle-Musigny, from the Côte-de-Beaune to the Côte-de-Nuits, to meet Christophe Roumier at his estate. The domain is still called "Georges Roumier," the name of his grandfather, who began to manage his wife's family domain in 1924. Though he didn't start to bottle his own wines at the estate until 1945, he was among the first proprietors to do so. His son Jean-Marie succeeded him in 1961, and Christophe, his grandson, twenty years later. The wines of Georges and Jean-Marie were respected, but the wines of Christophe have earned him a place in the pantheon of star vignerons of our time. And yet like his friend Jean-Marc Roulot, he does all he can to avoid the wine limelight.

After crossing the snowy courtyard of the handsome but modest stone buildings of the estate, we head into the office. While Christophe's sister, Delphine, works at her computer, he launches us into an animated discussion before we can even take our coats off. "Tradition," he says, "is something that we're re-creating every day. And our intentions today can't be that different from before. Only the methods have changed. Tradition is more a state of mind than a gesture."

I look at Christophe: transparent and yet full of depth and mystery, absolutely down-to-earth, and yet with an elegance that is unforced, the mirror of his wines. On the assumption that what we say in front of our peers always will be shaded differently, I repeat a question from the previous day, a question that usually proves to be a trap for my fellow filmmakers.

"Do you innovate?" I ask him.

"Not me. I don't think so. I try to avoid mistakes once I've made them. I look to progress. What I've had inculcated in me is enough. Even if I add a little something here or there. I think Dominique is more the revolutionary type."

"But your wines aren't like your father's."

"No, but my '95s aren't like my '90s, either, because my way of working has changed a little. I didn't wait for the same maturity in the vineyard before, for example. It's often a question of happy accidents. The idea of ripe fruit has marked my generation more than both the previous and the subsequent one, because of global warming. Now we tend to harvest earlier, but with even riper grapes."

His response doesn't surprise me. Many fashionable filmmakers who produce gimmicky stylistic tricks to call attention to themselves will be the first to reveal how groundbreaking they are, while the truly innovative simply pursue their sense of aesthetics as if it were a natural and not unusual gesture. Even Orson Welles, one of the most radical and flamboyantly experimental of artists (from the noir opera *The Lady from Shanghai* to his dissonant soap opera version of *Othello*) once told fellow director Peter Bogdanovich that he never thought what he did was unusual. "I just place the camera where it seems most interesting to tell the story," he said with uncharacteristic modesty.

Laure was struck by the "cool Cistercian purity," as she said, of the '95 Bonnes Mares we'd drunk at the previous day's lunch. So I ask Christophe if he's religious. He laughs. "No, I never wanted to be a monk. We were brought up in the conventional, conservative Catholic ethos. Which means that they taught us more about the trappings of religion than the substance. They taught us to go to mass, and the rest was supposed to happen on its own. In fact, I've never really been religious. I'm not a believer. But how many people who go to church are devout? In the rural world, going to mass gives you a social position. But is it an inner need? Often, it's just superstition. But all that doesn't mean that wines can't be monastic . . . I wonder if you can say that, 'monastic wines'? Well, my '95 was like that. Monastic. It wasn't an easy year. But I've always been happy with how the '95 turned out. I've made better wines, but I love it because it's got complexity. It's an alert wine, a bit austere. It's not a fashionable wine. I like that."

Again I try to pick up the themes and questions from the previous day to see if the answers will come differently today, while we're alone. "Do you feel overwhelmed sometimes by the weight of the *terroir*?" I ask him.

"No," he says flatly. "Burgundians aren't overwhelmed by *terroir*. They compose themselves in relation to it. What is inscribed in each parcel. I'm not an artist. I'm a farmer. I'm in charge of a plant that I have to help grow, whose fruit I harvest, which then has to be transformed into wine."

"But there's a name on the label that distinguishes you from your neighbor."

"I'm not convinced that if you gave me the same grape twice I wouldn't make two different wines. I work by instinct. All the sensory elements of a wine aren't necessarily calculated. There's a whole aspect of a wine that's made without us. The result can be a surprise. There's nothing artistic in that."

I laugh. "You couldn't be more wrong. No real artist would tell you that his work was entirely intentional. They speak the same way you do. There's always an intention, but you don't know where it will lead you."

"Maybe you're right. But look at the reality. Yesterday we were talking about spoiled children. How many vignerons receive the same wonderful gift of vineyards on the Côte?" Then he adds dryly: "I don't think that all the vignerons here are artists."

I ask him what the most crucial decisions are for him in determining the character of a wine. "First, there's the health of the vine," he responds with enthusiasm. "That has to be monitored. The vine can't be given too much fertilizer, or it will be too vigorous. The grapes need to be concentrated, especially for the reds, though not excessively. To best express *terroir*, the juice-to-solid ratio is very important. But I don't worry about the yield [the number of hectoliters per hectare]. A small yield doesn't necessarily mean a great wine. That's malarkey that some vignerons recycle for credulous journalists."

"Like an intense actor will not necessarily provide the viewer with an intense experience. Intensity can easily become histrionics and nothing more," I suggest, conscious that the parallel extends further; histrionics in actors is often what gets them undiscriminating journalists' highest kudos and awards.

Christophe nods his head in agreement: "Yeah, wine journalists like to talk about dramatically low yields as a measure of greatness. But it's equally spurious. There's rapidly a point of diminishing returns with low yields. What counts is to control the vigor of the vine by pruning. But the most critical factor is deciding when to harvest. Before that you determine the personality of the wine through the philosophy of the estate: the use of herbicides or not, organic farming practices without submitting to doctrine, biodynamism, whatever you choose. Although I'm essentially organic in my practices, I'm not doctrinal. I use organic pesticides, but I will use a chemical product if, for example, I have a risk of mold at the beginning of the growing season."

"It sounds like believing in homeopathic cures up until the severity of an illness may require the exceptional use of antibiotics."

"Exactly," says Christophe. "I really love having that kind of latitude. But I'm very careful about what I use, very mindful of preserving the life of the soil. Biodynamism is about the life of the soil in perhaps a more profound way, but there are a lot of things I don't yet understand. Dominique has embraced it with a passion. It's an interesting option for the future for me."

Transmission of Taste

Christophe remains standing, very still and tranquil but emanating a quietly powerful energy. I think about the singular effect his wines have on me: a liquid full of life and energy but that is reserved, that gives the impression of enormous interior stability. There's doubtless a Zen aspect to Christophe's methods and to his wine. I'm not surprised that he appreciates the culture of Japan so much. I ask him about the passing of the generational torch at his domain.

"You know, the passing of responsibility from father to son is very difficult in our field," he says, glancing at his sister, who apparently never manifested—or was encouraged to manifest—any ambitions to succeed their father. At any rate, she doesn't look up from her secretarial chores at the computer. "It's not easy to transmit to someone else your way of expressing yourself your whole life. For my father, making wine was what gave him his sense of self-worth. What happens if his son wants to work in a different way? Fathers often have trouble passing along what is admirable in their actions as a vigneron. I was lucky, despite the inevitable friction."

Christophe's thoughts seem to move away and return in rapid succession. "The transfer of responsibility always causes sparks. The 1982 vintage was huge, the biggest harvest I'd ever seen. Things got away from my father. He was already not well. So I took the initiative. We did two harvests, two weeks apart. I made wine from the second wave, with the less prestigious vineyards. My father was exhausted, so he let me do it. I took my time. By chance I was able to show him that there were other ways to work. In the beginning, the wines I vinified were better. But with time, the breed of the first batch of vineyards showed their superiority, despite the stylistic differences in the vinification. And this in itself suggests that the hand of man, even if well applied, is ephemeral in relation to the underlying force of the *terroir*."

After standing for so long, Christophe invites us to come into the kitchen. I note that neither the office, nor the hallways, nor the kitchen contains the customary display of prizes, medallions, and other mementos of glory that are visible in most estates, renowned or not. I tell Christophe that I remember that in New York in the 1980s I began to hear people talking a lot about the Domaine Roumier. It was then that the concept of winemaker stars gained currency. The *Wine Spectator* and a multitude of other magazines in Britain, France, Germany, Italy et alia were gaining wider readership for a new generation of socially ambitious but (vino) culturally innocent consumers. The magazines needed to create celebrities and personalities so they could inscribe themselves in the general celebrity culture.

"It's too bad, really," says Christophe, sighing. "We're just vignerons. Our work is very basic. That kind of stuff distorts, falsifies everything."

"You're considered a star in the wine world," I say. His face whitens.

"I never wanted that. And it's made a lot of demands on us, on the estate. On me. It isn't in my nature. I don't like to flaunt myself in public. I'd prefer it if people admired the wine rather than the person."

"But you do rock-star tours in the United States."

"I'm obliged to. I'm going to do a tour with Jean-Marc and Dominique in January, to New York. We'll meet collectors at big dinners. That the wines are famous is one thing, but us! There are people who are really fanatical, who spend ridiculous amounts of money, horrifying amounts. What do you say we go taste some wines?"

He disappears into the cellar. Some old bottles are displayed above our heads, covered with mold and dust. I can barely decipher the labels. Christophe comes back quickly with two unlabeled bottles. He opens one of the bottles. It's the first wine he made entirely on his own, a 1982. Of course I'm moved by the gesture. It's like Pasolini showing a visitor his first Super 8 short that he's just pulled out of the closet. "It's a humble Chambolle-Musigny, a simple village wine from a very ungenerous vintage," he says. "You have to take it for what it is. I haven't tasted it for a long time. It's from the second wave of harvesting, which I did myself. I'm not exactly giving you a precious gift here. It doesn't have much body. But I'd imagined that a wine as light as the '82 would lose its substance very fast. I'm really surprised that there's even a little life in it."

The color is very delicate but with a complex orange and amber light. In the mouth, it's both austere and lively, with a mordant acidity. It is as Dominique described Christophe's wines yesterday: evanescent.

Christophe puts the bottle on the table next to two empty carafes.

I say that "I've always thought that decanting a wine an hour or more before tasting it is like people who make love only thinking about arriving at the climax of the act as swiftly as possible. I love discovering a wine the moment it's opened, in the first shock of contact with the air, and then tasting and retasting it over at least an hour or so."

"It's as if you were to miss the introduction of a film," he agrees. "There's a whole progression in a wine, too," he says as he pours the second bottle.

"This is from the same vintage: 1982. It's a Musigny." This is one of the rarest and most celebrated of the Burgundy *grands crus.* "I don't have a clue what it's going to be like. It should, under normal circumstances, be the fullest expression of what a great wine is: elegant and deep without being forceful or aggressive. This came from the first phase of vinification, overseen by my father. Dad was very active but sometimes in a too programmed way. That's the way he was brought up." Christophe sniffs the wine. "It's not exactly a transcendent nose. But what's surprising is that there isn't the overwhelming difference that you would find in a normal vintage between a Chambolle village wine and this *grand cru* Musigny. Still, you can sense the greater suppleness in the mouth. The tannins are more present than in the village wine, and you feel a certain suave serenity that lingers in the mouth despite the meagerness of the body. But it's funny. My father and I probably had the same idea of the *kind* of wine we'd like to make. It's just that our methods were different."

Despite the great fragility of these wines, we lose ourselves in the fascination that these two ethereal liquids exert on us. We sip and watch in silence. I'm moved by the transparency of this man who brought up two bottles from one of the most unflattering vintages of the last thirty years. Unlike most winemakers, who will open their more flattering (not necessarily their most prized) wines for even the least distinguished of visitors, Christophe Roumier has proven his mettle as an artist by my reckoning, preferring instead the excitement of discovery and exchange without any fear of revealing his flaws.

14

WITH DOMINIQUE LAFON

If **Christophe Roumier** suggests a certain Apollonian ideal among the great Burgundy vignerons, Dominique Lafon would be the Dionysian (minus the girth). Forty-eight years old, fair-haired and light-eyed, this tensile and muscular man has a face lined like the rows of earth manually tilled between his vines. Insisting on his peasant side—he's happiest, he tells me, on his tractor or when handling the vines—he is also a man who knows how to take pleasure from all cultural expressions. Now a legend in the world of wine for his Meursaults and his single *grand cru* Le Montrachet, Dominique has traveled the world from the Copacabana Palace in Rio, at the invitation of an extravagant Brazilian wine collector, to the luxury hotels of Tokyo, where he is received like a pop star. I imagine that I can see these same opposing qualities in his wine: unabashed richness and sensuality in the fruit, balanced by a surprisingly taut and minerally acidity. He is a frank peasant and an artisan of the greatest sophistication—and someone who never seems to be afraid to speak his mind, a rare quality in a man with so great a reputation to protect.

When I ask Dominique to show me what he holds closest to his heart in Burgundy, he doesn't hesitate to drive us eighty-five kilometers from Meursault to Mâcon, at the southern border of Burgundy. It's a very "Dominique" choice. The reputation of the Domaine des Comtes Lafon is based on their prized Meursaults and Montrachet. The recent venture in Mâcon, one of the humblest and least regarded appellations in Burgundy, is a small personal project of Dominique's, far removed from the glamour of the Côte-de-Beaune and the Côte-de-Nuits, a refuge of sorts from the complex pressures of a highly lucrative and public family business.

The Sunless Highway

Under a moody slate sky, we meet Dominique in a parking lot at the off-ramp of the major north–south highway. We climb into his pickup truck and head to southern Burgundy on the rarely sunny Autoroute du Soleil. "It's a real paradox," says Dominique. "I hate driving, but I have to do it to get to Mâcon. I go twice a week, unless I'm traveling."

Anticipating that we'll be tackling more serious issues, Dominique starts us off on a gossipy note. Laughing, he asks me if I had any experience shooting with Jancis Robinson, probably the most influential critic in the world after Robert Parker. "I actually filmed with her once," he says, "and it was a ridiculous experience. It's too bad, because she's talented and was one of the first woman 'masters of wine' [the most reputable and rigorous training program for wine tasters in the world]." I explain to Dominique that in fact I had a number of encounters and exchanges with her, going from bad to silly.

"I interviewed her in London for *Mondovino* because I'd been following her since the beginning of her career," I say to Dominique. "She had been someone I appreciated enormously, because when she started out she wasn't afraid to blow the whistle on dubious industry practices and all expressions of pretension and foppery in the wine world."

The very British Jancis Robinson is in fact an extremely cultivated and intelligent woman, author of countless books (including the excellent reference guides *The Oxford Companion to Wine* and *The World*

Atlas of Wine, in long-standing collaboration with the great wine historian Hugh Johnson). She is also head and shoulders above Parker, both intellectually and as a taster. But considering the trajectory of her career, it's a bit like (to dare an outrageous comparison) comparing Colin Powell to Donald Rumsfeld in the run-up to the Iraq invasion. Did we forgive Powell or loathe him more intensely than Rumsfeld for his superior qualities—because we knew *he knew* better—as he tried to persuade the world with calculated fabrications? But having lost track of her for a number of years leading up the shooting of *Mondovino*, I went to see her because I hoped that this sophisticated journalist would offer an alternative view of the wine universe to her better-known, gunslinging rival Robert Parker. Alas, after filming with her for six hours, there wasn't a single phrase that I could use. Where was the fearless wine warrior I'd known in the 1980s and early '90s?

The critic who greeted me at her North London house spent an hour-long taxi ride and an entire lunch in a South London restaurant worried that I would film her while eating (or in any unflattering action) and seemed most concerned by neutralizing her "old English nanny" appearance with flashy designer clothes and consensual comments. The media-savvy presenter of countless wine television programs constantly censored herself, ferociously protective of her image. It was probably the most stiflingly self-censored conversation I had with anyone in the wine world over the course of four years of filming. How could this be? Surely a critic is the one person who could be relied on to speak freely about any industry's machinations. But with her much-followed "Jancis Robinson" website and cottage industry of products associated with her name, she has apparently transformed herself from a journalist into a brand.

I explain to Dominique that she sent me numerous sympathetic e-mails during the editing period and when the film was announced for Cannes. But once she found out she wasn't in the film, she didn't disguise her anger. Still, when the film came out in Britain after an enthusiastic reception in France, she published an article in the *Financial*

Times that was a bit sour and petty, but positive overall (though it concluded with her fretting about the brand of shoes she'd worn the day we filmed!). However, in a third reversal a few months later, once the film was perceived by wine world potentates as a (pesky) threat to their close-knit power network, she published an article defending the integrity of Michel Rolland, attacking the film as manipulative and false. She lavished praise specifically on the wines of the New World as guided by Michel Rolland. Of course, I thought, she couldn't bad-mouth all these wines because she makes too much money recommending them. New World wines and imitations of Old World wines by Michel Rolland are the ones that drive the market in England. So she has no choice but to intervene in a positive way, in order to maintain her weight in that market. That's the trap for successful critics in the wine world. They can't question the system because they're profiting from it. If they started telling the truth about the huckster wines that predominate, they'd lose the advertising pages—among those critics and magazines who accept them; and for those who don't (like Robinson and Parker), they'd simply lose their highly lucrative positions of authority in a market largely determined by these wines.

Dominique laughs. "She's formidable. She knows where she wants to go. I had quite an experience with her once. In 1994 she told me she wanted to make a film about the grape varietals of the world. She came to interview me about Chardonnay in Meursault. It was during the harvest, when I'm horribly busy. She asked me to comment on a colleague's wine that I was supposed to taste blind. I told her it wasn't my job to do that; it was out of the question. The 'master of wine' should taste, not me. Anyway, the last day of her filming, we were in the winery, by the fermentation tanks. She had a purse with a bottle of wine sticking out of it. She took it out, poured a glass, and asked me what I thought of it. So I picked up the glass before I could think to say no. I smelled it. The nose was unremarkable, but in the mouth it was the worst corked bottle I'd ever tasted. I ran out of the room so I could spit it out. She kept the scene in her film, but without sound, saying, "I had Dominique

Lafon taste a wine produced by the big Australian Chardonnay industry, and this was his reaction to it. He refused even to spit it out inside
his winery." Everyone thinks it's a funny scene, but I'm furious, because
I have nothing against the wines of this producer, who I didn't know.
The bottle was corked, that's all."

I laugh, both horrified and somehow not surprised that this was
the act of a journalist who accused me of being manipulative when I
edited *Mondovino*. I ask Dominique if he's not wary of the wine press in
general.

"The press doesn't like being kept at a distance. When Parker
comes . . . well, actually he sends Rovani, his longtime 'associate' in Burgundy, since no one wants anything to do with him." (In fact, this associate has since left Parker's employ and become a wine merchant.) "I
ask him what he wants to taste. But he's much more concerned if I've
read his reviews. I tell him I never read press reviews of my wines. They
don't interest me at all. What would I get out of them? Most of the time
I don't even understand them."

"Fantastic. The vignerons themselves can't make sense of the critics'
language."

"Everyone knows that between good scores and bad scores, there are
errors in judgment. And if someone comes to your cellar, that's already
better than a lot of them. But they come only for a part of a single day,
whereas we observe our wines changing constantly from one day to the
next. What definitive judgment can they make of an unfinished wine if
they don't take the time to return? There are days when all the wines in
the winery are not showing their best. If the guy comes on that day—
well, we're screwed. You can't be naïve. It's not that the wine's bad, but
it's still developing, in the process of being made. It's especially ridiculous when a wine is tasted very early in its life. Any commentary is
always very fragile, very suspect, like our snap judgments about people
whom we know only glancingly."

The Mâconnais

We reach the Mâconnais after an hour on the road. It's much wilder and more pastoral than the Côte-d'Or around Beaune. It really feels like the country: rolling hills and tiny villages of modest stone houses. Dominique turns off the country road near the village called Chardonnay and drives up a dirt road toward the top of a gracefully curving hill. "I wanted to show you this, the Clos de la Crochette," he says. "With its southern exposure, it's one of the most singular and beautiful *terroirs* in the Mâconnais. We've worked it organically since I bought it. In the spring it's covered with yellow flowers." He stops to look at the lightly snowy winter landscape. "We placed bees in the vines. I wanted to create an animal universe; it's a crucial concept of biodynamism. Next year we'll have our first honey production." He continues with the same enthusiasm as the car pushes through the squishy earth trail: "See the broken stones underfoot? Along with the deep clay underneath, it makes the soil aerated, perfect for drainage. The vines don't do well with their roots soaked in water." He stops the car and looks out with proprietary pride at his clos (a clearly delineated enclosure). "This was one of the first vineyards planted by the monks of Cluny, who were well aware of the soft caress of the sun in its southern exposure. Look! There's my star vineyard worker."

We stop and get out to greet an employee of Dominique's who is pruning the vines even though it's snowing. In his fifties, an ex-fisherman from the Saône, Paul has worked with Dominique for a little more than a year.

He turns to us: "I won't tell you about the hassles we've had to confront with these vines. It's as bad as the hardships I faced as a fisherman. Here, I'm pulling off the branches Dom has pruned."

Dominique puts his arm around Paul and explains, "We try to prune during the waning moon as much as possible. Biodynamism takes into account an environment that goes from the nearest element to the most distant. If you only think about rainfall for instance, without considering the movement of the planets, it won't work. The energies are inter-connected."

Paul calmly continues his labors while Dominique gives him a word or two of advice. Even with the snow turning to rain, the landscape is majestic. "Beautiful places make for good wines," says Dominique. Soaked, we take refuge in the car and drive on toward the winery.

"Paul's something of an intellectual. He's very aware, very informed. But his social position is complicated. He was out of work and over fifty. So he was considered finished. Unemployable. You can't imagine how happy I am to work with this guy, because he's passionate about what he does, because he's never at a loss for words. When something doesn't work, he says so. He brings in new ideas—like the bees, for instance. People like him are indispensable. If someone works here without love, your wine will suffer. This work [the pruning]—if it's not done with precision, you can destroy the vine for the rest of the year."

As we drive through a quiet, pretty village, Laure looks around and says, "The nearby abbey of Cluny is the historic source of the vineyards in Burgundy. But the region is suffering economically, isn't it, Dominique?"

Dominique shakes his head. "When you see the prices, it's nothing. Today, one hectare of planted vines here in Mâcon is worth sixty thousand euros. One hectare back home in Meursault is worth eight hundred thousand euros. With the Meursault you're going to find much more finesse, more length in the mouth, more class, more longevity. It's a question of rarity also. The effect of its rarity increases the cumulative price effect of the wine's quality. Mâcon is a delicious wine: tasty, generous, but not rare. It's a cheerful wine. This is the area of Cluny. And compared with the Cistercians (of the abbey of Cîteaux, back in the north of Burgundy) the abbey of Cluny led a flamboyant life. Here, the temperament of the wines is relaxed, festive. When I first came here, people treated me like a foreigner. But I never felt like one."

I ask him why he came here to the unfashionable—and less lucrative—southern end of Burgundy. "Because I love things that are on a human scale," he answers. "And here there's no distance between the owner and the man who works in the vineyard. People talk together. I also pitch in with the manual labor. The family estate at Meursault doesn't have that kind of humanity. I didn't want to go to the south of France, where I don't know the grapes or the culture. I wanted to have an intimate knowledge of the place I was going to be working in. Here you have the same types of land, the same geological origins as in Meursault, which made it easier for me to understand the process quickly. And I'd been working in Meursault for fifteen years. I needed— once I turned forty—to reconsider my position, to take a risk. Here my business isn't financed by Meursault; it's entirely borrowed from the bank. I've got a very tight, bare-bones budget. Every time I achieve something here, it's a real victory. In Meursault, if we need a tractor, we just buy a tractor."

We arrive in the village of Azé, with its majestic twelfth-century church. The light is magnificent, as it is anywhere in Burgundy, perhaps the most complex and changing light I've ever seen. Obviously as a film director I'm sensitive to the importance of light, but I feel that it's one of the explanations for the complexity of the wines. It's a light that gives energy. I ask Dominique if this notion seems silly to him.

"Not at all. Luminosity throughout the growing season is a key factor—often more important than sunshine—in determining the character of a vintage. In '96, for example, it was cold all year, but the Pinot Noir ripened because there was a dynamic light. Olivier de Serres, one of the first theoreticians of *terroir*, wrote in the sixteenth century that *terroir* is the alliance of soil, a complex network of plants, and of light."

In fact, the medieval village and the surrounding countryside are bathed in multiple lights. The *lights* are in fact plural, ranging in tone from warm to cool gray, pink and violet, to a series of blues from icy cobalt to a warm cerulean. It looks as if multiple paintings from different centuries have been superimposed on one another as far as the eye can see.

We drive on to nearby Berzé-la-Ville. Dominique wants to show us the Romanesque church that contains a Christ on the cross, which he visits regularly when he comes to the Mâconnais. But the church is closed. Dominique shrugs. "Too bad. Because depending on the light, you don't see the same things from inside the church."

It strikes me as ludicrous, as I stand outside this church with Dominique, that many wine critics and journalists—especially in the United States and Australia—deny the importance of historical *terroir*. They refuse to believe that the tastes of wine that issue from a *terroir* are linked to the civilization—in all of its expressions—that created it. How can anyone who drinks the wines of Burgundy and has visited the region not feel that there's a link to the surrounding civilization? It's right here in front of us. It isn't in the past. It's a living thing. And though most locals—especially those who don't have the privilege of leisure time—don't pay that much conscious attention to many of the aspects of the culture, they don't need to. It's part of them.

We finally arrive at Dominique's winery, in Milly-Lamartine. There's nothing romantic about it. It's a nondescript semi-industrial hangar. Everything is functional and minimal. We go in to taste his deliciously bright and vigorous Mâcon whites, samples drawn straight from the vats because the fermentation is not quite complete at the end of November. Dominique plunges us immediately into a discussion of his passion: biodynamism. "Both domains are biodynamic," he explains. "I started implementing it in Meursault in '95. For me it's a logical agricultural model. It springs from Rudolf Steiner's teachings in his 'Course for Farmers,' from 1924, in which he stated that you can't separate any living element from the surrounding natural elements. Everything in nature interacts. The principle of life is more complex than we allow in general."

I ask him about the use of plant and animal compounds that are distributed in homeopathic doses to the soil.

"It's astonishing. We give a real dynamism to the soil. But what we do is based more on empirical observation than theories. Biodynamism places a great importance on observation and on the notion of a harmony of all active elements. I spend an enormous amount of time simply observing my vines."

Dominique takes the long glass cylinder known as a "thief" and extracts the pale yellow wine from an oak barrel (a *used* oak barrel, with none of the vanilla Botoxing effect of new oak). There's an amazing stillness in the relation between the thief, the glass, the man, and the liquid. After a long pause, in which he observes Laure and me with a subtle twinkle in his eyes, he says, "But it's always very hard to explain what we do. How can you really talk about the life of plants to city folk who've never observed the behavior of a plant in their life?"

15

WITH JEAN-MARC ROULOT

Before we go to his vineyards up and down the slopes of Meursault, Jean-Marc Roulot and I have breakfast in his kitchen. He's slightly less reserved than he was during lunch with his wife and their vigneron friends. I want to take advantage of this to better understand the relationship between his commitment to *terroir* and his work as an actor. The latter activity remains, for the vignerons of the Côte, weird and incomprehensible. Watching Jean-Marc—six foot four, strong, with a very long aquiline nose and a gaze that is intense but so discreet that somehow his entire aura borders on timidity—I have the impression that he was that boy in school who is respected but who always feels a bit separate and alone.

We drink multiple cups of coffee to prepare us for the biting cold outside. Jean-Marc explains how he got the acting bug. "In the late 1960s, Becky Wasserman, when she started exporting wine, often went to my parents' house in Meursault. They were good friends with her husband, Bart, also an American. She liked us a lot, and in the early seventies my sister and I used to go have dinner at her house every Monday night, so we could learn English. I'd take trips with Bart, who was a painter, to visit museums all over France. I even went to Cologne and to

London, where his work was being exhibited. I was seventeen years old and this world, so radically different from my parents' nonintellectual, rural existence, made a big impression on me. I did theater in high school, but I never told my parents how much I loved it. It was so alien for them. Bart encouraged me a lot. Then I decided to make the move to Paris. In the late 1970s in rural Burgundy, a son who left home to act . . . Even though I didn't feel guilty, I saw that I was causing them pain. My father cried the day I told him of my decision to study theater instead of remaining at the family domain. It was a catastrophe for him. But I was lucky. After two or three years of hell in Paris, I got selected for the Conservatoire [the prestigious national theater school]. Symbolically it was very helpful—very reassuring for me. I found out after my father died that he'd been proud of that, that he'd talked to people about me. But he never said anything to me. He got sick at the beginning of my second year at the Conservatoire, but he still came to see me at the end-of-the-year performance. That eased his worries. But of course, he never knew that I ended up coming back to the domain."

"You came back when he died?" I ask.

"No. Under French law, you have to announce your plans for succession in a family business within six months. We had meetings here in Meursault, with my mother, my sister, the accountant, the legal advisor, the notary. I told everyone that I wouldn't be taking over. So they decided to appoint an estate manager. I came back to the domain several years later."

"Your father had no idea about his succession then. Do you think of that now, when you make the wine?"

"My father was sick for nine months. I told the Conservatoire about it, because things had to be kept going. So I'd spend four days here and three in Paris. He saw that I wasn't just going to let things fall apart. But I only came back in 1989, ten years after I left for Paris. I was thirty-four years old. I was lucky enough to be able to do what I wanted, but I had also gathered all the knowledge from my father that I could by the time I was twenty years old. When I think of my father, I think of work. I learned things just by watching. I never had him on my back, like a lot of other sons, telling me to do it this way or that way."

I ask if he thinks that has given him a certain liberty in relation to the *terroirs*.

He pauses for a few seconds before responding: "For me, you've always got to seek enrichment elsewhere. People were always at me to choose between one thing or the other, acting or wine. Okay, so maybe I'm not working as an actor as I'd like to. That's for sure. But it was critical not to just follow blindly in my father's footsteps. For me, the theater was a place of freedom, and it still is. With time I became flexible enough to go back and forth between the two worlds."

"Do you think that notion of freedom is the basis of an actor's craft?"

"There are other things, too, that are more ambiguous, like the desire for recognition. I haven't had the recognition yet as an actor, but I love being in someone else's skin, blending into different situations."

"You don't have the same liberty with wine?"

"No. It's complementary. Here, it's about digging into your own roots, and theater is about others, what's around you. Your relationship with the world. When people taste your wine, it's true that this quality is also there."

We get into Jean-Marc's car and drive toward the slopes of Meursault. For any wine lover, this is a place of enchantment, especially as the gently undulating hills are blanketed today in a layer of freshly fallen snow. Even people who don't care about wine couldn't be indifferent to this landscape. And since I believe the landscape is inscribed in the wine . . . We leave the village proper behind us and drive along the base of a hill. We stop in front of some vines. Here and there, stone walls or gates separate the parcels. Jean-Marc drinks it in with me. "I like what we can see from here because I have the feeling that it's faithful to the landscape from a long time ago. There are lots of stone walls in the parcel known as *tessons*, in front of us, with its special walled vineyard, the 'Tessons, Clos du Mon Plaisir' ['Tessons, Enclosure of My

Pleasure']. The name isn't accidental. It's often the wine that gives me the most immediate pleasure. To our right is the 'Petits Charrons' and to the left the 'Grands Charrons,' which is the best parcel because the slope is the steepest." This means, among other things, that drainage will be best and that more bunches of grapes will catch more of the precious, fleeting northerly sunlight.

I ask Jean-Marc if he thinks his generation is the most actively engaged in organic farming and biodynamism. "Yeah, I think so. Frédéric Lafarge in Volnay, Anne-Claude Leflaive in Puligny, Dominique here. They've been the pioneers of biodynamism, which is the pioneer for all organic practices. I work organically, but even though I believe in biodynamism, I'm not there yet. Probably one day soon. Already converting to pure organic farming was a big step for me. And there's no question that the individual identity of each plot of vines has been more strongly expressed because of it."

Here in the middle of these autumnal vines, the view is breathtaking. I feel like I'm wrapped inside a Breughel. The russet vines are crisscrossed by pockets of green grass underneath the snow blanket. And although the sky is an icy gray, there is a shimmering luminosity that throws all the tones into clear relief. Everything feels both precise and softened, thanks to the gentle ebb and flow of the hills. In the same way, when I drink Meursaults of quality, I get the feeling of an enveloping roundness that is never dull or flat, that always has a sharp, topographical relief.

We walk back down a little. Jean-Marc looks behind us. "You see, when you want to get a better view of the hillside you need to step back. Here we're at five hundred meters.

"It's from the plains that you get the best sense of the hills. When I bought the section of the Bouchères vineyard in '96, I went to a village two kilometers away one night with Hubert de Montille. I wanted his advice. But we hid inside the car so nobody would see us. When vines are for sale here, you can't be too careful." I imagine the bald pate of Montille, illuminated by moonlight, and Jean-Marc's folkloric nose in silhouette, the two men trying to go unseen by their curious Burgundian neighbors . . .

We climb the hill, following a path that crosses the sea of vines.

"When you take into account the topographical accidents of nature, you understand why the paths exist where they do, separating the different parcels. Between the Poruzots and the Bouchères vineyards, the slopes create the form of a little wave that exactly mirrors the differences between the two wines the vineyards produce. Every little shift and bump in the topography finds its expression in the taste of the wine. Above the wall over there are the Poruzots, the beginning of the *premier cru* vineyards. Fifty meters higher up there's another stone wall, separating the lower Poruzots from the upper, where there's even a finer distinction of flavor, because they don't catch the same light. You see that swell over there; it looks like Emmanuelle Béart's breasts thrusting out. In her natural era. Before all those plastic surgeries. Then there's a cavity. And the wine falls off in quality, too. The formation of the hillside created a speedier erosion there than in the Poruzots below it. So there's little earth in the Bouchères, and the vine suffers more quickly as a result. You have to pay attention with the date of the harvest because the Bouchères grapes can quickly become overripe. But how can you explain something like that to a customer waiting expectantly in a restaurant for his pleasure? And yet Burgundy is exactly what all this is."

I ask Jean-Marc who were the first to make these distinctions in making wine here. He smiles. "The old-timers. It began at least with the monks of the Abbey of Cîteaux in the Middle Ages, who took note of the differences, though the Romans who planted many of these vines must already have had some sense of it. But the monks weren't as precise as [the historian Dr. Jules] Lavalle in the nineteenth century who created a classification of quality and who put words to the experience of previous centuries. In the midthirties the *Appellation Contrôlée* system was introduced as law, and this further defined the parameters, though they are always subject to review. Over the *long term*. I have the deepest respect for the system of classification here because it's the result of such a long tradition of observation and empirical experience. On the other hand, I get really pissed off by instant classifications and hierarchies, especially those that spring from some self-proclaimed expert wine taster with twenty years' experience."

Jean-Marc has expressed to me one of the fundamental truths of wine, and one of the principal reasons why we're in trouble today. This system of delineation in Burgundy is the expression of a detailed, evolutionary empiricism. It existed latently in the geography and then cumulatively across the work and experience of active history, of thousands of years of civilization: a testament to what man can do positively on this planet by working with nature and introducing his own eccentric genius. This is the polar opposite of the current fashion for creating spuriously authoritative hierarchies based solely on the taste of individuals, whether critics, sommeliers . . . or film directors who write books. These are systems of classification based solely on the criteria of personal taste, of personal preference. Obviously this has inherent value—for and by itself. But however honorable, indeed necessary as a personal exercise, it becomes highly suspect, if not pernicious as a public imposition of a "truth" as valuable as—or superior to—*any* other. These are solipsistic constructions with no link to any empirical communality. Jean-Marc and the hills of Meursault are a precise counterdemonstration.

We continue back down toward the plain, where the most humble of Meursault's vineyards lie, those that are neither *premier cru* nor *lieux-dits* (i.e., historically delineated and named parcels), which are sold under the simple label of "Meursault." But it should be noted that if those vines are healthy and handled by a vigneron of talent, they can produce wines of depth and character, if perhaps with less detail and complexity. As we pass by the dozens and dozens of different parcels further subdivided among hundreds of proprietors, it's clear who uses chemical herbicides and pesticides and who farms organically; the earth is either a barren brown or a surprisingly resonant green from grass that persists through this season. Up close, the vines themselves are either droopy and tattered or vigorous and glistening. Jean-Marc points out a resplendent parcel of Dominique's vines in the aptly named Meursault-Charmes vineyard: "Biodynamism is a way to create a signature for your work in the vineyard just as one develops a signature for one's wine in the cellar. One of the things that most attracts me to the idea of biodynamism is that the various treatments allow you to personalize your vines."

I'm reminded of what Jean-Louis Laplanche, the former proprietor of the Château de Pommard and batty Freudian psychoanalytic philosopher, said in an episode of the series version of *Mondovino*. He stated flatly (petulantly, in fact) that there is an opposition between the *terroir* and the vigneron's signature or personal style, in which he believes—contrary to most Burgundians—that the signature is paramount. "I think that opposition is false," I say to Jean-Marc.

"One without the other is impossible," he agrees. "The grapes of a *terroir* can—and, alas, too often do—produce a truly shitty wine. However, if you make a purely 'personalized' varietal wine—predicated on facile fruitiness and an ostentatious display of power—rather than a *terroir* wine, it's easier to give a quick comparative assessment [hence the delight of many wine journalists]. But you've erased a sense of place, a sense of origin, a deeper identity than just your own. That impoverishes all of us."

This is a critical paradox, it seems to me. In order for us to exist fully as individuals, we must inscribe ourselves in a larger narrative than our own. Otherwise, in affirming a wholly sui generis individuality, we are detached from any communal (historically based) safeguards against the omnivorous culture of marketing. The culture of taste—hence personality—is thus reduced to a collision of dangerously manipulated market forces and a Darwinian economic struggle: the inexorable reduction of us all into wholly malleable consumers. This is simply a more subtle and contemporary engine of brainwashing than the fascism of the 1930s, but no less perfidious in the long term. And if the current economic crisis reaches a more critical point, the differences between the two forms of oppression may become further blurred. It must be said that the current practitioners of marketing are often congenial figures with no wish at all to subsume us in any evil design. But those who preach the cult of the individual nonetheless are contributing to the erasure of our collective culture and therefore, ironically, of our individual identities. The (*historically* mutable) delineation of Burgundian *terroirs* and their highly idiosyncratic interpretation by people like Jean-Marc, Dominique, and Christophe seems to me a very graceful (if infinitesimally minuscule) response to this threat.

PART IV

The Taste of Authenticity

16

AUTHENTICITY, *TERROIR*, AND IDEOLOGY

A Fly in the Gazpacho

I came back from Burgundy feeling profoundly encouraged. While I may not have discovered the Grail of limpid winespeak, the daily contact with craftsmen of talent, conviction, and humility had restored my faith in the deeper beauty—and communicability—of wine. The wines I drank there and the vignerons' accompanying words, reflected every measure of the wines' origin and their makers' complexity and authenticity (however contentious and unfashionable the latter term). What a contrast with the way wine is perceived and discussed in the city, any city: Paris, London, New York, São Paulo. The human dimension and the agricultural dimension of wine were always in sight during my few days in and around the village and vines of Meursault. Now I braced myself for a return to the urban maw, where wine is a commodity, a solipsistic expression of one's sense of power (or taste), a bargaining chip in the metropolitan struggle to assert an identity, to survive with a competitive advantage.

On my return to Paris, it brought to mind a passage from Evelyn Waugh's *Brideshead Revisited*. The narrator, Charles Ryder, an art student in Paris in the mid-1920s, is invited by a rich and somewhat boorish businessman to dinner. In exchange for suffering his company, Charles insists on choosing the restaurant and the wines, including a white and a red Burgundy: "a 1906 [Grand Cru] Le Montrachet and a 1904 [Gevrey-Chambertin Grand Cru] Clos de Bèze, only a few years older then than Rex." Charles savors his meal while Rex prattles on:

> "Jolly near a hundred thousand in London. I don't know what they owe elsewhere. Well, that's quite a packet you know for people who aren't using their money. Ninety-eight thousand last November. It's the kind of thing I hear."
>
> Those were the kinds of things he heard, mortal illness and debt, I thought.
>
> I rejoiced in the Burgundy. It seemed a reminder that the world was an older and better place than Rex knew, that mankind in its long passion had learned another wisdom than his.

In the hope of softening the return to city life and its discontents, I headed straight to the Quai des Grands Augustins. For me, one of the most joyous eating experiences to be found in Paris today is at a Spanish restaurant, El Fogón, on the quai. The cuisine of forty-year-old Galician Alberto Herraíz is a wholly authentic expression of *terroir*—and yet there is no more radical and innovative food to be found in Paris (a testament as much to Parisian lethargy as to Albert's inventiveness, to be sure). In fact, El Fogón manages to embody all the paradoxes that exist between modernity and *terroir*. Or, rather, this "Spanish" restaurant abroad, certainly inflected by French products and culture, reveals the specious conflict between modernity and *terroir*, an extension of the specious debate between signature and *terroir*. El Fogón is far removed from the (in)famous Catalan Ferran Adrià and his deconstructed, theoretical cuisine. Yet, Alberto Herraíz has been able to employ aspects of Adrià's postmodern techniques in creating pleasures that are deeply ancestral, sensual, and humanist. You don't go there to admire the chef's work. You go there for the tapas menu (I'm less a fan of his paellas) and the pleasure of eating.

You're welcomed to Herraíz's restaurant with a gesture that is unthinkable with Adrià or other vanity chefs: a plate of ham. And not just any ham: vintage Belota Pata Negra ham, aged in the restaurant for several years, a pronounced expression of the possibilities of (porcine) *terroir*. The tapas tasting menu will then ensure a flow of ten appetizer-size dishes (for about the price, incidentally, of a single tapas at Robuchon's L'Atelier). The starting point is frequently a single platter holding six small glasses, each containing a different kind of gazpacho—cauliflower and clam, for example, or arugula and anchovy, or beet and mint. Each sip feels like the quintessence of each ingredient, in a semi-liquid form but not so deconstructed that it has lost its textural and gustatory origin.

Herraíz, a man with twinkling eyes and a direct, almost brusque warmth, creates new menus every day with a polyphony of flavors and original presentations, but simple in the expression of each product of the earth. Once again, I'm reminded of my friend Juan Pittaluga's maxim of "the tension between the savage and the sophisticated." The dining room is unusual for Paris: airy, cheery, with bright but flattering light, sleekly modern in its lines, but with most decorations and furnishings made from softer, more classical materials. Above all, the banquettes are spacious and autonomous enough to allow each table a minimum of privacy while enjoying the quietly humming public spectacle.

Of course, even in this glimpse of gastronomic paradise—a truly egalitarian expression of refinement—there's a hiccup. In search of a coherent expression of *terroir* between food and wine, or simply out of reflex nationalism, El Fogón is trapped in the rupture between the Spanish culinary revolution and the viticultural one. You could even call it a Spanish gastronomic civil war. To accompany the playful and innovative reinvention of Spanish dishes that provoke and delight the palate, the wine list offers one catastrophic destruction of your taste buds after another: a showcase for the disaster that has befallen the Spanish wine industry in the last fifteen years. With two notable exceptions (the bitingly dry Manzanilla sherry and the venerably oxidized

twenty-plus-year-old vintages of Tondonia Rioja Blanco), the whites
are alcohol-heavy, lacking any balancing acidity, cloyingly fruity, bat-
tered and Botoxed by new oak. The reds are overconcentrated, overripe,
saccharine, syrupy, and also artificially wrinkle-free (again with the
exception of some aged Tondonia reds). Given the delicacy and vitality
of the food, I find these wines undrinkable, unfit, in fact, for any culinary company.

Two Modernities Opposed: The True and the False
(BUT WHICH IS THE AUTHENTIC?)

The deadly force of these vinous assault weapons now completely dom-
inates the Spanish wine market. This makes the grace and subtlety of
the Tondonia white even more exceptional. Though it is made by one of
the larger wine producers in the Rioja region of north-central Spain, a
firm that makes more than five hundred thousand bottles a year, Tondonia is among the most complex and profound white wines in the
world. Despite never being put on the market until half a dozen years
after their birth (a costly means of ensuring that the wine will have sufficient complexity when sold), the price of these wines is laughable, as
little as twelve to fifteen euros a bottle. The family-owned company is
run today by Maria José Lopéz de Heredia, a young woman firmly
anchored in the present but whose wines, overseen by her brother, Julio,
bear the traces, in texture, style, and flavor, of the nineteenth-century
wines her forebears fashioned—out of preexisting traditions—when
they founded the estate. The reds are less crystalline and original than
the whites, in my opinion, but are also expressions of a singular relation
to time and space. The presence of the 1976 and 1981 Tondonia reds
and the 1964 and 1981 whites on the Fogón list are amply suggestive
that the *terroir* from which they come contains tales that go beyond the
immediate self. At the time that the 1964 Tondonia white was made—a
wild and oxidized enchantment that suggests the wines of the Jura but
with the elegance of the great whites of Burgundy—almost all the other
producers of Rioja also made white. Today there are fewer than a hand-

ful who continue to make this unrepentantly unfashionable white. Guillermo de Aranzábal, the owner of an admirable neighboring estate, La Rioja Alta, confided to me sheepishly that they'd abandoned their own white "because it's too hard to make this style of white comprehensible to the international consumer. And even in Spain, our consumers have become 'international' in their needs."

It seems terribly sad to me that the generosity of the El Fogón menu cannot be matched by a corresponding wine list. But is Alberto Herraíz to blame or are his hands tied by the situation in Spain? I believe it's the latter. Indeed, it's not accidental that the professional marketers of Spanish wine now proclaim that "Spanish wine is the New World in the Old." But what's happening on the other side of the Pyrénées that is so different from French, Italian, and German responses to wine globalization? Though the question is inherently ironic given that each one of these four countries, the four most important wine-producing lands in the last thousand years, are all themselves direct products of a Roman globalization two thousand years ago. In France, many regions are filled with wines that have ceded little or nothing to the homogenizing demands of the globalized marketplace, from Anjou to Touraine, from the Chablis to Champagne, from Alsace and Burgundy to the Rhône, Provence, and the Jura. While Bordeaux and the Languedoc have re-created their dominant styles in the approximate image of the interchangeable global god, it's possible even in those areas to find numerous wines of individual character and *terroir*. Italy offers even more hope, despite the fact that throughout the 1980s and '90s they capitulated to the homogenizing international style with as much alacrity as anyone. But today, from the Friuli to Umbria, from the Piedmont to Sardegna, there are movements even more active than in France not just to preserve a relation to their *terroirs*, but to resuscitate *terroirs* and styles that have disappeared outright. In Germany, the record among serious growers is the most impressive, with very few concessions to globalization of any kind (although wags would point out that Germany's postwar ostracism by the international community was the principal reason for this).

And what of Spain? For a long time it existed on the fringes of the international market, filling a discreet niche for fine wine lovers with a taste for ethereal old Rioja at very modest prices. Throughout the period of Franco's dictatorship, from the 1930s to his death in the mid-1970s, there was little incentive and little new initiative on the wine scene, keeping the wines parochial, to be sure, but also distinctive from other cultures' production. Ironically, with the opening of the country following the installation of a democracy, Spanish wines have embraced the globally interchangeable, identity-free style of wine with a vengeance, seemingly jettisoning each year, from each region, those qualities that could distinguish them from the international vat pack. And of course the more these wines mimic the syrupy sweet clone of planetary success, the more they garner high scores from the likes of Parker, the *Wine Spectator*, and Jancis Robinson, and the more their prices become ludicrously speculative, the famous €803 Pingus from the Robuchon L'Atelier at the forefront. Many of these international-styled wines are emerging from regions with little viticultural history (thereby truly meriting the moniker of "New World in the Old"), like Manchuela or the Balearic Islands. Instead of histories, these products have had stories invented for them by marketing teams, stories that were subsequently recycled by obliging journalists. Just between 2000 and 2005, the export of Spanish wines tripled, from one million cases to three.

What relationship can we understand, then, from the fall of Franco and the rise of these new wines? Is it the product of a simple enthusiasm for the new world economic order of the 1980s and '90s? Is it in fact a new democracy and liberty of self-expression that only reactionaries, inveterate snobs, and Francoist apologists could decry? Is it simply the logical accompaniment to the astonishing technology-driven revolution in Spanish cuisine that has produced a greater number of inventive chefs than in probably any other country in the past twenty years? Or is it the opposite of all these notions? Is it, in fact, a logical extension of the Francoist regime, the passage from one form of extremism to another, a coherent transition from the repressive dictatorship of the Generalissimo and its controlled oligopolistic markets to an economic and cultural system much less democratic than it appears? Perhaps the current global economic crisis will bear out the latter notion more decisively in time.

Today thousands and thousands of new winery owners and investors in Spain have gotten in on the wine game, skillfully marketing their apparently artisanal status. There has been a flood of thousands of new labels of Spanish wines with local and foreign grapes (mostly the latter) and an apparent choice for the consumer at every price point, from €3 to €803. Who could deny that this is not democracy at work?

Before attempting to assess the taste of the wines themselves, let us consider their makers, which often amounts to the same thing. The majority of owners of these new "boutique" wineries throughout the world, from Spain to Chile to Napa, are people who've recently made a fortune in another line of business—in media, finance, real estate. Doubtless many are motivated by an Arcadian dream, but we can't ignore the fact that winemaking is now a globally recognized path to social recognition, as tempting a target for worldwide arrivistes as the acquisition of works of art have proved since the Medici in Renaissance Florence. In Spain the Remírez de Ganuza estate in Rioja is perhaps emblematic of this movement. A successful real estate dealer, Fernando Remírez de Ganuza bought his lands and created his brand in 1992. Already with his 1998 Rioja, he managed to collect ninety-five- and ninety-six-point scores from Robert Parker for wines so dense and black they compare favorably with a jar of blackberry jam. When I met him at the Madrid branch of Lavinia in 2006, Ganuza explained to me cheerfully that "Rioja is a brand name, not a *terroir*." He seemed delighted of course that his success was instantaneous, and wondered what could possibly be objectionable about that. He had no interest, he said, in waiting generations to explore a relationship with the soil or even with wine itself. Of what use was it, he asked, to calibrate his efforts—and hard-earned money—in a relationship to time, history, the evolution of Spanish culture, and civilization? I understood his point. He is of course obliged to search out an immediate response to his dreams in the global marketplace. From his perspective, why shouldn't he look to Parker or the local equivalent, José Peñín, for the appropriate parameters of taste if it leads to success? It's logical that Remírez de Ganuza and others like him will seek out the services of the facilitators of this taste, consulting enologists like Michel Rolland (who's very active all over Spain) and locals like Telmo Rodriguez, who turns the neat trick of sometimes employing unusual local grapes to give the wine a badge of authenticity, while its flavors and character are magically transformed into the instantly recognizable global taste.

If we imagine peasant wine producers who have struggled for generations simply to survive, we can easily understand the attraction for them if one fine day a new person shows up, makes a wine in a certain style, and finds instant wealth and success. This, after all, is one of the principal attractions of a market-based democracy. For those who believe that modernity has finally arrived in Spanish wine, the proof of its democratic nature is precisely in the thousands of new viticultural projects that have exploded throughout the country in the last fifteen years and the conversion of equal numbers of "traditionalists," peasants and industrialists alike, to the cause of free (falling) market wine.

Victor/Victoria: The Triumph of Power

On a visit to Madrid and Barcelona for the Spanish release of *Mondovino*, I came face-to-face—in an appropriately virtual way—with one of the quintessential hucksters of the new wine world order. His name is Victor de la Serna. What's strange is that Victor and I have a lot in common. We're both a polyglot mixture of the European and American. He's a journalist of international politics. I'm the son of one. We both are passionately devoted to wine, and yet, Victor, in writings from the United States to Spain, has decided I'm an undesirable member of the community of wine lovers. He wrote in *El Mundo* (the second highest circulation daily in Spain) in March 2006: "In terms of intellectual honesty, Nossiter doesn't hold up. His film at the end of the day is an outright fraud, a work of fiction, a Michael Moore–like paroxysm."

I first came across Victor de la Serna's name in 2004, after *Mondovino*'s release in France, when he posted an entirely invented diatribe on the website of his friend Robert Parker. The U.S. wine press pays especial attention to the goings-on of this board. When *Mondovino* was released in the United States in 2005, a number of newspapers, including *The New York Times*, picked up on what became a nearly hundred-page post, initiated by Parker's attack dog of the time, Pierre Rovani, and dozens of his acolytes. In a delicious ideological confusion, *Mondovino* and I were denounced as an unforgivable expression of "left-leaning antiglobalization," unable to sympathize with a character in the film who "accurately states that Mussolini did many positive things for Italy before his formal alliance with Hitler" (in the words of Rovani), and simultaneously guilty of ruthless Gestapo-like interviewing techniques (this charge made by a reactionary Austrian living in California—other than Schwarzenegger). The far right association culminated in a later post by the grand poobah Parker himself stating unambiguously that I and my "ilk [are] the scary wine Gestapo."

Among the hundreds of hostile postings was one from a certain Victor de la Serna from Madrid, accusing me of avoiding Spain in my film because it didn't fit my thesis and of deliberately misrepresenting the portrait of the august wine consultant Michel Rolland. From a week of shooting in vineyards all around Bordeaux, he claimed I so manipulated my edited footage that all we saw of the eminent Rolland was a jet-speed round of winery visits via chauffeur-driven Mercedes. As even Rolland has had to admit, we in fact shot on a single October morning with him, from 8:00 a.m. to 1:00 p.m., and, at his insistence, we never left his Mercedes for more than a few minutes to go inside the wineries, never once going near a vineyard. These facts didn't deter Victor from asserting that "the horrors of the modern, homogenized times are only figments of Nossiter's imagination—or of the heavy, heavy chip he carries on his (left) shoulder."

Curious about the author of these virulent ad hominem attacks, I quickly discovered that Victor de la Serna is more than a mere wine critic. For decades he's been an internationally noted journalist of world affairs and is currently an editor at the powerful *El Mundo* news-paper. He also finds time for regular political commentary on Radio Cadena COPE, a station sponsored by the most doctrinaire wing of the Spanish Catholic Church. This highly influential figure also happens to be a man of self-proclaimed journalistic ethics.

When I went to Madrid to help my wife, Paula, shoot a short film on Spanish wine for the DVD release of *Mondovino* in Spain, she was curious to interview him. According to my feistily independent Catalan distributor, Sagrera, not only did he refuse her request passed on by my distributor, but he also informed them that, in his position as a deputy editor at *El Mundo*, he was canceling all *El Mundo* interviews with me. Although he's not a film critic, he added that he would even write the review of *Mondovino* himself. Luckily Sagrera raised such hell about censorship at the newspaper that *El Mundo* was obliged to run a short article and assigned a legitimate film critic to write a parallel review to Victor's. In an act of surpassing chutzpah the next week, Victor made a fresh post on the Parker website, claiming that I had fabricated a story that he'd tried to censor my film at *El Mundo*.

Reading the (Bitter) Tea Leaves

All this is a tempest in a wine cup, of course. But the dregs of wine, like tea, can often be parsed for larger meanings. In the case of Victor, it revealed Spain's position at the crossroads of the current global con-flicts. The base of his argument was that "Spain wouldn't have snugly fit Nossiter's preconceived ideas: 30 years ago the wine business here was dominated, as it was 100 years ago too, by a handful of huge négociant-type producers and co-ops, both in Jerez and in Rioja. On the other hand, now there's an explosion of small producers the likes of which never existed in this country's 4,000 years of winemaking. So much for wonderful old artisanal traditions being swept away by globalization and standardization."

This assertion is false in multiple ways. First, I owe most of my wine education to one of my greatest friends, Louis Broman, the president of

Wines from Spain in the United States until he died in 1995 from AIDS at the age of thirty-eight. The joys of complex, aged whites and reds from Rioja, new-style, sleek Albariños from Galicia, and the recovered traditions of artisanal Finos from Jerez all formed my palate thanks to Louis's elegant guidance, as did, for instance, a profound conviction that the Mosel Rieslings of Germany are among the world's most distinctive pleasures. Alas, I didn't shoot in Germany, either. Why? Because after five hundred hours of footage accumulated over four years on a shoestring budget, it was simply impossible to shoot anymore. Moreover, as *Mondovino* is a film and not in any way a journalistic investigation, I felt no need to be encyclopedic.

More telling is the affirmation that the Spanish wine scene does infinite credit to the neoconservative view of world trade, all the while being culturally responsible in such a way that no skeptic of the homogenizing forces of globalization might object. Ever attentive to the gaze of the Robert Parker website, Victor added: "Estate wines, *terroir*-driven wines have only sprouted up in very recent times, after 150 years of industrial, mass-produced wines. This directly contradicts [Nossiter's] view of the lamentable standardization or globalization of wine due to dastardly characters like Rolland or Parker." It's certainly true that there are many winemakers and an enormous number of non-wine people turning to winemaking in all regions of Spain, mobilizing significant financial resources and a great deal of passion to participate in this multibillion-dollar global industry. But are they all artisans just because they own less than fifty hectares? And are they all producing wines that are expressive of cultural, regional difference? Conversely, just because you're big doesn't mean you make industrial, anonymous products. Spain has long been distinguished by large companies in Rioja such as López de Heredia's Viña Tondonia, La Rioja Alta, Marqués de Riscal, and Marqués de Murrieta who have made superb wines, expressive of a Spanish and Riojan distinctiveness, at extremely reasonable prices, and almost uninterruptedly for over a century. But a deeper examination of Victor de la Serna's position leads us to the crux of the false debate between modernity and tradition in wine as well as one of the most blatant examples of conflicts of interest I know of in a wine world fraught with them. Not only is he one of Spain's most influential wine journalists, but since 1998 he has also been the owner of a winery, Finca Sandoval, in Manchuela. Indeed, two years after starting his "artisanal" winery, he co-founded *elmundovino* (no relation to my film but yet another uncanny doubling), the newspaper's wine journalism subsidiary and hugely influential for Spanish wine across the globe.

Janus Drinks from the Wine Cup(s)

In a delicious irony no screenwriter would dare concoct, none other than Victor de la Serna was one of the first to denounce one of the principal global conflicts of interest that mark *Mondovino* (the film, not his website), an example, in fact, that gives the lie to the notion that small is always good, big is bad. In 1997, before he became a "boutique" winery owner, Victor, wearing his hat of crusading journalist alert to the dangers of standardization, wrote the following in an article titled "Parker Seen from Europe":

> For a long time we've known [Parker] has other, local "assistants" whose names don't appear in Parker's *Wine Advocate* but who are crucial in screening, pre-tasting wines for him and directing him to some and away from others . . . and it may be leading him down some wrong alleys. In Bordeaux, his shadow assistant and a very, very important person is winemaker Michel Rolland. Rolland's influence has grown immensely through RP (Robert Parker), and Rolland-styled wines are basically the same thing as RP-styled wines nowadays. Wineries throughout the world know this, and the fact they're turning to Rolland to re-style their reds (and, they believe, to ensure high RP ratings) is perfectly tell-tale. Rolland, with his high-extract, hyper ripe (overly matured at times), low-acid wines, can improve products made from middling-to-good terroirs and turn them into very sound, quite attractive commercial products. But—how is this overblown style applicable to very great terroirs? I have my doubts.

Remarkably, only nine years later, he would flip-flop and become an impassioned defender of of both Parker and Rolland (logging over two thousand comments on Parker's board). And since by anyone's measure, Parker's and Rolland's power has grown exponentially over the past decade, it's startling that Serna would now mock anyone for imagining that "there's a Parker-Rolland power structure." Is this about-face related to the fact that he is now a winery owner himself, making wines very much in this "globalized" style, a classic example of the so-called "artisan" winemaker contributing, in fact, at the boutique level, to the worldwide multibranding, monostyling of wine? At any rate, his newfound sympathies are certainly paying off. Victor's winery appears on two hundred separate threads on the Parker website, and Parker has assured Victor of economic success throughout the world by giving smashing reviews to his wines—those crafted in exactly the same high-extract "overblown style" that Victor denounced only a few years ago.

Gerry Dawes, noted independent critic in the United States of Spanish wines, explains some of the background to this story: "De la Serna's mother's property is in Manchuela [La Mancha], where no wine of any credible significance had ever been made. They decided to plant grapes out there, and de la Serna began trumpeting the 'great promise' of the region in articles in *El Mundo* as early as 1998." This was a good idea, since "he invested his savings and bank loans in the place." And the message was hammered home repeatedly by his subordinates at the newspaper and on his website. For example, in the *El Mundo Sunday* magazine of November 15, 2002, there appeared an article on Victor's emerging La Mancha region with the subheadline: "Did you know that the reds of Léon, Murcia and La Mancha are triumphing throughout the world, part of the Spanish wine revolution? And that some of the bottles top 100 euros! Watch out Rioja!" Or consider an *El Mundo* piece exactly three years later, titled, with biblical portentousness, "Desert Region Converted into Great Wines." In it, we learn that "the astonishing modern wines of Finca Sandoval [of Victor de la Serna] are the greatest the region has produced in its entire history . . . with an ensemble of novel grape varietals."

De la Serna, adds Dawes, used his status as a leading wine writer to call in powerful wine consultants, "advisors like the Eguren boys, Mariano García and god knows who else." In fact, it turns out "god knows who else" included none other than Michel Rolland (one hopes Michel never read Victor's earlier article), albeit on a "friendly" basis. De la Serna then found his way, possibly through these connections, to Parker's main ally and friend in Spain, importer Jorge Ordonez.

Jorge Ordonez is a Boston-based Spaniard and a very interesting example of vertical integration within the wine business. Having been exclusively an importer, he turned his hand in the 1990s to making wine himself throughout Spain and, says Dawes, "Over the past five years, Ordonez has systematically gone about letting go of many the wineries he represented for more than a decade and has replaced them with his own wineries, his own winemaking team and brands of pure invention (often without region or even varietal mentioned on the label). Without Parker rubber-stamping his efforts, I believe that would be impossible. In my opinion, Robert Parker, working with such importers, has turned a wine world of independent winemakers making *terroir*-based wines that were identifiable by their origins, into a consultants', importers' and reps' game, where wines are literally tailored just for one palate."

Ordonez, whose wines are reviewed with greater frequency and more favorably by Parker than any other Spanish importer, quickly became Victor de la Serna's agent for Finca Sandoval in the all-critical U.S. market. "Victor went with Jorge to Monkton [Maryland, home of Robert Parker] to meet the man and present his wine personally. He got 92 points and has been omnipresent on Parker's website ever since," reports Dawes. In fact, de la Serna proclaims on his own El Mundo website that the ninety-five points he got for his 2003 Finca Sandoval TNS was the highest rating Parker has ever given a wine ("Man"?) from La Mancha. Dawes continued: "And to think Victor once lectured me for not calling him for a quote when I wrote about his penchant for overblown wines in an *Alta Expresión* piece, [a phenomenon] for which El Mundo (i.e., Victor) single-handedly helped whip up a frenzy in

Spain. One would think that he had learned something about ethics in journalism when he went to Columbia University."

Unquestionably there's a new tide of excellent small winemakers in Spain, from Quim Vila's superb Rioja "Paisajes" to Clos Batllet in Priorat. These are winemakers' expression of local identity (even when they're not locals themselves, as is the case with Quim Vila), and yet they're resolutely innovative and modern (reflections, in fact, of the sometimes scintillating new Spanish cuisine). But they are exceptions. There are many more carpetbaggers, arrivistes, and status-mongers like de la Serna who've understood the global game of standardized taste and insider networking to reap rewards of money and status. De la Serna's case is profoundly expressive of the false claims to modernity, the free market, and universal democracy (ideological confusions mistakenly associated with conservatives) of the Rolland/Parker/*Wine Spectator* establishment. Because, of course, de la Serna has nothing to do with modernity, if by this we mean progress and ethical innovation. What he has newly created—a region, a winery, a taste in wine—has no substantial, communal future, since it's unrooted in any gesture other than an individual's grasp for power. On the other hand, while he claims to be an agent of modernity, he also holds himself up as a model archconservative. But he is clearly interested in conserving nothing— like his brethren in the New Right across the globe—other than gestures that enhance his own power. He has nothing to do with the free market, since he is dependent on the cronyism and classic conflicts of interest that make the market anything but free. Could it be that this concentration of bad faith and slickness can be understood in the concentrated artificiality and contrived taste of his wines? The taste of power comes full circle.

17

AUTHENTICITY: THE REMAKE

Alta Expresión, Alta Poder

The Spanish branding of the Rolland/Parker globalized style is known as *alta expresión*, which Dawes explains like this:

> Scores of powerful, highly concentrated, new-wave wines have cropped up all over Spain like the saffron crocuses that proliferate in La Mancha every October. These intensely extracted, international style wines encompass a bewildering array of newly minted brands that vary widely in quality and seriousness. Lumped together under the controversial term vinos de alta expresión ("high expression" . . . wines . . .), these potent wines depart sharply from the traditional, mellow, age-worthy style for which La Rioja, the country's premier wine region, is famous. Winning high praise in some circles and vociferous criticism in others, alta expresión wines have pushed Spain smack into the center of the brewing international debate between winemaking traditionalists and advocates of the high-octane New World approach.

My only caveat with this view is that I don't see an opposition between traditionalists versus modernists. Quim Vila, for example, is a wine world equivalent of El Fogón's Alberto Herraíz, a modernist innovator with clear roots in the past. A Catalan—a people known for their fierce independence of spirit—this multitasking wine merchant/wine agent/wine producer considers himself an outright modernist. And I believe he is. As a *caviste*, his tastes are catholic. In his Barcelona wine shop, Vila Viniteca (one of the greatest I've ever seen in my life, for breadth and depth of selection and ethics of pricing), there are wines from *terroirists* such as Tondonia and half the great vignerons of Burgundy and the Mosel; to dozens of Michel Rolland's international ventures; right back to Victor's Finca Sandoval. As an agent and distributor, he represents Vega Sicilia, the Romanée-Conti of Spain, and Pingus, the ultra-trendy €800-a-bottle Parker concoction, also from the Ribera del Duero region. And like Robert Vifian of Tan Dinh, he is friendly with the entire spectrum of these people.

Though a Catalan and therefore a virtual foreigner in Rioja, he cofounded the Paisajes winery in this north-central region in 1998. Paisajes, for me, is one of the most exciting red wines of Spain—and a fine model for the future. A Rioja that has a *terroir* core of determinedly earthy, acid-driven flavors in an elegant body, it has nonetheless been rendered more supple and fruity than its longer-established local counterparts. In a further irony, although he acts as agent for perhaps the two most gratuitously expensive new wines of Spain, Pingus and Clos Ermita, he prices his own bottle at around eighteen euros. Yes, indeed, the ebullient, feisty, impish peacemaker Quim Vila is an exception in all ways to the trends.

In the independent U.S. publication *The Rosengarten Report*, we can read about circumstances that led to the general *alta expresión* phenomenon:

> The style I knew so well from tasting Riojas made in the 1940s, 1950s, 1960s, 1970s, and 1980s was unique in the world of vino—delicate, ethereal wines, brick-red with just a little age, kind of fragile, but with

more aroma and flavor per milliliter of wine than any other fermented grape juice I know. Part of the unique magic is that red Riojas were traditionally released after extensive aging at the winery, maybe 5–7 years.

Then it happened. Wine writers, mostly American, decided that traditional red Rioja didn't taste enough like California Cabernet, didn't fit into their world oeno-view; they had no idea what to make of wine that wasn't purple, massively fruit packed, forceful, brutish, lethally engorged on alcohol, painful with tannin, and framed with more new oak than a dotcommer's just-erected ski chalet in Aspen. The day that *The Wine Spectator* published their first extensive notes on red Rioja—giving scores in the 70s to wines that should be worshipped, and scores in the 90s to wines that were desecrations of the noble tradition—was, in my opinion, one of the most tragic days in the history of wine. For Spanish winemakers knew full well the clout that wine publications like this one have, the taste-making power they carry—and, like winemakers everywhere who read about their traditions being trashed, began to change their wine styles in hopes of pleasing people who haven't a clue about their wines in the first place.

While David Rosengarten and his occasional collaborator Gerry Dawes are certainly right to raise alarms about the general dominance of *alta expresión* wines, the exceptions to the rule, like Quim Vila, are almost more illuminating. They lead us to interesting questions about authentic identity in Rioja and what meaning the authentic can have in the current culture. On the one hand, there is Quim, son of a modest Barcelona delicatessen owner, creating sui generis a form of true modernism, firmly centered within the sphere of *terroir*. On the other hand (or, rather, the other side of the same hand), there are long-established wineries such as Maria José López de Heredia's Viña Tondonia and Guillermo de Aranzábal's La Rioja Alta, which have found a way to fuse their resolutely Riojan identity with a progressive outlook. It should go without saying that both styles are "authentic," if by *authentic* we

understand an *ethically* constructed—hence evolving—identity (as opposed to the reactionary impulse to permanently fix identity).

Unlike the Catalan merchant Vila, both López de Heredia and
Aranzábal are from the landed gentry with deep roots in the local soil in
Haró. On the other hand, like him, they are anything but insular, constantly traveling the globe in search of new markets and new stimuli.
They are perhaps all classic conservatives in some ways and fearless
progressives in others, each one providing his own variation on this
healthily paradoxical theme. Part of what fascinates me about the
courtly, cosmopolitan, and immensely civilized Guillermo de Aranzábal
is precisely how his own notions of local identity that once were the
concerns of reactionaries have become, through changes in the culture
of the world at large, expressions of an outlook that has (traditionally)
been associated with the Left. Though I suspect he'd be the first to be
surprised by this assessment.

Over a dinner in Madrid with Rioja producers for my wife's film
Mondoespaña, Jesus Madrazo, winemaker at Contino spoke of "Riojitis"
to describe the aversion that critics like José Peñín (the Parker of Spain
in terms of local influence and ratings), *elmundovino*, and de la Serna
have for Rioja as a region. Closer to Bordeaux in size, geography, and
direct historical influence, Rioja nonetheless is a wine that can most
resemble Burgundy in its subtlety, detail, and grace. But this style of
wine, expressed in Rioja Alta's "Viña Ardanza" or Tondonia's old "Reser-
vas," has been virtually banished from the Spanish and international
press in the last ten years. It's no surprise that a recent rating of Peñín's
top sixty wines from Rioja didn't mention a single one from these producers and that among his highest scored wines are those identical to
Parker's: the radical "*alta*-ista" Artadi and Remírez de Ganuza with his
thick, gooey, black-as-night wine appropriately named "Trasnoche."
These prophets of the "new order" (let's inter their specious claims to
modernity), when they do speak of the region's roots, disparage "traditional Rioja." The dismissive use of the word *traditional* is a perfect
echo of their U.S. counterparts' attempts to discredit *terroir* as the
defense mechanism of Luddites and disingenuous reactionaries. In the

introduction to his wine guide, Parker accuses those who evoke notions such as *"terroir,"* "tradition," and "classic vintages" of willfully misleading the consumer with mumbo jumbo and creating undrinkable wines that are "hard, acidic [the latter a negative quality in his lexicon], angular, compact and tannic from under ripe fruit" . . . or "from grapes that never matured, some even rotted . . . *Terroir* triumphs again!" he concludes with frat-boy sarcasm.

In response to these sorts of attacks against La Rioja Alta as a large-scale producer of mediocre, "old-fashioned" wines (in contrast to "modern, artisanal" winemakers like Victor de la Serna's Finca Sandoval and Remírez de Ganuza's Trasnoche), Guillermo de Aranzábal, director of the company, responded at the same dinner with Madrazo: "I'm offended by accusations that we are an 'industrial' winery. I'm the fifth generation working in the winery and the only thing I ever heard from my father and grandmother from the time I was little has been about having respect for the wines, for the region, for the personality of each bottling . . . at any cost. We have reinvested in the winery since its foundation and still today more than 95 percent of the profits go back in for reinvestment toward quality. We are not here for the money. We're not here for the glamour of the business (it wasn't glamorous when my family started). We are not a multinational, nor are we a financial group. And calling us 'mass-producers'—as de la Serna has done—is simply unfair."

Guillermo, who got an MBA in the United States, actually started his working life in his family's foundry, since the winery wasn't even economically viable until the late 1970s. The more I got to know him the more I regretted not having filmed in Spain for *Mondovino*, principally because he gives the lie to the mistaken notion that large-scale producers always make brand wines and not wines of *terroir* and, as we've seen with Finca Sandoval, small doesn't necessarily mean beautiful or authentic. Guillermo and I began an increasingly personal correspondence after my trip to Madrid, speaking often about the death of our mutual friend Louis Broman ("un caballero," wrote Guillermo, a caballero himself) and about the influence on us of our deceased fathers. Guillermo explained to me that "I lost my father a few months ago. He died at seventy-six, last April in fact, from cancer. He taught me almost everything I know today: ethics, the respect for your history and identity, but also the need to investigate new ways to do things, to look at the future without complexes. My father was a businessman of Basque origin and Basque feelings. That means that the concept of *terroir* has always been present in anything we have done, a love for the place and its people. But because of all the decades here in this country, when everything you are or have may be used against you—I'm talking about terrorism also—whatever we do, we do thinking about its impact on our society at large."

Nationalism and Terro(i)r

Guillermo believes that the fierce independence of Basques—and Catalans, for that matter—is an expression not of exclusionary nationalism but of the assertion of difference to allow for the tolerance of others. Both Basques and Catalans powerfully resisted Franco and, the barbaric separatist group ETA aside, now resist many of the excesses of global homogenization (surely a better term than *globalization*). As he wrote, he's keenly aware of the dangers of associating *terroir* with nationalism, especially for a Basque because of ETA's murderous terrorist activities of the last decades. Up through World War II and its aftermath (until the 1970s, really), progressives opposed almost all forms of nationalism because of its association with totalitarianism and repressive and imperialist causes. With the exception of the radical Left advocating nationalist insurgencies in colonial situations, the Left itself could be said to have been fundamentally antinationalist. But Guillermo's comments made me think how the tide has shifted in the wake of the new totalitarianism, which is economic and cultural, post-ideological, and (for now) transnational.

Today the "progressive" position has been inverted. At least in most of the West, the progressive impulse is now to seek out and give value to national and regional expressions, since the great threat is homogeniza-

tion and no longer a splintering nationalism. There are of course obvious exceptions, notably in Africa, where "national" identity is generally
a postcolonial invention. However, it's worth considering that the wiping out of regional, national, or tribal differences and the attempt to
impose transcultural "unity" is as dangerous as the glorification of
Croatian or Hutu identity. It's also a given that the line between one
group's conception of a separate identity (*terroir*, if you like) and that of
a competing larger force can often be arbitrary. Just like the drawing of
lines between some Burgundy *premier* and *grand cru* vineyards. The
only defense for affirming separate identities in both cases is where
there is a historical richness that attests to one culture's distinctiveness
from its immediate neighbor. One thing, at any rate, is clear. If we abandon the fierce defense of regional difference, we abandon an essential
notion of human identity in the face of transnational marketing and
homogenization. Trasnoche, indeed. The inexorable logic of those who
seek to subjugate cultural difference for personal profit—whether a
multinational corporation or a carpetbagging "artisan"—is to transform us from citizens asserting our tastes to consumers fooled into an
illusion of choice as an expression of taste.

If we fail to identify with historical identities (not to imitate them
but to locate ourselves in a larger narrative context), then we become
unmoored and we will fulfill the worst fears of Huxley and Orwell.
Without *terroir*, we will all lose all freedom and individuality.

Left Is Right. And Contrariwise

It's also instructive to consider the relationship between problems of
authenticity and the ideological confusions of the last twenty years
between the Right and the Left. One of its most interesting manifesta-
tions is the inversion of who can be deemed more *conservative*, the Left
or the Right. Up until 1980, the Right held a virtual monopoly on the
discourse of conservatism, and the Left dominated (often equally vacu-
ous) discourses of change and revolution. With the arrival of a real revolution at the heart of world power, the Reagan-Thatcher revolution, all

this changed. The Reagan government destroyed decades-old safe-guards against monopoly and oligopoly control of industries. Most notable for me was the reversal of the 1947 Paramount antitrust laws, which had prevented studios from vertical integration, from rigging the market by controlling production, distribution, *and* exhibition of films. It's enough to consider the overnight transformation of Hollywood from its 1970s experimental golden age (Cassavetes, Monte Hellman, early Scorsese, early Coppola, Arthur Penn's *Night Moves*, inter alia) to 1980s Reagan-era production (and distribution and exhibition) of exclusively profit-driven, corporate-sponsored, acultural "entertain-ment products." Decades of uneven but thoroughly vital and idiosyn-cratic Hollywood *terroir* was thus undone in the space of less than a decade. And things have not improved since. By opening the floodgates of unbridled greed, of the unapologetic quest for money and power as laudable civic values, the Reagan and Thatcher revolution destroyed any possible link between the Right and true conservatism. Few power brokers on "the Right" in the United States, England, France, Italy (including French president Nicolas Sarkozy and Italian prime minister Silvio Berlusconi), or elsewhere seem interested in conserving any aspect of our communal culture. There is now a systematic, global destruction of our relations to the past.

But as if to confirm the death of traditional ideological distinctions (and to confirm that Blair and Brown's Labour Party in England, for example, is the rule not the exception), repudiating the past has been blood sport not just for the Right but also for the Left and Center. Think of François Mitterrand: not just his gradual abandonment of all principals historically associated with socialism but also his active con-cealment of his own collaborationist past. Or consider Bill Clinton with his failure to create any meaningful link to the progressive past of the Roosevelt Democratic Party and so effectively severing the party from its historical identity, unmooring it from its base of providing a dissent-ing vision of American life. (At the time of this book's writing, it's still unclear how far President Obama will be able to reestablish those links.) Or consider Brazil's President Lula—and countless other leftist leaders across the world. Lula fought for decades for social and economic justice while in the opposition, but immediately capitulated to all of the conventional powers once he achieved power himself, instantly dissolving his Workers' Party ideals. It's no surprise then that his government has gone serenely unpunished despite proven cases of fraud and corruption. In a climate where the past has no meaning, what you said or did even the previous day is no longer relevant. This is why *terroir* is such a threat to these dangerous carpetbaggers, Left, Right, and Center, because respect for *terroir* demands an ethical responsibility to the past (which itself demands a constantly evolving reappraisal of its uses and meanings). Cultural expression, transparency in the media, the general social welfare, civic responsibility, the political and economic necessity of full employment (as my father argued in his perspicacious call to a return to Keynesianism in his 1990 book *Fat Years and Lean: The American Economy Since Roosevelt*), all collapse when we lose our sense of history, of our communal bonds.

What's Authenticity Got to Do with It?
(WITH APOLOGIES TO TINA TURNER)

With so many people proclaiming the necessity of authentic, organic wines, from the countercultural organic "salon" of the Le Verre Volé wine bar in Paris to the corporate-shadowed sommelier for Alain Senderens's temple of gastrodemocratic luxury, it's worth asking the question "What is authentic?" Or, rather, "Who wants the authentic? Why do we crave it?" Or maybe we should also ask, "Why do others *not* need it, thriving instead on the purely novel, hybrid, artificial, sui generis?" Though that's perhaps not the most accurate opposition. Because the "authentic" is not the "pure," the "virginal," or the "traditional." Unrepentant postmodernists (whose great academic project of the last thirty years has been to deny the existence of the authentic), relativists, and the cunning profiteers of self-marketed (self-medicated?) "progress" are all happy to smear as a pathetic, reactionary traditionalist any quixotic fool foolish enough these days to openly defend the authentic. Ironically, those people traditionally considered right wing or conservative are usually in lockstep on these attacks. Although the cultural reflex remains to associate the "Right" with conservatism, we've seen how this has become one of the most grotesque oxymorons of our time.

So what is the authentic? Why is it important to care about authenticity? We live in a world, after all, where everything, from our photos to our bodies to our moods to our minds, can be artificially altered in a matter of seconds. So why not go with the new reality (and relativism) and say all is fine and equally valuable and true and worthy?

To those who say, "Authentic is what I say it is," I'd respond that the notion of the authentic, of the "natural" is intrinsically linked to the sanctity of individual dignity. Each one of us is not only *entitled* to differentiate ourselves from all others, but *must* differentiate ourselves. A dangerous corollary of the refusal to accept the authentic is the unrestrictedly solipsistic invention of an identity, a creation, a product or position. It is the means by which we will bring an end to thousands of years of communal civilization.

The mischaracterized "modern wine" is just such a portal, from its *alta expresión* Spanish version to its Californianized Bordeaux château variant in France to its 16 percent alcohol Argentinean incarnation. It is a construct that asks only: "What can I like without thinking and what do I want now?" Whereas a wine of *terroir* asks you to wonder about it—and about yourself. "Who am I? Where do I come from? What stories from a land, from history, from nature, can be told?" Those who argue for the mythical "free market" and for wines or other cultural expressions ex nihilo are narcissists. The defense of wine larger than the self, of wines of *terroir*, is an expression of adult, communal taste. The other is infantile.

Terry Theise, the pioneering American importer and defender of German wines of *terroir*, has this to say in his 2005 catalogue:

> Here's what I think we're after: a point of utter receptivity because we're seeing only the wine instead of seeing ourselves seeing the wine.

Oh it's all very Zen. But I am ever more persuaded it is the way to pleasure and sanity. If we don't see past ourselves, our discrete palates, we can't get past *What am I getting from the wine.* The process starts and ends with "I." What am "I" getting? What do "I" think (how many points will "I" give this wine), and all I can say is if you drink wine this way I sure hope you don't make love this way, because your partner's going to be very bored.

The Past Is the Future. And Always Was.
(BUT WILL IT STILL BE TOMORROW?)

Since 1992, Peter Sisseck, an intrepid young Dane, has made the über *alta expresión* wine called Pingus in the Ribera del Duero region of Spain. Nothing can—or should—stop him from inventing any price tag he wants. And he has. His bottles appear wherever instant "I" is sold, for €800 to €1,000 a bottle. It is a pure invention of Parker's world. It was Parker's one-hundred-point scores and a mysterious, fortuitous marketing "event," involving the loss of almost an entire vintage in a shipwreck—thus enshrining its market and media rarity—that catapulted Sisseck to fame. Setting these exorbitant prices, playing Parker and the market with consummate skill, he clearly has no interest in seeing himself and his wine in a larger narrative context. Conversely, what leads Dominique Lafon and Jean-Marc Roulot in Meursault or the Sottimano family in the Piedmont to keep their wines at half, even one third, of the potential asking price—even though they are none of them so wealthy that they have no economic worries? After a live sighting of bottles of Pingus in the Madrid Lavinia, my wife asked Dominique about this. He seemed surprised by the question: "We have no interest in creating a financial meaning for our wine that ruptures the continuity of our relations with each other, with other people in Burgundy, with our clients," he told her. He could have added that he didn't want to create a rupture with his past and therefore with the future.

I'm not a prelapsarian dreamer. I don't think things were better "in the past." I think the problems we face today bear a startling resemblances to those of our parents (alas, alas). I found plenty of wine to love and drink twenty-five years ago. I still do. Maybe more. But the Parker/Pingus/de la Serna association reminded me of what Edward Bradley, my ever-engagé professor of Homeric Greek and Latin from Dartmouth College, told me while I was researching *Mondovino*:

> We don't have a monopoly on the destruction of local cultures. The Romans were expert. Like us, they destroyed as much as they created. But it's very hard for us to measure the costs of the Romanization of the West because the costs have been buried by the accretions of time. And buried by the absence of testimony that records the pain of the loss of local cultures. We don't know all the amazing birds and flowers that have disappeared forever. We can only imagine something of the pain caused when we hear of fifty thousand Gauls who had their hands chopped off, and that Caesar sold at least half a million of them into bondage. But the enormity of the Roman conquest in terms of human suffering is largely lost to us. In theory, what distinguishes us today is our ability to bear witness—I'm thinking of Primo Levi, for instance. If we have any purpose as a culture, it's at least in part to bear witness to the costs of the losses today.

And just as we have an infinite variety of wines available today, so, too, we have an infinite variety and infinite means of bearing witness to the pain of the loss of local culture. This virtually limitless ability to record testimony, in conjunction with a historically unprecedented rate of change, are probably the two crucial qualities that distinguish the time in which we live. But this also means that we can eradicate not just culture but cultural memory at an unfathomable pace.

With this in mind I asked Professor Bradley to imagine a society one hundred years from now in which there was no more history, in which historical memory has disappeared. I asked him to imagine what he could possibly say in an address to these ahistorical humans of the near future to explain why a sense of history was a necessity.

As if he'd somehow thought of the same lugubrious scenario, he responded before I'd finished my thought:

> I would say to them, "Do you have a father? Do you have brothers, aunts and uncles, a grandfather? A home from which you come?" Personal historical memory is the establishment of the individual in his fuller, larger, deeper sense. Without these links, one has no moorings. One is lost in the darkest depths of solitude forever. An awareness of our collective history is that phenomenon writ large.

How wine expresses memory is varied. It can be as simple as the bottle that I had in my New York cellar for many years and recently shared in my garden in Rio, over a barbecue, with talented local film director Sandra Kogut and her American husband, Thomas Levin, an ebullient Princeton professor of a postmodernist bent (and hence a ferocious, if ever genial, skeptic of the nostalgic impulse). The wine was a 1978 Monsecco Gattinara from Le Colline.

Unaccustomed to drinking an Italian wine of this age, my otherwise voluble friends were speechless as they sipped the strange and beguiling brick-orange liquid. Not only was the wine old but it was made in a style that will not be duplicated today, with a wild, exhilarating acidity and raw but filigree tannins. This was tasting a wine, in all respects, from another era. But as much as I was moved to know that not just this bottle but this style of wine was disappearing, I didn't feel nostalgic about it (pace the watchful Tom), *saudades*, as the Brazilians say. I felt no *passéiste* desire for someone to reproduce the wine today. This would be patently inauthentic, I told Tom. As inauthentic as if a contemporary French filmmaker tried to remake a Fassbinder and—even more kitschy—pass it off as a postmodern "homage." This would be an unethical relation to the past, not respecting the integrity of a discrete historical moment. The current fashion for "quoting" in art is as bankrupt as those who ignore the past, pace culture-killing Tarantino.

As I drank the old Piedmontese red, I was reminded of Frances Yates's classic text on the art of memory, and the ancient Greek custom of constructing a virtual house within the mind in which each room is furnished with the distinct narrative elements that eventually will allow for the pinpoint recital of a lengthy tale. I imagined we were gliding through a living, liquid museum, even as the rooms of that museum gradually dissolved from our sight with each sip we took, as the bottle's contents were consumed and lost forever. I was aware that at nearly thirty years old, the wine had body, textures, flavors that were radically different from what they must have been in its youth. But its character—tart, acid, bitter, savory, resolutely adult—must surely have been there from the start. We were stepping back into the context of 1978 as we drank, when fashions didn't demand McDonald's-style sweetness. This bottle afforded us a glimpse of an era, from a *happily ephemeral* vantage point.

18

THE SPECIAL OLYMPICS OF WINE

New Is Always Better

Wine critic Cyrus Redding writes that "the wines of the moderns are, there is no doubt, much more perfect than those of the ancients." The words of this intrepid, globetrotting Englishman are to be found in his *History and Description of Modern Wines*, published in 1833. Just as every generation produces commentators on the unequaled cultural poverty and decadence of its era, it also produces, for those involved in any aspect of commerce, the belief that the products of their era have never been better. And both sides are surely always right. Merchants of any object that involves a question of taste and their yapping subcontractors, the Critics, always have a vested interest in believing that the newest is the best. How else can they sell their wares, after all? For the last twenty-five years our merchants across the globe have been selling a style of wine that is the direct result of an accidental blind tasting. This tasting, which took place thirty years ago, is less the reason that tastes changed than an expression of how changes in taste are always expressions of shifts in power. And blind luck.

The so-called 1976 Olympics of wine tasting is one of the most celebrated events of recent wine history. There are very few American winemakers and critics who don't cite it as a watershed event. It marked the shift in power away from Europe and toward the United States and the rest of the New World. It's spoken about in such reverential tones in America that it could be read as a cross between the wine world's equivalent of proving Newtonian gravity and the Second Coming. But this time it wasn't so much water turned into wine as wine turned back into grape juice. In my opinion, it's one of the greatest catastrophes that has ever befallen the wine world. In the spring of 1976, in Paris, Steven Spurrier, a well-to-do young Englishman, was at loose ends. He'd just bought a wine shop and begun giving wine courses in English, mostly for American expatriates. But business was slow. As a stunt, really, he decided to stage a promotion for his classes. No one took American wines seriously at the time, but Spurrier came up with the farsighted (or blindly lucky) idea of doing a comparative blind tasting of these unheralded Napa Cabernets with the top châteaux of Bordeaux and, for whites, California Chardonnays alongside some of the better (but not all of the best) white Burgundies. So absurd to most people was this notion that only one journalist showed up, and that was at the last moment and by accident. This was George Taber, *Time* magazine correspondent. Many years later Taber wrote an unapologetically jingoistic book about what he witnessed—and helped create—titled *The Judgment of Paris: California Versus France . . . the Historic Tasting That Revolutionized Wine.* Alas, in some ways, he's right.

Though it could have equally been titled, in my opinion, *(Sometimes) There Is No Judgment in Paris.*

The judges of this ersatz competition, French winemakers, critics, and merchants, were asked to give numerical scores to all the wines they tasted blind. These numerical ratings were then tallied, and the winners were, to everyone's astonishment, an American red and white. Taber's breathless piece in *Time* magazine proclaiming Americans as the new David of the wine world set off a wave of press coverage around the globe. This happened to coincide with the arrival of the singularly wealthy American consumer and wine producer into the global market.

Newly self-anointed American critics such as Parker happened to catch the wave. Indeed, Parker is a classic case of the right (or wrong) guy at the right place at the right time. With all of five years' experience simply *drinking* wine, he ingenuously proclaimed himself an expert consumer advocate. He was precisely that half step in front of the neophyte American wine consumer of the time that allowed him to gain a foothold in their conscience, without fear of (mutual) embarrassment. With no substantial knowledge but brimming with the enthusiasm and self-confidence of the onset of the Reagan era (whose autographed pictures adorn his study), he could lead the fearful masses without the inconvenience of actually knowing where he was going. Within less than ten years, the Napa palate, American critical support for that palate (based on reflex taste and chauvinism), and the wealth of the new American consumer were dictating changes in winemaking and drinking across the globe. While Spurrier's blind tasting can hardly be faulted for opening this Pandora's box, it's fair to say that the legend that grew up around this tasting conferred an utterly specious legitimacy on the notion of objective, mathematical, empirical judgments in wine.

How did this happen? First, the fact that the Napa wines were unknown outside of the United States contributed to the considerable quality of the wines at that time. This was the last period of nonmarket-constructed California wines. These unselfconscious products of newly discovered *terroir* were made by passionate wine lovers with little prospect of fame and fortune. Just like in Hollywood at the time, the California wines of the 1970s were rough around the edges but intense, filled with a vitality and an authentic energy peculiar to the postwar American spirit. The grain and texture of Cassavetes's inimitable *Killing of a Chinese Bookie* or Coppola's *The Conversation* and *The Godfather*(s) or the brilliant, unfettered invention of Monte Hellman's *Two-Lane Blacktop* (the "authentic" version of *Easy Rider*) all found their echo in the edginess and gutsiness of Ridge Zinfandels, Montelena Cabernets, and even Mondavi Chardonnays. Ironically, what happened in the 1980s to Mondavi's wines is not dissimilar to what happened during the same period to the films of Francis Ford Coppola, their eventual neighbor and fellow winemaker. Mondavi's eventual corporate self-destruction in this decade is equally symptomatic.

Though I'm deeply skeptical of the place that the California wine industry (driven by the Napa Valley) has now arrogated for itself—at least in the eyes of American consumers—I have a great affection for the wines of California, the Pacific Northwest, and New York State, and I'm equally sure there is an interesting future for the vine in places like Virginia and New Mexico. Some of my happiest wine memories are of Finger Lakes Rieslings, Anderson Valley Gewürztraminers, Washington State Cabernets, and rabble-rousing Zinfandels from Lodi. I believe profoundly in their value and the eventual determination (after many generations) of significant, resolutely American *terroirs* in all these places. But there was a profound shift in the culture in the 1980s that derailed the necessarily humble search for *terroir*. It produced a sense of instant entitlement and self-worth. Instead of patiently exploring the potential for *terroir*, California winemakers suddenly proclaimed that they *owned terroir* every bit as legitimate as any snotty old European—that is, in those cases where they didn't deny it existed. Suddenly the styles and prices changed radically. Wine became a vanity piece, an expression of power. The Reaganite—and then Clintonite—nouveaux riches flocked to Napa to buy wineries and emblazon their names across labels. Ever more outrageous claims were made for American wines based solely on money, power, technology, and the twin marketing monster of ads and—consciously and unconsciously—co-opted journalists. Perhaps one of the benefits of the current economic (and political) crisis will be to bring American winemakers back to Earth (planet Earth), reassessing their place in the spatial and temporal cosmos and leading them to search once again, as they began to do in the 1970s, for joyously heterogeneous American tastes. In my opinion, this holds equally for the wines of Australia, South Africa, and Argentina, which have become the playthings of the Anglo-Saxon- and Asian-dominated international market. In all these countries, there is still a profound journey that can take place with dignity and humility toward the gradual uncovering of their *terroirs*, as numerous current winemakers, from Mendocino's Lazy Creek winery to Australia's Jim Barry, already prove.

But back in 1976, the singular quality of California wines of that time shouldn't have been enough to sway judgment in the presence of wines of the caliber and sophistication of Max Ophüls's *Earnings of Madame de . . .* , or Bresson's *Au Hasard Balthasar* (with the latter I think of the 1973 Meursault made by Jean-Marc Roulot's father that was in the competition). So how were these American wines judged superior? First of all, the wines being tasted were two, three, at most four years old. Bordeaux of that period were made in such a way that they were tannic and withdrawn in their youth, unflattering. The California wines, on the other hand, although much more savory, dryly tannic, and edgily acidic than the fruit (suicide?) bombs made today, were nonetheless infinitely fruitier, sweeter, and more immediately appealing than the young Bordeaux.

To the tasters, who included the ever-courteous Aubert de Villaine of Romanée-Conti, these Californian sweet-juiced wines were a seductive novelty. And of course they seemed more compelling. How could Audrey Hepburn possibly win a Miss World competition when surrounded by more carnal choices? How on earth could her ethereal charms and class be shown to advantage, parading up and down a stage in a bikini? This is to take nothing away from the appeal of the fleshy American wines but merely to suggest how patently absurd the notion of a wine competition is. You can imagine, though, how a blind tasting featuring Brigitte Bardot in 1976 could lead to the culture of Pamela Anderson twenty years later. This absurd British schoolboy's exercise, to which naïve French professionals unwittingly lent legitimacy, was then transformed by American nationalism and economic self-interest into an event of significant repercussions. These repercussions included the creation of a world market set up around wines that would be designed to overpower tasters in these artificial competitions and pseudoscientific point systems, which would continue to confer legitimacy on Schwarzenegger and Anderson wines. Kermit Lynch, American importer of great Burgundy and Rhône wines (and Joguet's Chinons) since the 1960s (and resident of California), has the final word on the value of such tastings. He said, "Blind tasting is to wine what strip poker is to love."*

Alas, this blind tasting arrived at the right moment, when the American-dominated world culture wanted results, concrete success, pseudoscientific explanations. This movement was compounded with the emergence of the United States as the sole superpower in the early 1990s. California wine, like Hollywood, already had been spurred to massive growth under Reagan in the '80s. With the unbridled pursuit of wealth, individual gain, and economic advantage held up as lodestar goals, the stage was set for the imposition of the American taste on the world market, in wine, in cinema, wherever culture could be sold. California became the standard everywhere, a patina of warm and fuzzy humanism in the movies (or its evil twin, unmediated violence and destruction), seductive roundness (or staggering power) in the wines. But each expression trailed behind it an underlying standardization of feeling, thought, and ideology. Power, of course, has always provided the tit that taste can suck on. But it's a tit with as much poison as milk.

Taste of Childhood

How free are we when we taste? How independent are our palates? What does it mean to taste? Do we all have abilities? Do people across the world really want all these alcoholized soda pop concoctions, or are they conned and bullied by marketing and the collusion of the market itself into submitting to them? And, then, do they gradually grow accustomed, and consider this a legitimate norm? Are our tastes shaped by free will and free market forces, or are we victims of the phenomenon of imposing the lowest common denominator and calling that

---

*Spurrier restaged the 1976 tasting in 2006. Once again the American wines "won." But given numerous peculiarities to the tasting (such as Jean-Marc Roulot refusing to send Spurrier his wines for the competition or that the majority of judges were American and British—including Jancis Robinson—and thus with palates inclined toward a certain style, this hardly "proved" the superiority or superior ageability of the wines. Nor of course did it disprove it. All things being equal (which they often are), it was just another game of strip poker.

democracy? Randall Grahm, a genial, renegade winemaker in Santa Cruz, is the rare successful Californian winemaker eager to decry the Napa power structure and the fraud of many Californian wines. He explained to me on a visit to his *Charlie and the Chocolate Factory*–style winery that "Man's primitive instinct for sweetness and fat is reflected not just in a Big Mac but also in the rich, ripe, sweet, alcoholic wines that are easy to produce anywhere in the world and at any price category. The more the same wine is made rich and smooth, the easier it is to market it as a luxury version of the monolithic fruit bomb standard. And this is what California does to perfection. We live in an age when fat and sugar are highly prized." It's tempting to say that not since Neanderthals depended on fat and sugar for survival has mankind been so enamored of the two laziest, least dynamic of alimentary elements.

Michael Pollan, nutrition and food writer at *The New York Times* has been following this trend—which obviously extends beyond wine—closely. Citing an article in *The American Journal of Clinical Nutrition*, he wrote:

> One dollar spent in the processed food section of the supermarket— the aisles in the middle of the store—will buy you 1200 calories of cookies and snacks. That same dollar spent in the produce section on the perimeter will buy you only 250 calories of carrots. Similarly, a dollar spent in the processed food aisles will buy you 875 calories of soda but only 170 calories of fruit juice. So if you're in the desperate position of shopping simply for calories to keep your family going, the rational strategy is to buy the junk.
>
> . . . we are driven by our evolutionary inheritance to expend as little energy as possible seeking out as much food energy as possible. So we naturally gravitate to "energy-dense foods"—high-calorie sugars and fats, which in nature are rare and hard to find. Sugars in nature come mostly in the form of ripe fruit and, if you're really lucky, honey; fats come in the form of meat, the getting of which requires a great expense of energy, making them fairly rare in the diet as well. Well, the modern supermarket reverses the whole caloric calculus:

the most energy-dense foods are the easiest—that is, cheapest—ones to acquire.

This phenomenon runs across all aspects of society. At a dinner, for example, at the house of Alexandra de Léal, the guardian angel landlady of the loft in which I edited *Mondovino*, I was seated next to a "Monsieur Kahn," introduced to me as her "neighbor, distinguished Freudian psychiatrist, with many patients from the movies." After I left off wondering about the intentionality of the seating arrangements, I was able to concentrate on Monsieur Kahn's words. He was speaking about the current culture's dependence on behavioral drugs like Prozac and Xanax. "More and more of my patients—and not just movie people," he said, looking deeply into my eyes, "feel obliged to take these drugs just to endure the normal events from a life cycle. To go through a period of mourning, for instance." He explained that "it leaves less and less room for the completion of a passage to adulthood." It occurred to me that wine, like people, needs to undergo a certain hardship in order to progress. A wine must go through all the stages of development, especially the difficult ones, in order to reveal its identity, its singularity. A wine that ages without scars will never achieve the complexity of one that's allowed to age naturally. Ever more ubiquitous Dorian Gray–like techniques such as microoxygenation (a process designed to instantly make a wine's tannins more supple, mimicking the ageing process) and the use of new oak ageing ("New Age oaking"?) allow wine to achieve an immediate user-friendliness, an instantaneous patina (a conscious oxymoron). As Dr. Kahn concluded (with a hint of perverse pleasure?), "we live in an age of perpetual infantilization."

Our culture encourages us in every way to remain infantile, not to assert our adult tastes, to conform. Meanwhile, this same culture celebrates an entirely false notion of individuality, the ultimate corporate-statist ruse. We live the Huxleyan fantasy that we are happy and free: new oak, sweetness, round tannins; Prozac; unearned, unironic happy endings in films. Sugarcoated lives in consumer hell. As if taking *Brave New World* one step further, we've administered soma to ourselves, fully conscious of its design. Wine experts everywhere—dependent on the global business for their livelihood—assure us that we are living a moment of the greatest democratization, with the best-quality wine universally accessible at all price ranges from China to Africa to Paraguay. But of course we're being hoodwinked. The Prozac, sweet, fat wine style (*alta depresión?*) is easier to reproduce in either its mass market or its boutique version because of improved technology, and global warming that allows picking grapes riper and sweeter at less and less risk. But without relentless marketing, increasing market collusion, and journalistic complicity, this Orwellian conception of democracy could never exist. We are transforming ourselves from political citizens into predictable consumers of a single, transnational, unified non-ideological body politic. The global citizen is now the global consumer of sweet and easy things.

Taste and Empire

Classics professor Edward Bradley believes that we weave our personal stories, our narratives, from the time we identify our own name (and where that name and those people associated with it come from). This, he argues, is the Homeric notion of weaving our narratives from a skein of larger ones, past and future, as Odysseus does orally throughout his *Nostos*, his homeward (*terroir*-driven) journey, and as his wife, Penelope, does each day—in an inverted sense—with her literal undoing of the tapestry. It is this act of situating the self in a larger narrative context that gives us purpose. The threats to *terroir* are an expression of the tendency today to sever one's own narrative from the larger weave. The contemporary expression of this movement began in some senses in the 1930s, with fascism, and has continued to the present through the more anodyne but perhaps even more corrosive agents of "saturation capitalism." Corporate worship, marketing priests.

But is this different from what Edward Gibbon described in his late-eighteenth-century masterpiece *The Decline and Fall of the Roman Empire*? Roman civilization collapsed during a period marked by a surfeit of goods and leisure, by a general acquisitive, consumerist spirit, by a voluntary abdication of civic responsibility (and concomitant abdication of freedoms), and a descent into the ex nihilo construction of personal "narratives." The end of empire was also marked by the gradual confusion of expressions of power for expressions of taste, until all taste became not much more than an expression of power. And that power, as we know, collapsed rather brutally.

Epilogue

THE FONSALETTE MYSTERY—SOLVED

I'd Really Like to Stay but I Must Be Going

It's my last evening in Paris before taking a midnight flight back home to Brazil. I have to discuss our upcoming movie one more time with Charlotte Rampling before I leave. She's filming, and tells me she'll meet me anywhere I like—as long as it's in the center of Paris. Exhausted by her day, she says she'll have only enough time for a glass of wine and a snack. I tell her to meet me at the Caves Legrand wine bar. The moment she steps through the Galerie Vivienne into the warm embrace of Legrand, her mood improves. At seven thirty in the evening the wine bar is quiet and nearly empty. All the ghosts of the nineteenth century are free to move about the place at ease. Still in makeup from the day's filming, Charlotte seems like a creature from another time.

"So, what are we going to drink?" she asks me with a big smile.

"What would you like?"

"It's cold. I'd like a red. But after twelve hours of filming, I don't want to make myself even more tired by drinking something heavy."

I understand. The doctor recommends a light Burgundy. I ask Gérard, who's been looking out for her arrival, what he has in Marsannay, a small village in the Côte-de-Nuits. In general, Marsannay wines are light and airy, with a joie de vivre like a true Beaujolais, but more stylish. Not a bad idea for Charlotte, I think. Gérard picks up a bottle of 2000 Marsannay from Jean-Louis Trapet.

"No way, Trapet!" I exclaim. "Too squeaky clean for my taste."

"Trust me," Gérard says. "This is a good wine."

I'm not too inclined to trust him, because I think I know the producer's style. But not wanting to spend too much time dickering over the wine while Charlotte waits for me at the table, I acquiesce. Ten minutes later, I realize I'm already pouring my second glass. The wine is cheerful, delicious, refreshing. Gérard was right. I was wrong. Lucky me. Charlotte is completely transformed. No trace of fatigue. She's become as radiantly goofy as I've ever seen her.

The bottle makes me consider how lucky I am. I'm in one of the most seductive temples of wine in France. I'm drinking an utterly delicious wine, made doubly pleasurable by the fact that it overcame my prejudice. And I'm sitting with one of the most admirable and beautiful women in the world. The coincidence of so much beauty leads us easily to the subject of the role Charlotte will play in my film: a plastic surgeon in Rio. Someone who operates on others, but has sworn never to touch the stuff herself. Charlotte is absolutely luminous at sixty years old, thanks to Mother Nature and thanks to her courage in living every moment of her life, good and bad, with equal conviction. I can't help asking a question about her that resonates with the character she's to play in *Rio Sex Comedy*.

"Have you ever thought of your beauty as a burden?"

Charlotte looks at me sternly. And then bursts out laughing.

"Are you crazy? What a luxury. What a privilege! And I've taken full advantage of it all my life." She takes a sip of the wine and winks. "When you're beautiful, you can get away with murder."

Gérard, a man not indifferent to feminine beauty, sits down with us. I watch with amusement as he immediately deploys all his tools of seduction. Out of a sense of delicacy or, more likely, mischief, I get up so he can have a few moments to play his hand. I wander toward the front room of the wine shop to see what's happening. Clients are drifting in at the front for a guided tasting. An employee stops me in the hallway.

"Mr. Nossiter?"

"Yes."

"I wanted to introduce the vigneron to you who is doing a tasting with our clients this evening."

I shake hands with an open-faced young man of about thirty.

"Hello. I'm Emmanuel Reynaud," he says.

"Emmanuel Reynaud, of the Domaine Fonsalette? I don't believe it!"

"That's right."

"What an honor. I've been an admirer of your work and your uncle's work for a very long time. But what an amazing coincidence to run into you here. I've bought so many of your bottles in this shop." I pause for a second, wondering if I'll bring up the infamous Fonsalette incident with Gérard. And then I dive in: "Do you remember a bottle of Fonsalette white that was sent back to you from this shop last year? A bottle they said a client described as defective, but which they thought otherwise . . . I owe you an apology. I'm the client responsible for the mess in the first place."

He looks at me oddly. "No. No one ever sent me a defective bottle of Fonsalette from the Caves Legrand."

I stood there for a few seconds, gobsmacked. After all that fuss, they never even sent him the bottle?

I head back to the table, where Gérard is murmuring to Charlotte.

I will leave for the airport in twenty minutes. I came to Paris for a few weeks to find the narrative for this book, more than a year after the strange business of the Fonsalette blanc. Who would have thought that at this precise moment, on my way back to Rio, I would cross paths with the vigneron himself, in the exact place where the bottle was bought and refused? No screenwriter would have dared that twist. It's too bad, really, that it isn't fiction, because then I could tell the story without people wondering how much truth there is in it.

I catch Charlotte just as she's getting up from the table, retreating from Gérard's seductive advances with a discreet smile. I hear the last few words he murmurs to her: "Have dinner with me anytime, and the contents of my cellar are yours!"

Acknowledgments

Manuel Carcassonne, my editor at the original French publisher, Grasset, and his wife, Laure Gasparotto, were the midwives of this book. Through Manuel's prodding and then with Laure recording and transcribing months of conversations, I was able to reconsider my relation to wine post-*Mondovino* and to discover a desire to share that reappraisal with others. I wrote the majority of this book in French but found that some chapters came out more naturally in English. For this edition I underwent the out-of-body experience of returning all the words to my native tongue. This involved a peculiar process that began with my own furtive and sporadic translations, then rejections of the (often blameless) translation attempts of others, succeeded by my own comprehensive retranslation. The last phase, of course, generated a compulsory round of rewriting, because self-translation—in all senses—is an oxymoron. This surreal experience was shepherded with enormous talent, wisdom, and humor by Courtney Hodell at FSG. Bill Clegg's flair for art and commerce were also critical for this book's existence in English.

I'm grateful to Sonia Kronlund, Juan Pittaluga, and Alessandra and Lucrezia Fanari, who lodged me (both literally and figuratively) during several crucial phases of the research. Roberta Sudbrack, one of the greatest chefs in the world (as much for her human qualities as for her sublime restaurant in

Rio de Janeiro), unknowingly gave meaning to this project from its inception. I'm thankful for the translation efforts of numerous people, including Tina Kover, Jessica Green, and, from a logistical standpoint, Esther Allen. The book is deeply marked by the generosity of Robert and Isabelle Vifian, Yves Camdeborde, Danièle Gérault, Jean-Marc Roulot, and the Montille family, Dominique Lafon, Christophe Roumier, Les Caves Legrand, Charlotte Rampling, Luiz Schwarcz, Michael Greenberg, George Prochnik, Heidi Warneke, Adam Nossiter, Gerry Dawes, Guillermo de Aranzábal, Pascal Mérigeau, Charles and Monique Joguet, Quim Vila, Yvonne Hégoburu, Alberto Herraíz, Gérard Margeon, Ciro Lilla, Bruno Quenioux, Renato Machado, Edward Bradley, Sophie Borowsky, Pierre Demarty, Olivier Nora, and Jonathan Galassi.

I am above all indebted to my wife, Paula, who, during the initial writing of this book in Brazil—a fourteen-month period—gave birth to our three children, Miranda, Capitu, and Noah Bernard, and somehow, remembering the shared joy of searching for wine when we lived in Paris, found time to suggest the premise of the book's journey.

Rio de Janeiro and Espelho, Brazil
February 2009

Index